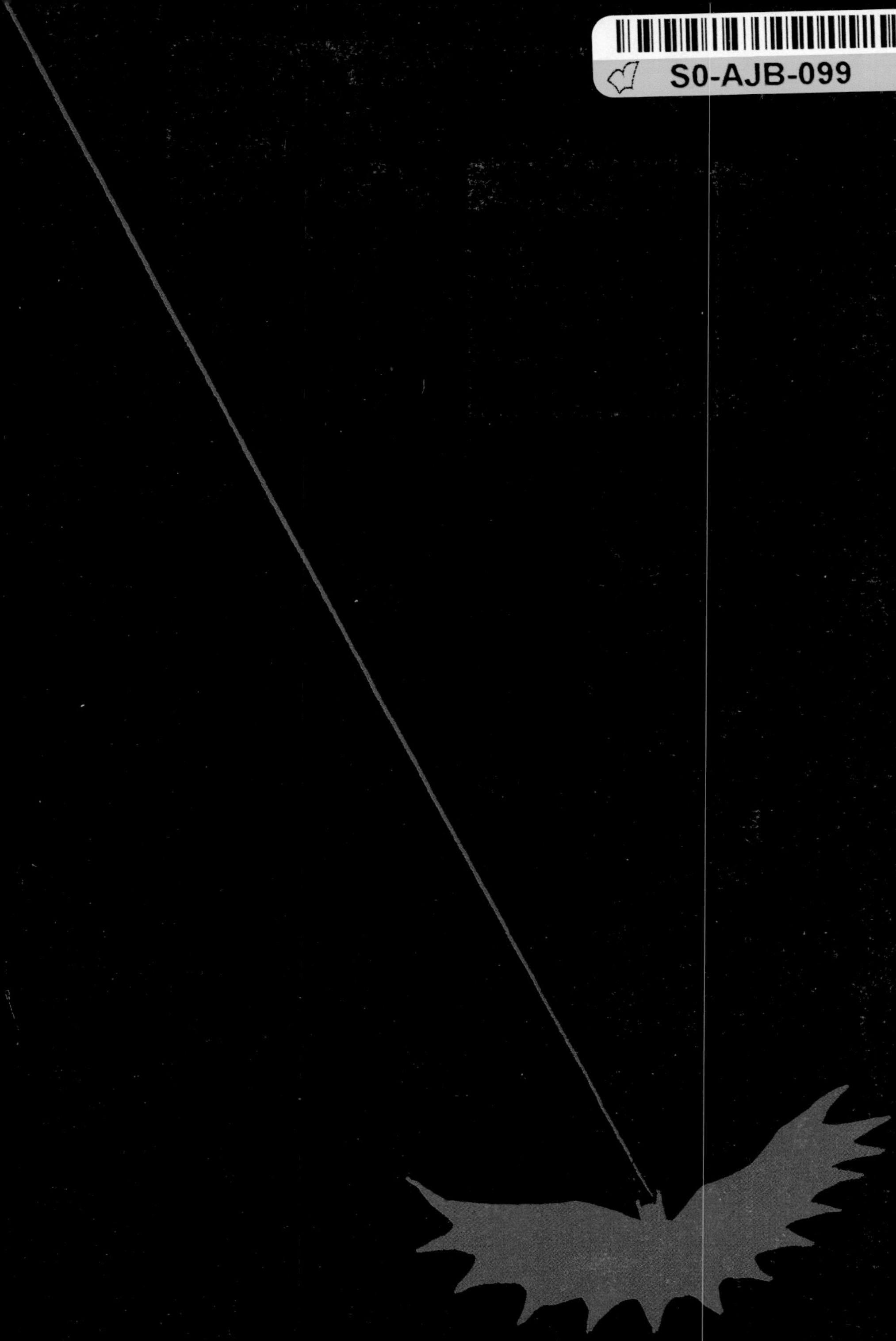

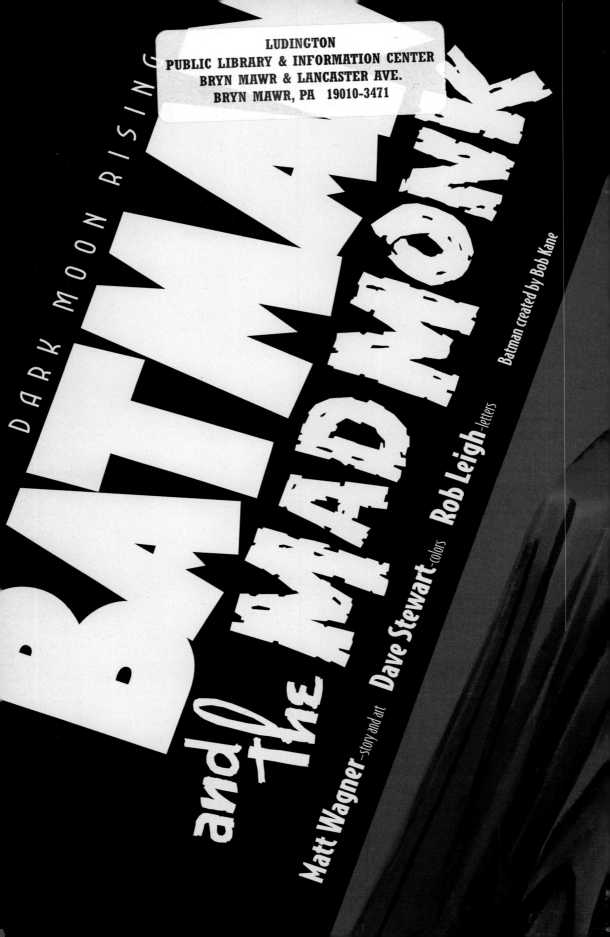

DARK MOON RISING

BATMAN
and the MAD MONK

Matt Wagner – Story and art   Dave Stewart – colors   Rob Leigh – letters

Batman created by Bob Kane

Dan DiDio Senior VP-Executive Editor   **Bob Schreck** Editor-original series   **Brandon Montclare** Assistant Editor-original series
Bob Harras Editor-collected edition   **Robbin Brosterman** Senior Art Director   **Louis Prandi** Art Director   **Paul Levitz** President & Publisher
Georg Brewer VP-Design & DC Direct Creative   **Richard Bruning** Senior VP-Creative Director   **Patrick Caldon** Executive VP-Finance & Operations
Chris Caramalis VP-Finance   **John Cunningham** VP-Marketing   **Terri Cunningham** VP-Managing Editor   **Alison Gill** VP-Manufacturing
Hank Kanalz VP-General Manager, WildStorm   **Jim Lee** Editorial Director-WildStorm   **Paula Lowitt** Senior VP-Business & Legal Affairs
MaryEllen McLaughlin VP-Advertising & Custom Publishing   **John Nee** VP-Business Development   **Gregory Noveck** Senior VP-Creative Affairs
Sue Pohja VP-Book Trade Sales   **Cheryl Rubin** Senior VP-Brand Management   **Jeff Trojan** VP-Business Development, DC Direct   **Bob Wayne** VP-Sales

Cover illustration by **Matt Wagner**

BATMAN AND THE MAD MONK

Published by DC Comics. Cover, introduction, and compilation copyright © 2007 DC Comics. All Rights Reserved. Originally published
in single magazine form in BATMAN:THE MAD MONK 1-6. Copyright © 2006-2007 DC Comics. All Rights Reserved. All characters, their distinctive likenesses and related
elements featured in this publication are trademarks of DC Comics. The stories, characters and incidents featured in this publication are entirely fictional. DC Comics does
not read or accept unsolicited submissions of ideas, stories or artwork. DC Comics, 1700 Broadway, New York, NY 10019. A Warner Bros. Entertainment Company.
Printed in Canada. First Printing. ISBN: 1-4012-1281-6 ISBN 13: 978-1-4012-1281-0

Previously...

A little more than a year into his crime-fighting career, Batman closes in on Sal Maroni, a high-ranking lieutenant in Carmine "The Roman" Falcone's gang. But without even knowing it, Maroni has become intimately entangled in all aspects of Batman's life.

Bruce Wayne is dating Julie Madison, a beautiful law student and the devoted daughter of wealthy Gotham industrialist Norman Madison. But to save his company, Norman borrowed large sums of money from Maroni, and his ability to pay him back is in doubt.

Another victim of Maroni's loan sharking is Professor Hugo Strange, a disgraced former psychiatrist obsessed with genetic engineering. Strange needs Maroni's money to carry on his experiments designed to create human perfection, but which have so far created only a trio of massively savage creatures—the Monster Men.

As Maroni squeezes the two men for the money, Madison becomes increasingly paranoid and with-drawn, concerned that the gangsters will hurt Julie to get at him. Strange, meanwhile, uses his Monster Men to slaughter gangsters gathered for a card game, and steals Maroni's own money to pay him back.

Batman investigates the massacre at the card game, tracing it back to Hugo Strange. Confronting him at his lab, he only barely escapes being fed to Strange's abominations. But using DNA that Batman left behind, Strange creates an even more advanced Monster Man, and decides to attack Maroni at the Roman's compound outside of Gotham.

At the same time, Norman Madison insists on being brought to see Maroni, arriving just as the Monster Men begin their violent raid on the compound. It's all Batman can do to contain the carnage and try to stop the genetically manipulated monsters before they slaughter everyone.

In the middle of the battle, Batman finds a shell-shocked Norman Madison. "This is no place for a man of your stripe," Batman tells him. "Go home, Norman."

Batman defeats the Monster Men, threatening to destroy Maroni with them unless he agrees to call off all Norman Madison's debts. Returning home, Bruce tells Julie that he's loaned her father money to pay back the gangsters and that everything will be all right.

But Norman's paranoid mind has found a new obsession: the Batman.

"He knew my name," he repeats to himself...

CHAPTER 1

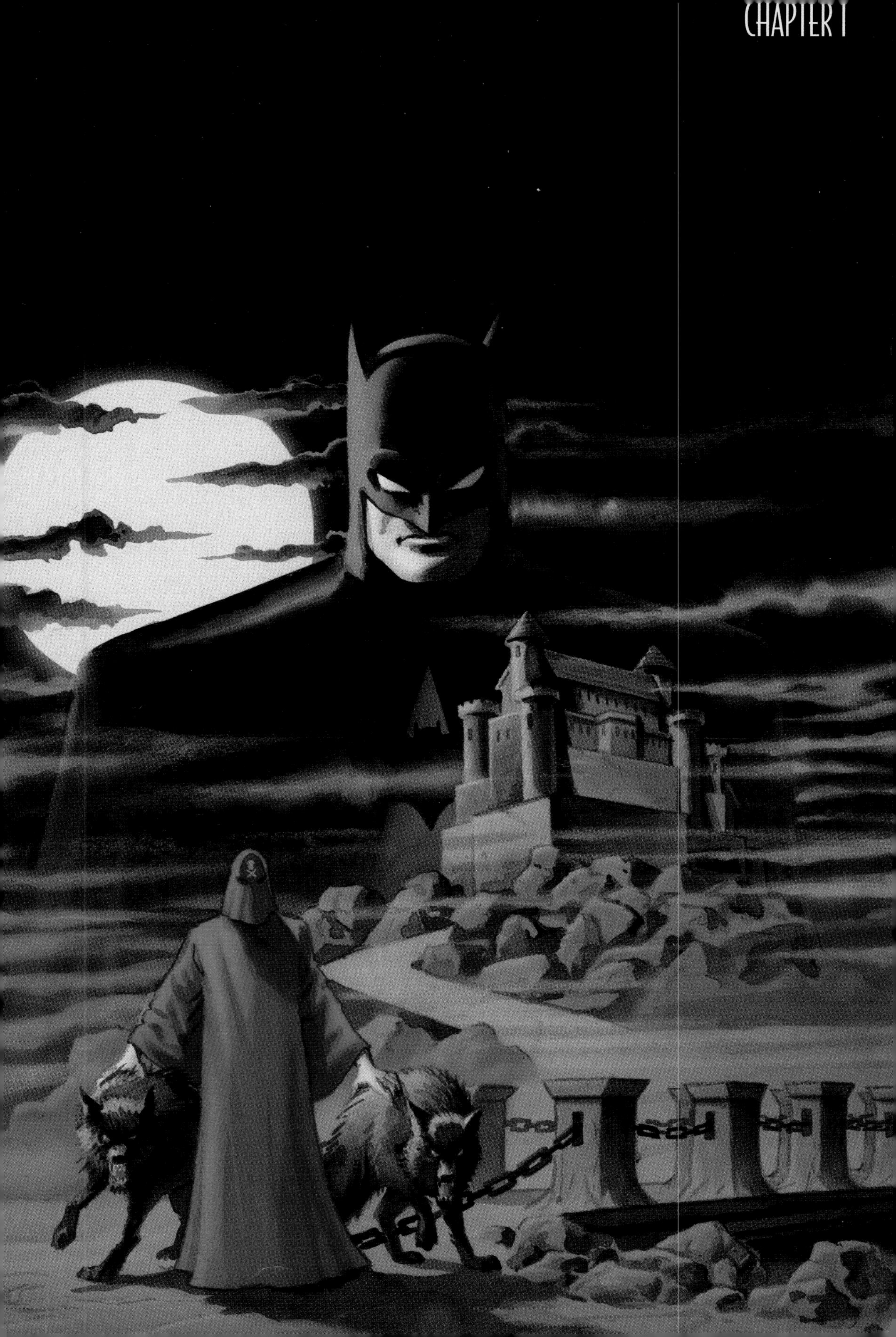

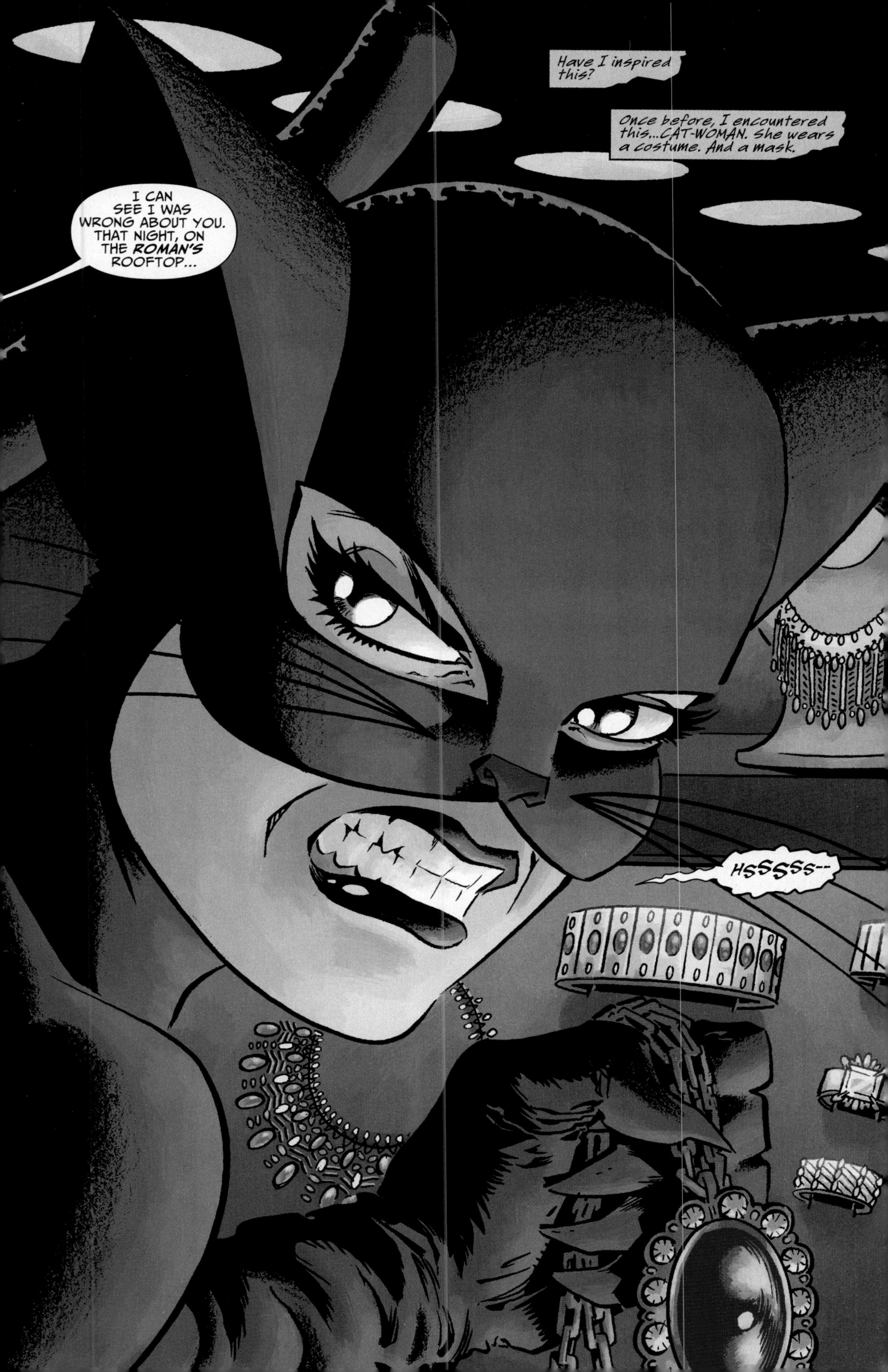
Have I inspired this?
Once before, I encountered this...CAT-WOMAN. She wears a costume. And a mask.
I CAN SEE I WAS WRONG ABOUT YOU. THAT NIGHT, ON THE ROMAN'S ROOFTOP...
HSSSSS--

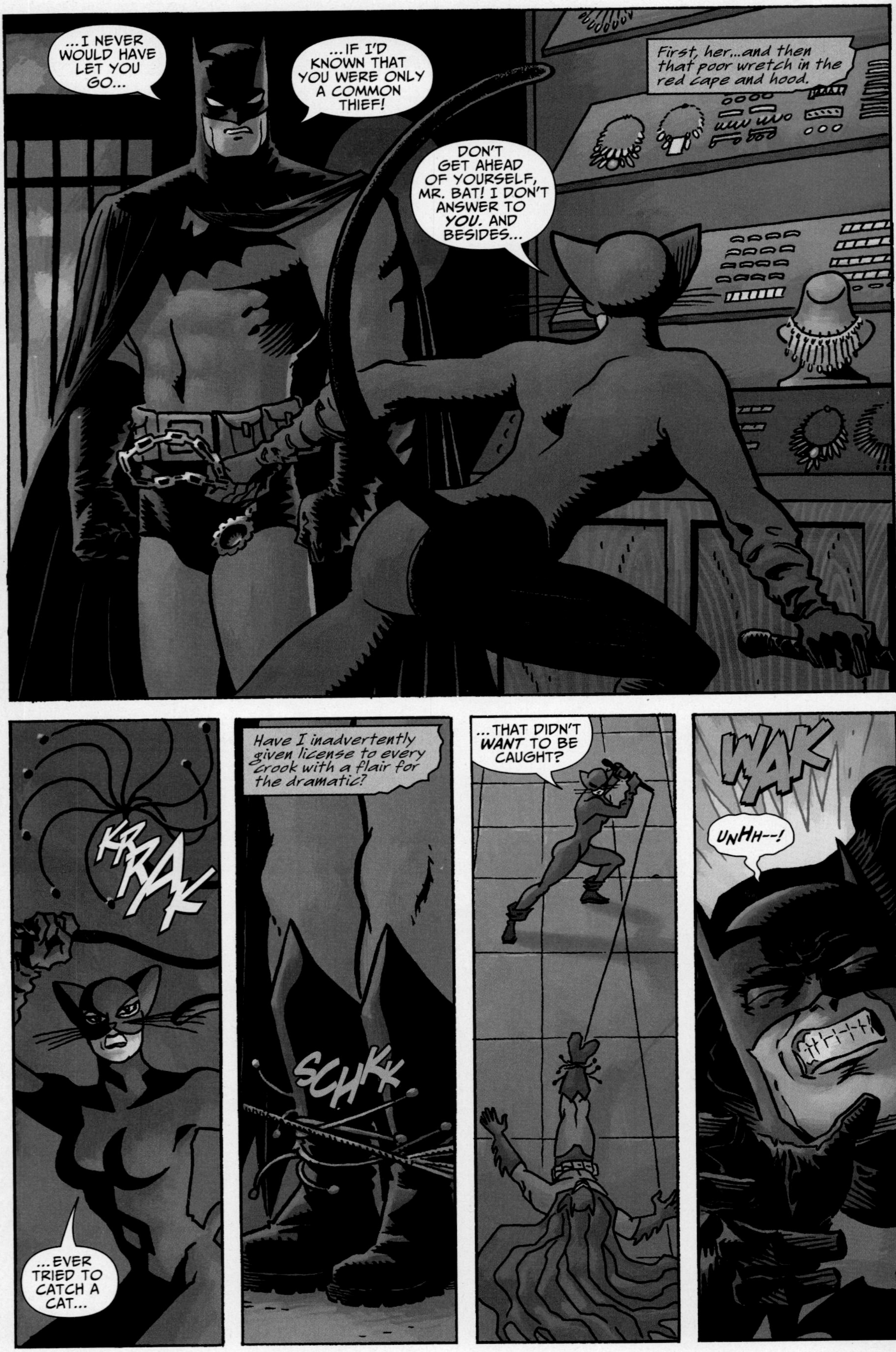
...I NEVER WOULD HAVE LET YOU GO...
...IF I'D KNOWN THAT YOU WERE ONLY A COMMON THIEF!
First, her...and then that poor wretch in the red cape and hood.
DON'T GET AHEAD OF YOURSELF, MR. BAT! I DON'T ANSWER TO YOU. AND BESIDES...
KRRAK
...EVER TRIED TO CATCH A CAT...
Have I inadvertently given license to every crook with a flair for the dramatic?
SCHKK
...THAT DIDN'T WANT TO BE CAUGHT?
WAK
UNHH--!

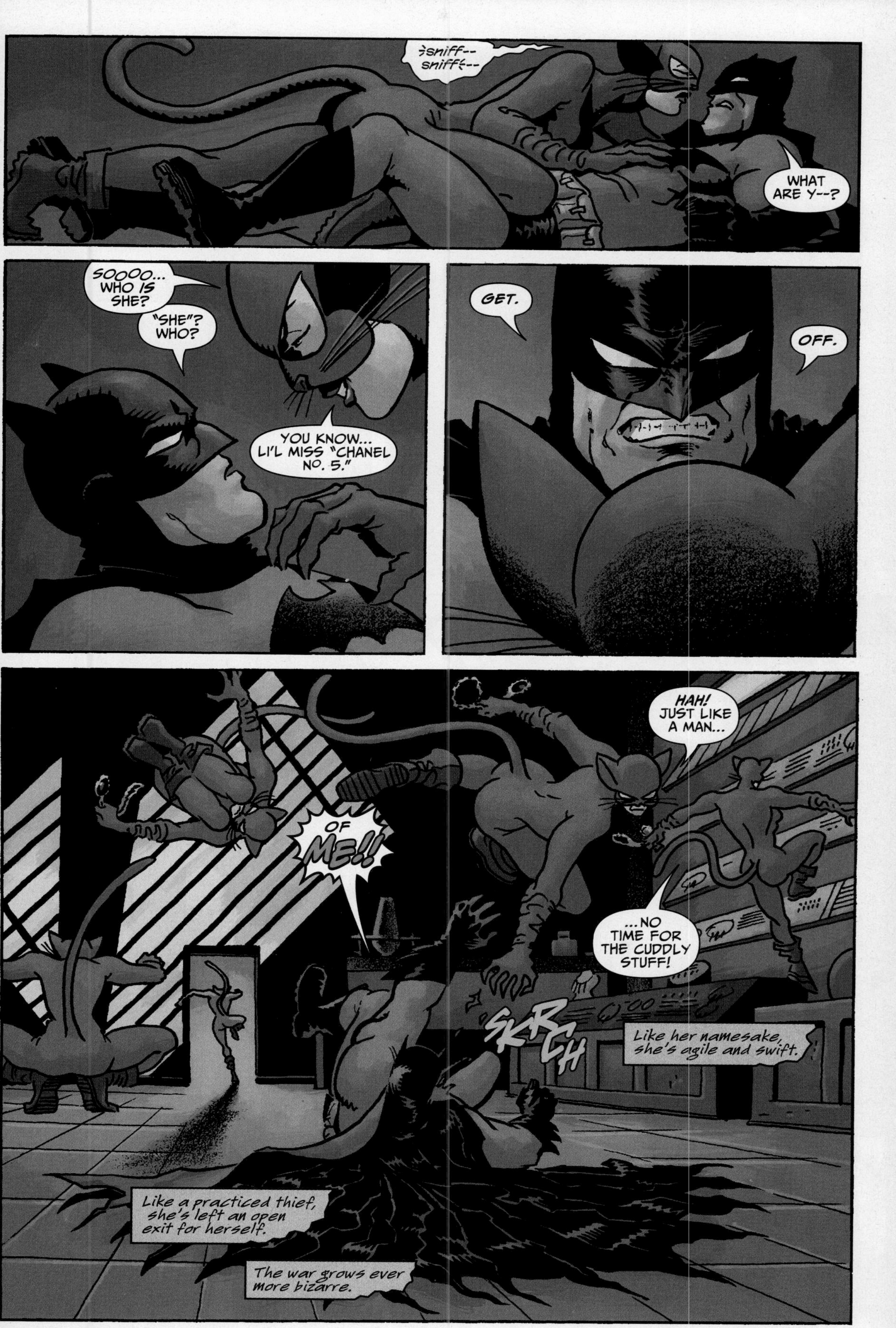

›sniff-- sniff‹--
WHAT ARE Y--?
SOOOO... WHO IS SHE?
"SHE"? WHO?
YOU KNOW... LI'L MISS "CHANEL NO. 5."
GET.
OFF.
OF ME!!
HAH! JUST LIKE A MAN...
...NO TIME FOR THE CUDDLY STUFF!
SKRCH
Like her namesake, she's agile and swift.
Like a practiced thief, she's left an open exit for herself.
The war grows ever more bizarre.

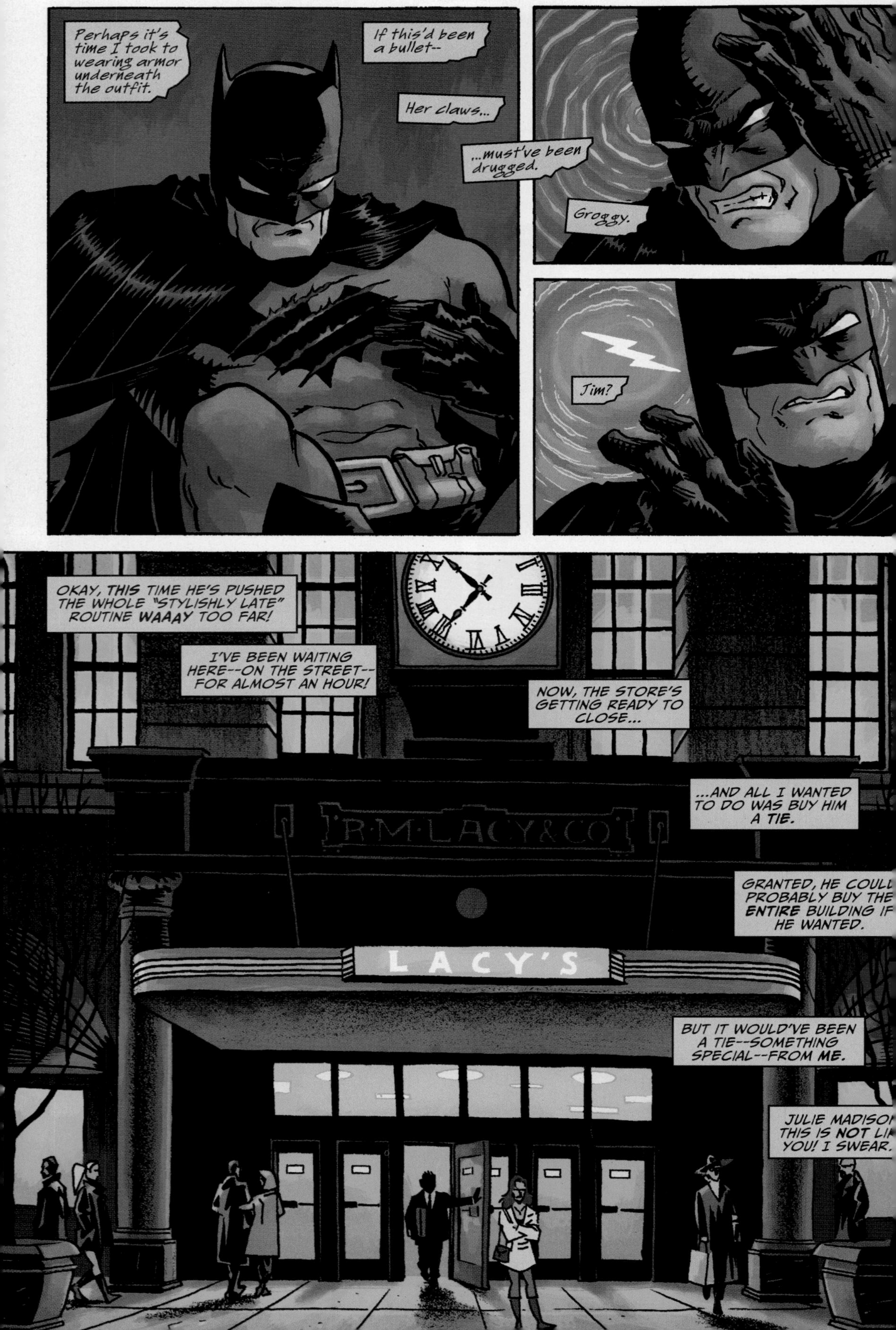
Perhaps it's time I took to wearing armor underneath the outfit.
If this'd been a bullet--
Her claws...
...must've been drugged.
Groggy.
Jim?
OKAY, THIS TIME HE'S PUSHED THE WHOLE "STYLISHLY LATE" ROUTINE WAAAY TOO FAR!
I'VE BEEN WAITING HERE--ON THE STREET--FOR ALMOST AN HOUR!
NOW, THE STORE'S GETTING READY TO CLOSE...
...AND ALL I WANTED TO DO WAS BUY HIM A TIE.
R·M·LACY&CO
GRANTED, HE COUL PROBABLY BUY THE ENTIRE BUILDING IF HE WANTED.
LACY'S
BUT IT WOULD'VE BEEN A TIE--SOMETHING SPECIAL--FROM ME.
JULIE MADISO THIS IS NOT LI YOU! I SWEAR.

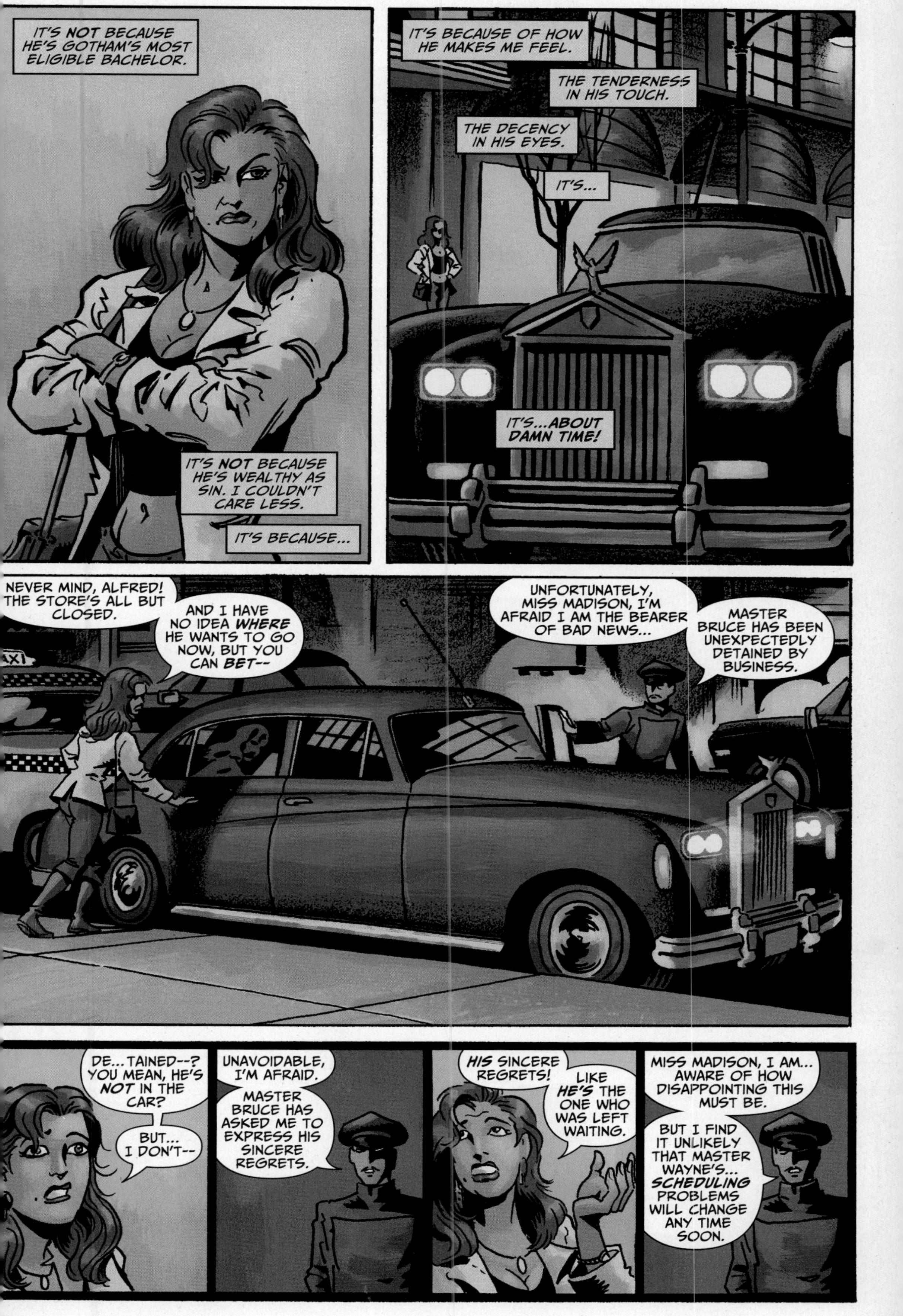

IT'S NOT BECAUSE HE'S GOTHAM'S MOST ELIGIBLE BACHELOR.
IT'S NOT BECAUSE HE'S WEALTHY AS SIN. I COULDN'T CARE LESS.
IT'S BECAUSE...
IT'S BECAUSE OF HOW HE MAKES ME FEEL.
THE TENDERNESS IN HIS TOUCH.
THE DECENCY IN HIS EYES.
IT'S...
IT'S...ABOUT DAMN TIME!
NEVER MIND, ALFRED! THE STORE'S ALL BUT CLOSED.
AND I HAVE NO IDEA WHERE HE WANTS TO GO NOW, BUT YOU CAN BET--
UNFORTUNATELY, MISS MADISON, I'M AFRAID I AM THE BEARER OF BAD NEWS...
MASTER BRUCE HAS BEEN UNEXPECTEDLY DETAINED BY BUSINESS.
DE...TAINED--? YOU MEAN, HE'S NOT IN THE CAR?
BUT... I DON'T--
UNAVOIDABLE, I'M AFRAID.
MASTER BRUCE HAS ASKED ME TO EXPRESS HIS SINCERE REGRETS.
HIS SINCERE REGRETS!
LIKE HE'S THE ONE WHO WAS LEFT WAITING.
MISS MADISON, I AM... AWARE OF HOW DISAPPOINTING THIS MUST BE.
BUT I FIND IT UNLIKELY THAT MASTER WAYNE'S... SCHEDULING PROBLEMS WILL CHANGE ANY TIME SOON.

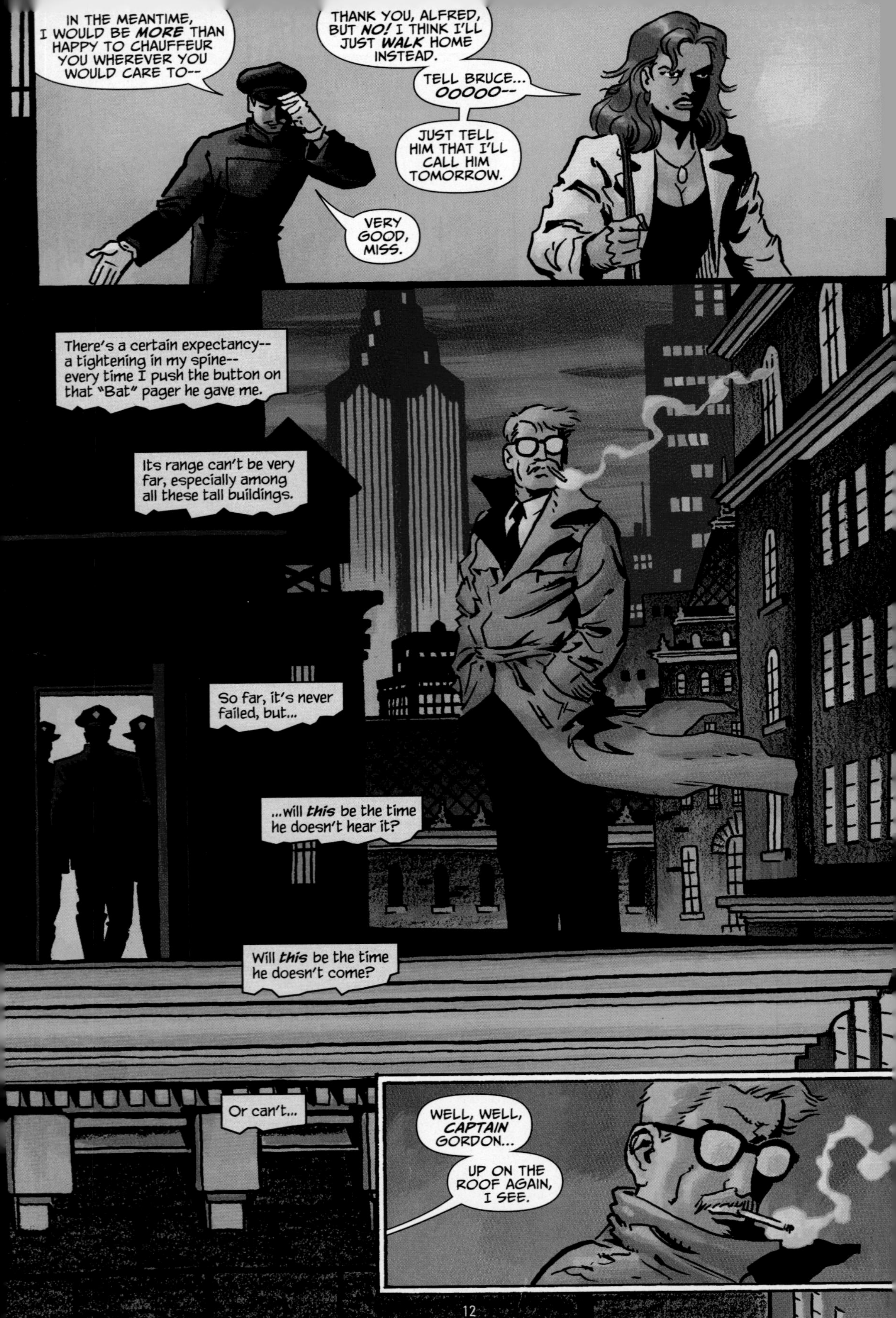

IN THE MEANTIME, I WOULD BE MORE THAN HAPPY TO CHAUFFEUR YOU WHEREVER YOU WOULD CARE TO--
THANK YOU, ALFRED, BUT NO! I THINK I'LL JUST WALK HOME INSTEAD.
TELL BRUCE... OOOOO--
JUST TELL HIM THAT I'LL CALL HIM TOMORROW.
VERY GOOD, MISS.
There's a certain expectancy--a tightening in my spine--every time I push the button on that "Bat" pager he gave me.
Its range can't be very far, especially among all these tall buildings.
So far, it's never failed, but...
...will this be the time he doesn't hear it?
Will this be the time he doesn't come?
Or can't...
WELL, WELL, CAPTAIN GORDON...
UP ON THE ROOF AGAIN, I SEE.

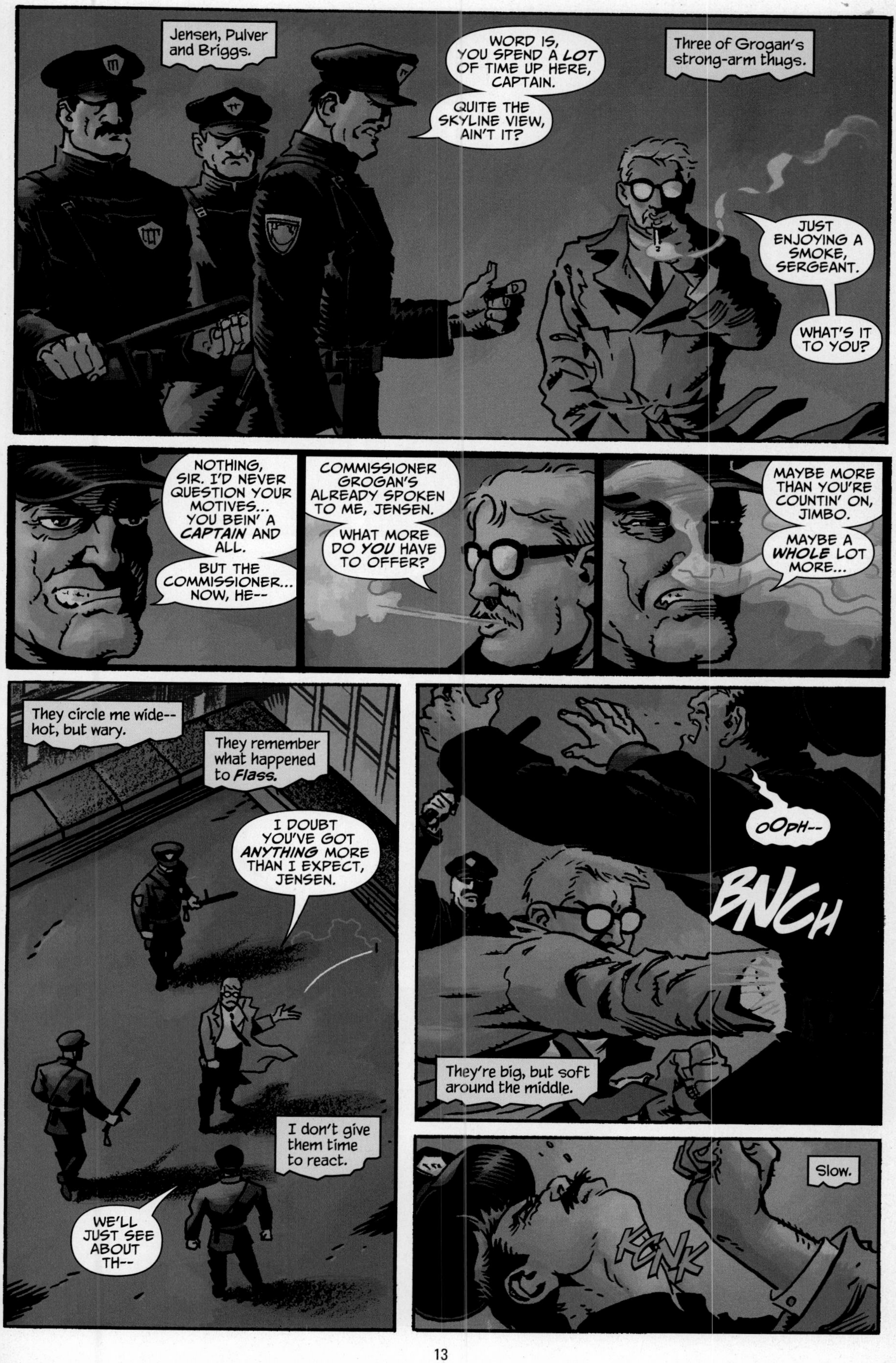

Jensen, Pulver and Briggs.
WORD IS, YOU SPEND A LOT OF TIME UP HERE, CAPTAIN.
QUITE THE SKYLINE VIEW, AIN'T IT?
Three of Grogan's strong-arm thugs.
JUST ENJOYING A SMOKE, SERGEANT.
WHAT'S IT TO YOU?
NOTHING, SIR. I'D NEVER QUESTION YOUR MOTIVES... YOU BEIN' A CAPTAIN AND ALL.
BUT THE COMMISSIONER... NOW, HE--
COMMISSIONER GROGAN'S ALREADY SPOKEN TO ME, JENSEN.
WHAT MORE DO YOU HAVE TO OFFER?
MAYBE MORE THAN YOU'RE COUNTIN' ON, JIMBO.
MAYBE A WHOLE LOT MORE...
They circle me wide--hot, but wary.
They remember what happened to Flass.
I DOUBT YOU'VE GOT ANYTHING MORE THAN I EXPECT, JENSEN.
I don't give them time to react.
WE'LL JUST SEE ABOUT TH--
OOPH--
BNCH
They're big, but soft around the middle.
Slow.
KONK

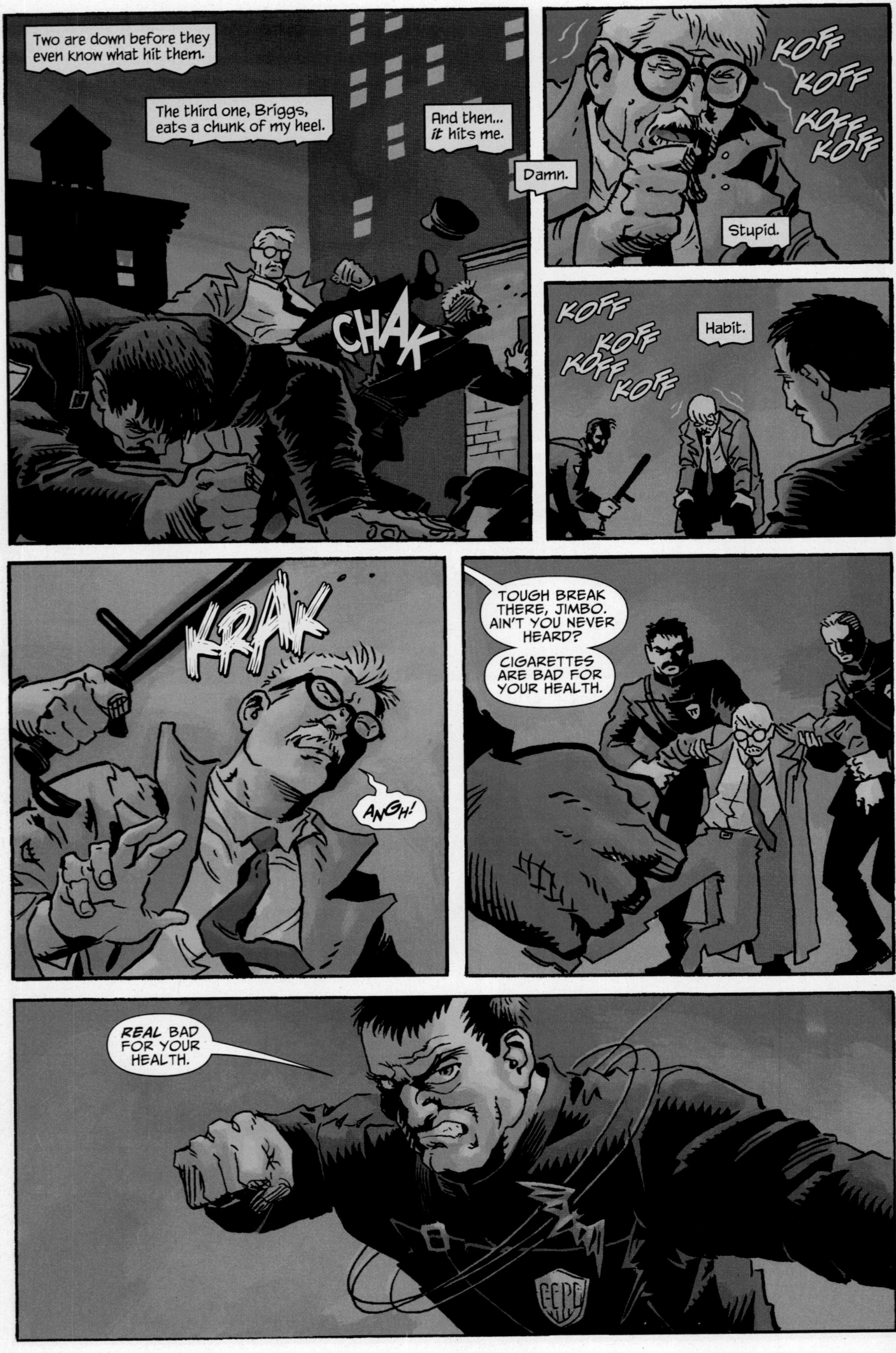
Two are down before they even know what hit them.
The third one, Briggs, eats a chunk of my heel.
And then... *it* hits me.
CHAK
Damn.
KOFF KOFF KOFF KOFF
Stupid.
KOFF KOFF KOFF KOFF
Habit.
KRAK
ANGH!
TOUGH BREAK THERE, JIMBO. AIN'T YOU NEVER HEARD?
CIGARETTES ARE BAD FOR YOUR HEALTH.
REAL BAD FOR YOUR HEALTH.

Happens so fast...

His screams seem to keep rising up and up.

Nothing after. No fall.

He just disappears into the night sky.

IT'S...IT'S *HIM!!* MUST BE!!

WHAT TH--?!

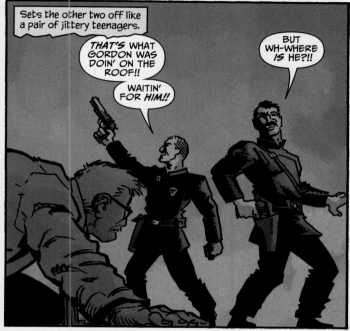

Sets the other two off like a pair of jittery teenagers.

THAT'S WHAT GORDON WAS DOIN' ON THE ROOF!!

WAITIN' FOR HIM!!

BUT WH-WHERE *IS* HE?!!

So hopped up they don't even hear him coming.

Truth be told...

OHHH, GEEZUZ! WHERE *IS* HE?! WHERE--?

SHUT UP!

DON'T--

...neither do I.

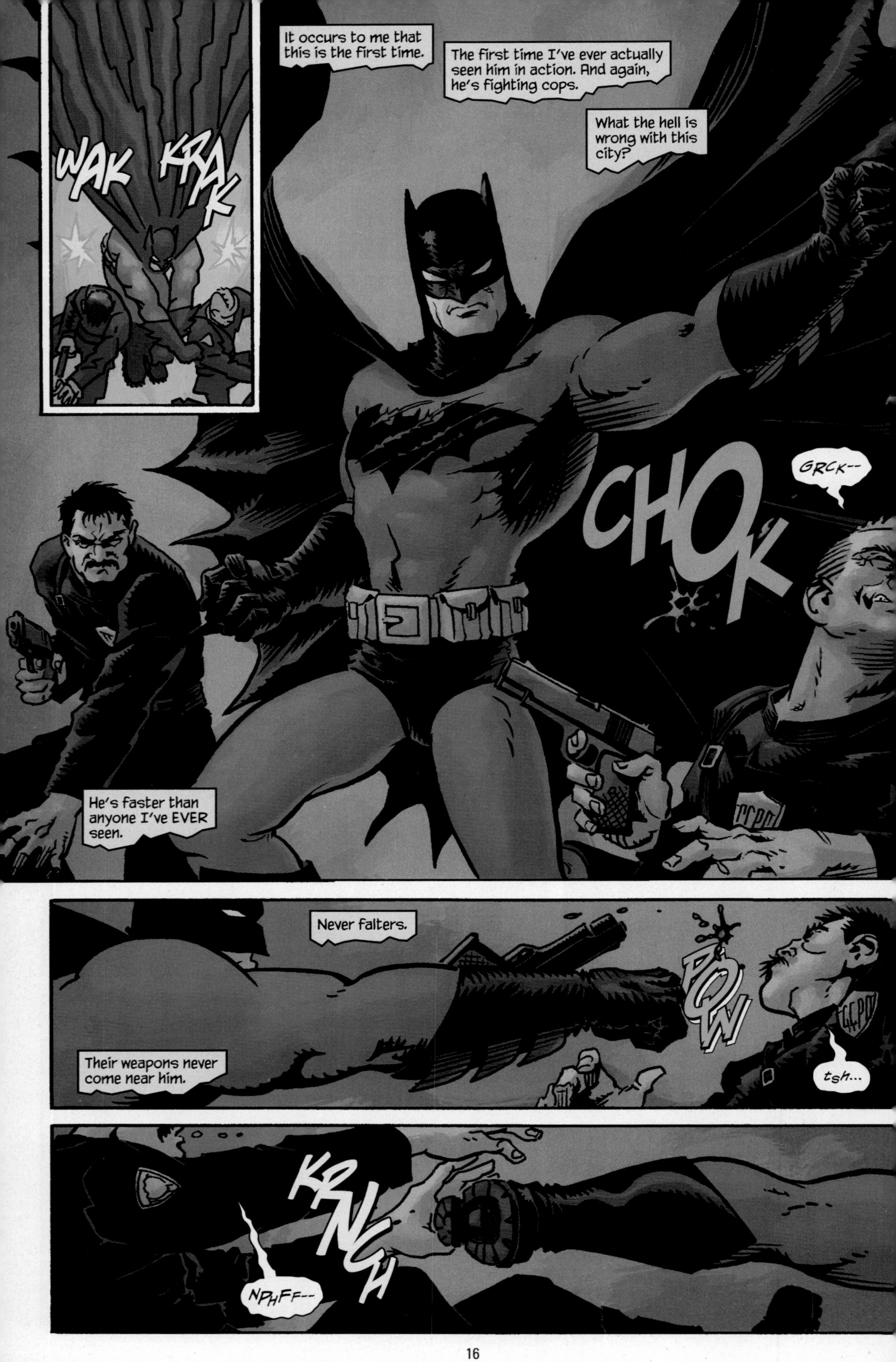

WAK
KRAK
It occurs to me that this is the first time.
The first time I've ever actually seen him in action. And again, he's fighting cops.
What the hell is wrong with this city?
CHOK
GRCK--
He's faster than anyone I've EVER seen.
GCPD
Never falters.
POW
Their weapons never come near him.
tsh...
KRUNCH
NPHFF--

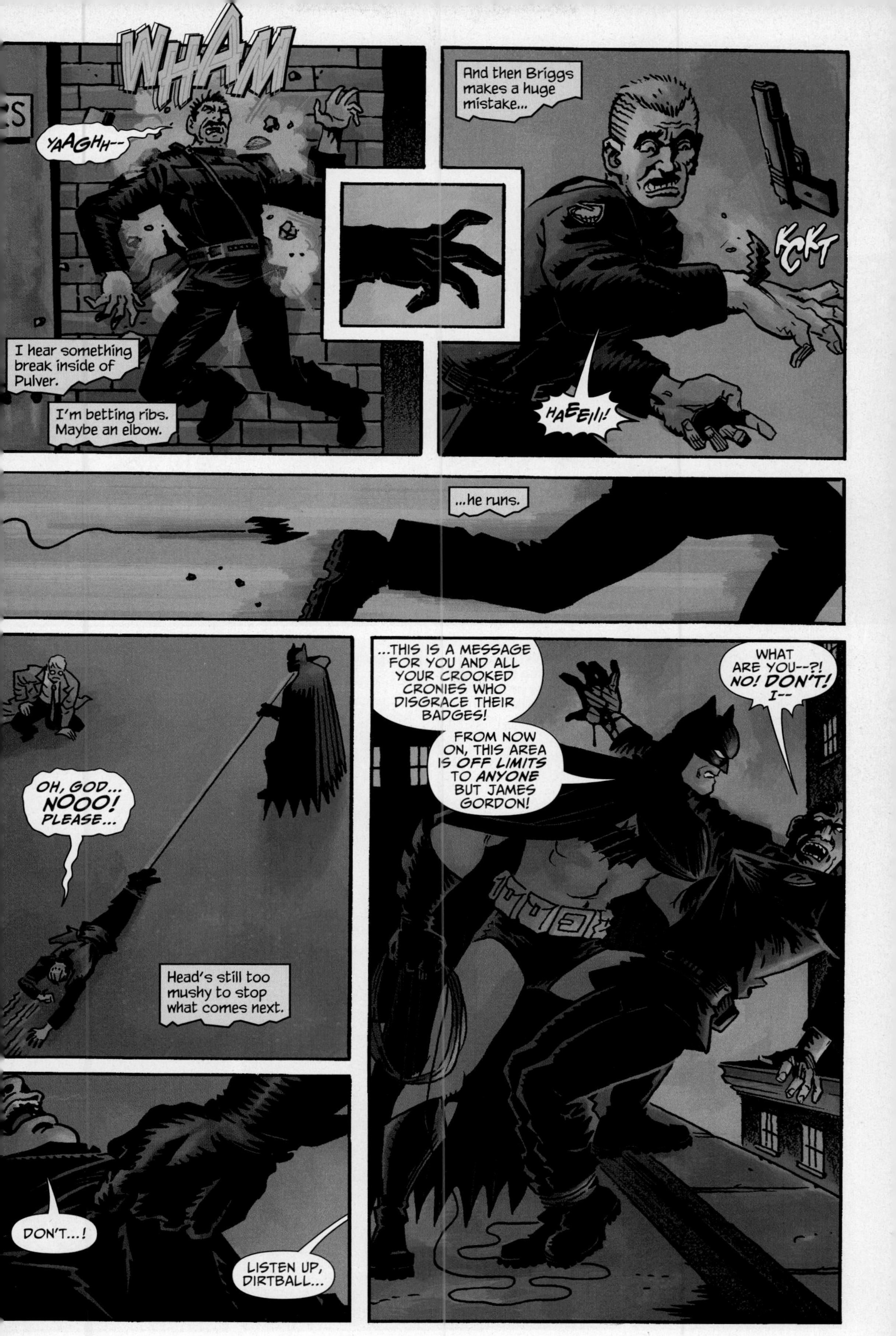
WHAM
YAAGHH--
I hear something break inside of Pulver.
I'm betting ribs. Maybe an elbow.
And then Briggs makes a huge mistake...
KCKT
HAEEIII!
...he runs.
OH, GOD... NOOO! PLEASE...
Head's still too mushy to stop what comes next.
DON'T...!
LISTEN UP, DIRTBALL...
...THIS IS A MESSAGE FOR YOU AND ALL YOUR CROOKED CRONIES WHO DISGRACE THEIR BADGES!
FROM NOW ON, THIS AREA IS OFF LIMITS TO ANYONE BUT JAMES GORDON!
WHAT ARE YOU--?! NO! DON'T! I--

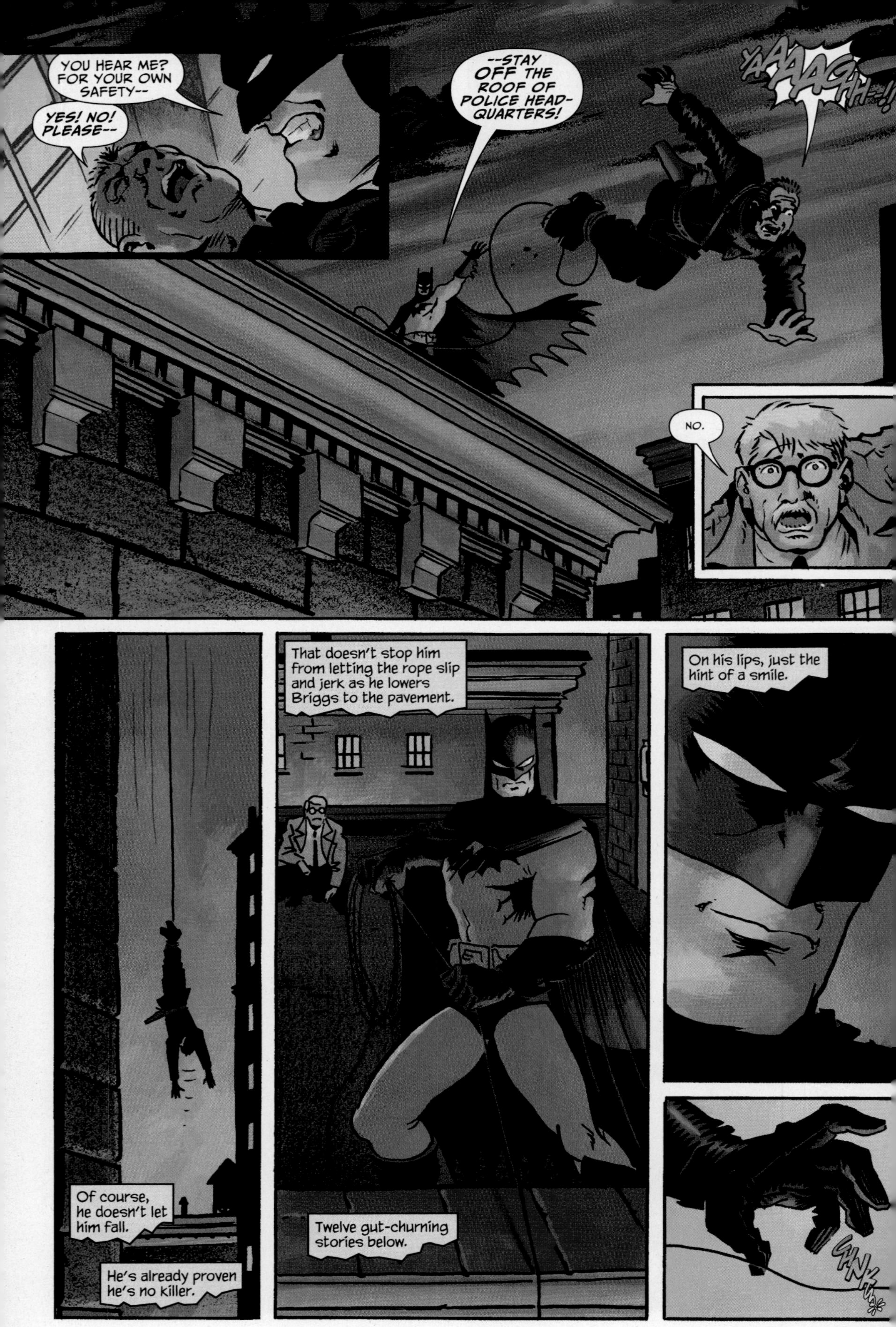
YOU HEAR ME? FOR YOUR OWN SAFETY--
YES! NO! PLEASE--
--STAY OFF THE ROOF OF POLICE HEAD-QUARTERS!
YAAAAGHH--!!
NO.
Of course, he doesn't let him fall.
He's already proven he's no killer.
That doesn't stop him from letting the rope slip and jerk as he lowers Briggs to the pavement.
Twelve gut-churning stories below.
On his lips, just the hint of a smile.

SORRY I WAS A BIT LATE. YOU OKAY?

I'VE BEEN WORSE. THANKS.

The Cat's drug still swirls inside me.

WHOA! THE QUESTION IS...ARE *YOU* OKAY? STEADY, MAN...

I'M...FINE. JUST--

Lucky fool. Taking on armed men with a head full of who knows what...

SO, WHERE'D YOU GET *THAT?*

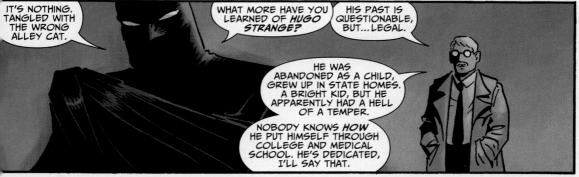

IT'S NOTHING. TANGLED WITH THE WRONG ALLEY CAT.

WHAT MORE HAVE YOU LEARNED OF *HUGO STRANGE?*

HIS PAST IS QUESTIONABLE, BUT...LEGAL.

HE WAS ABANDONED AS A CHILD, GREW UP IN STATE HOMES. A BRIGHT KID, BUT HE APPARENTLY HAD A HELL OF A TEMPER.

NOBODY KNOWS *HOW* HE PUT HIMSELF THROUGH COLLEGE AND MEDICAL SCHOOL. HE'S DEDICATED, I'LL SAY THAT.

LOOK, I KNOW I WASN'T QUITE ON BOARD WITH THIS AT FIRST, BUT AFTER SEEING THE STRINGS THE ROMAN HAS PULLED TO HUSH UP WHATEVER HAPPENED AT HIS COUNTRY ESTATE...

...AT THIS POINT ALL WE CAN DO IS KEEP A CLOSE EYE ON STRANGE. IF HE STEPS OUT OF LINE, MAYBE WE CAN NAIL HIM ON *SOMETHING.*

VERY WELL.

BUT THAT ISN'T WHY I CALLED YOU HERE TONIGHT.

SOMETHING...*NEW* HAS CROPPED UP THAT I'D LIKE YOU TO SEE.

WE NEED TO GO DOWN TO THE MORGUE.

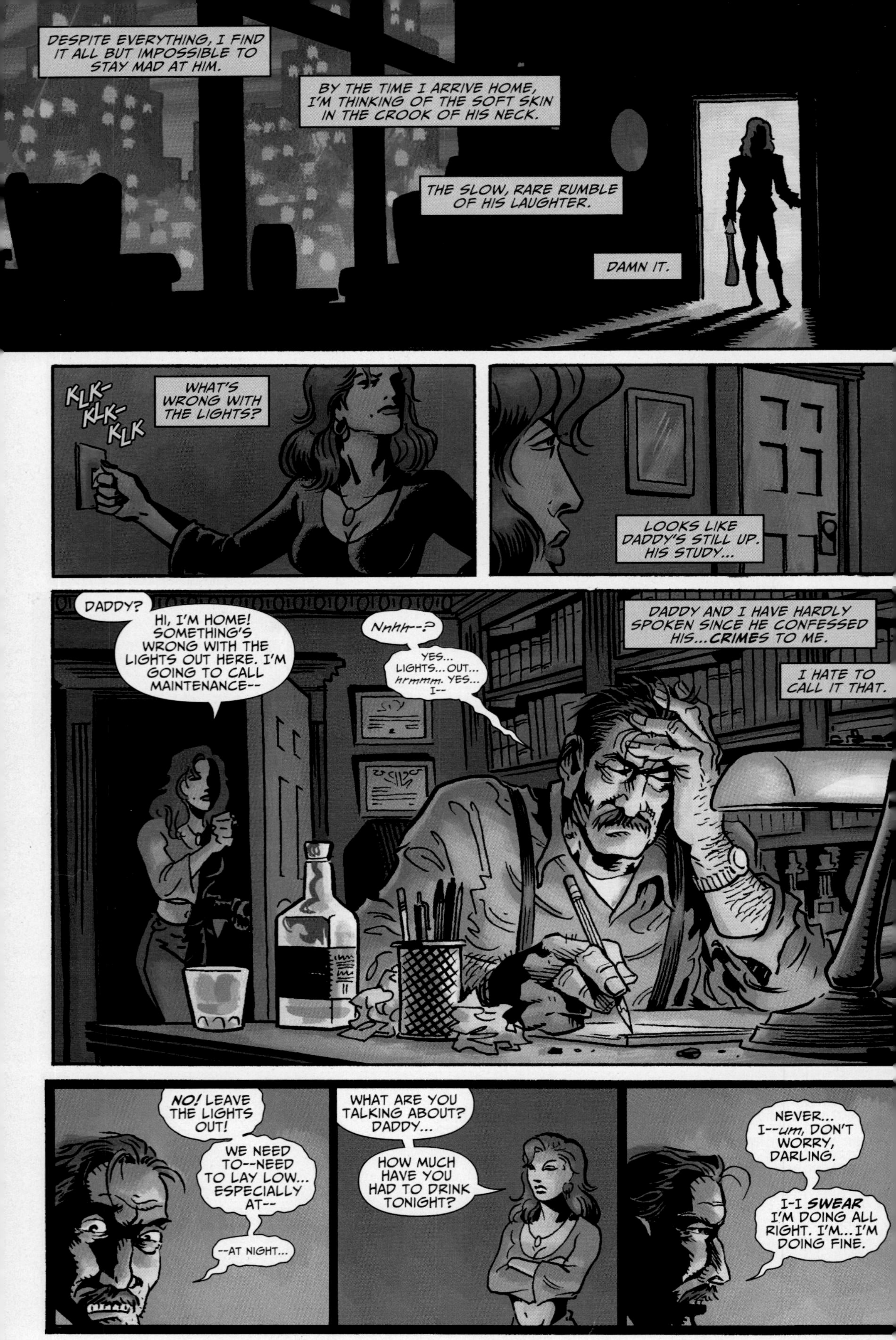
DESPITE EVERYTHING, I FIND IT ALL BUT IMPOSSIBLE TO STAY MAD AT HIM.
BY THE TIME I ARRIVE HOME, I'M THINKING OF THE SOFT SKIN IN THE CROOK OF HIS NECK.
THE SLOW, RARE RUMBLE OF HIS LAUGHTER.
DAMN IT.
KLK-KLK-KLK
WHAT'S WRONG WITH THE LIGHTS?
LOOKS LIKE DADDY'S STILL UP. HIS STUDY...
DADDY?
HI, I'M HOME! SOMETHING'S WRONG WITH THE LIGHTS OUT HERE. I'M GOING TO CALL MAINTENANCE--
Nnhh--?
YES... LIGHTS... OUT... hrmmm. YES... I--
DADDY AND I HAVE HARDLY SPOKEN SINCE HE CONFESSED HIS... CRIMES TO ME.
I HATE TO CALL IT THAT.
NO! LEAVE THE LIGHTS OUT!
WE NEED TO--NEED TO LAY LOW... ESPECIALLY AT--
--AT NIGHT...
WHAT ARE YOU TALKING ABOUT? DADDY...
HOW MUCH HAVE YOU HAD TO DRINK TONIGHT?
NEVER... I--um, DON'T WORRY, DARLING.
I-I SWEAR I'M DOING ALL RIGHT. I'M... I'M DOING FINE.

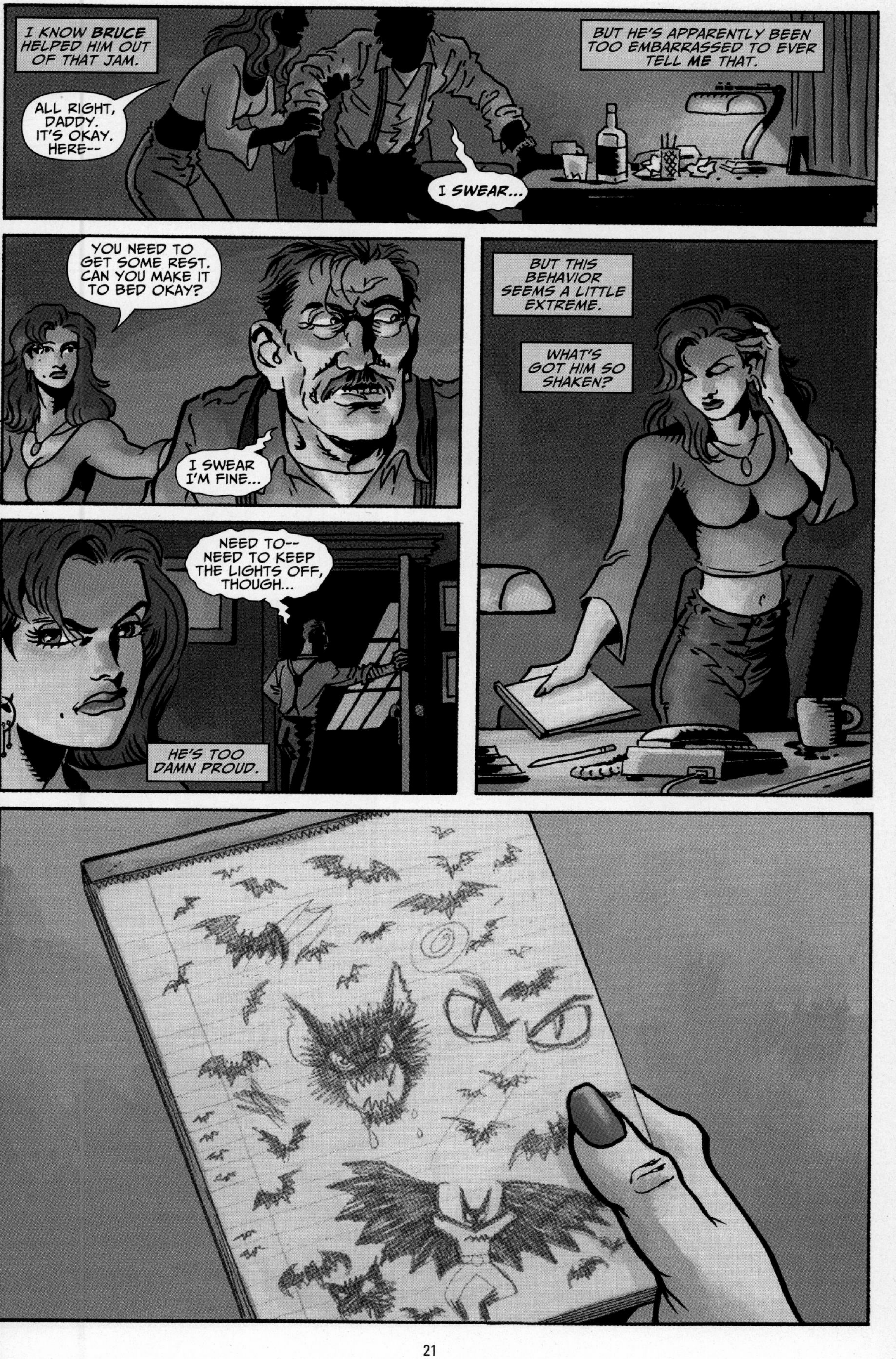

I KNOW BRUCE HELPED HIM OUT OF THAT JAM.
ALL RIGHT, DADDY. IT'S OKAY. HERE--
I SWEAR...
BUT HE'S APPARENTLY BEEN TOO EMBARRASSED TO EVER TELL ME THAT.
YOU NEED TO GET SOME REST. CAN YOU MAKE IT TO BED OKAY?
I SWEAR I'M FINE...
BUT THIS BEHAVIOR SEEMS A LITTLE EXTREME.
WHAT'S GOT HIM SO SHAKEN?
NEED TO-- NEED TO KEEP THE LIGHTS OFF, THOUGH...
HE'S TOO DAMN PROUD.

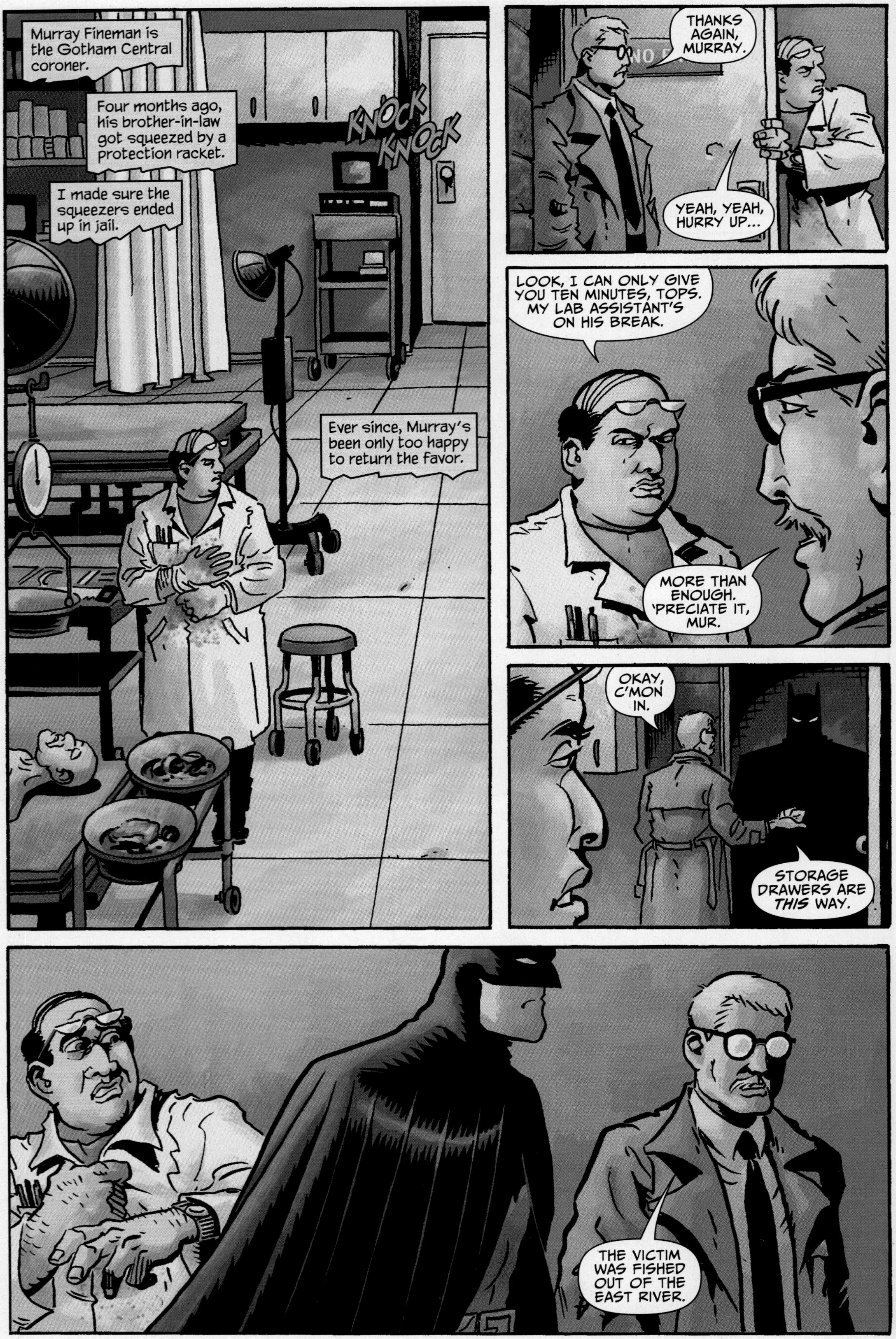
Murray Fineman is the Gotham Central coroner.
Four months ago, his brother-in-law got squeezed by a protection racket.
I made sure the squeezers ended up in jail.
KNOCK KNOCK
Ever since, Murray's been only too happy to return the favor.
THANKS AGAIN, MURRAY.
YEAH, YEAH, HURRY UP...
LOOK, I CAN ONLY GIVE YOU TEN MINUTES, TOPS. MY LAB ASSISTANT'S ON HIS BREAK.
MORE THAN ENOUGH. 'PRECIATE IT, MUR.
OKAY, C'MON IN.
STORAGE DRAWERS ARE *THIS* WAY.
THE VICTIM WAS FISHED OUT OF THE EAST RIVER.

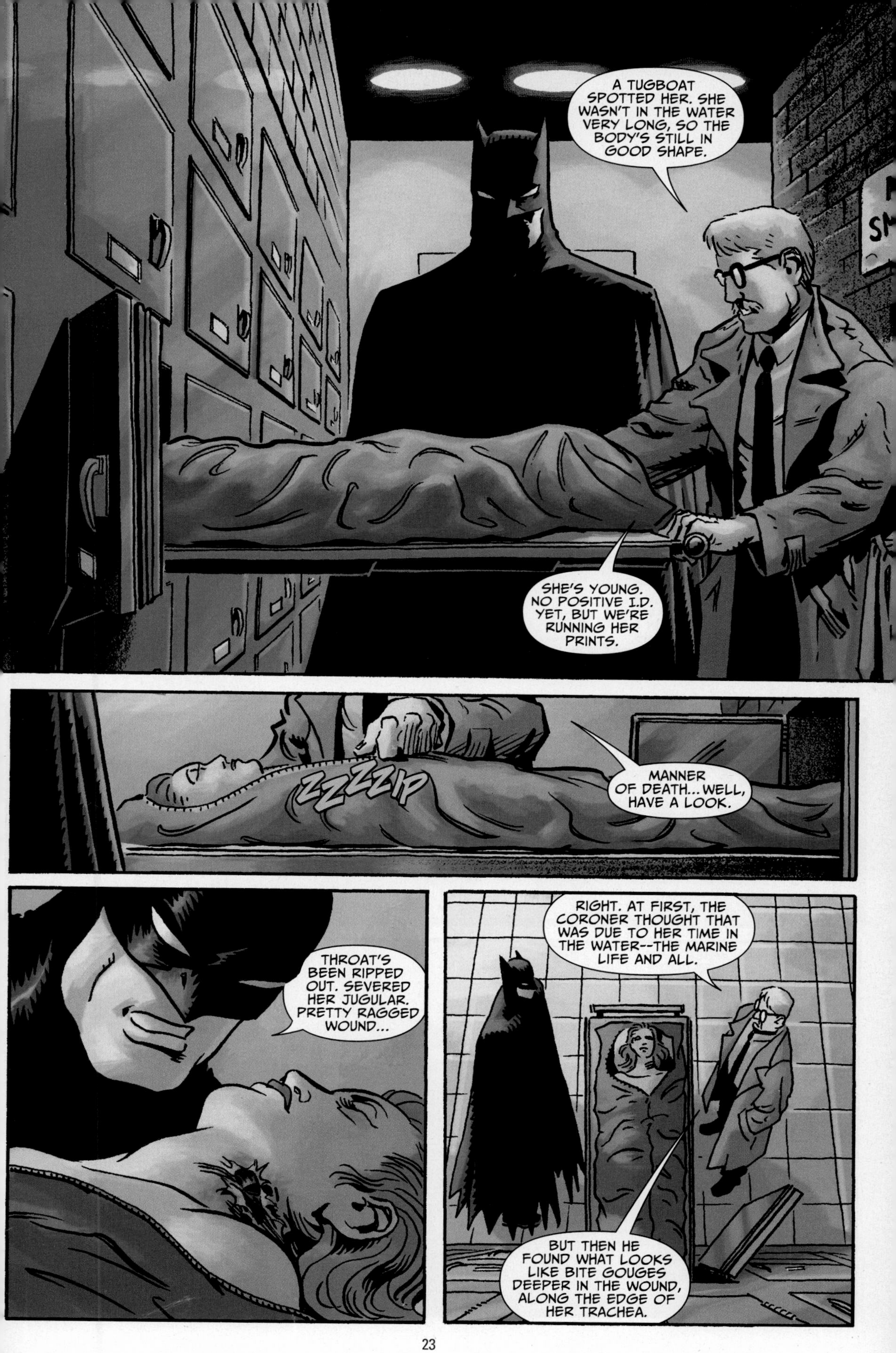
A TUGBOAT SPOTTED HER. SHE WASN'T IN THE WATER VERY LONG, SO THE BODY'S STILL IN GOOD SHAPE.
SHE'S YOUNG. NO POSITIVE I.D. YET, BUT WE'RE RUNNING HER PRINTS.
ZZZZIP
MANNER OF DEATH... WELL, HAVE A LOOK.
THROAT'S BEEN RIPPED OUT. SEVERED HER JUGULAR. PRETTY RAGGED WOUND...
RIGHT. AT FIRST, THE CORONER THOUGHT THAT WAS DUE TO HER TIME IN THE WATER--THE MARINE LIFE AND ALL.
BUT THEN HE FOUND WHAT LOOKS LIKE BITE GOUGES DEEPER IN THE WOUND, ALONG THE EDGE OF HER TRACHEA.

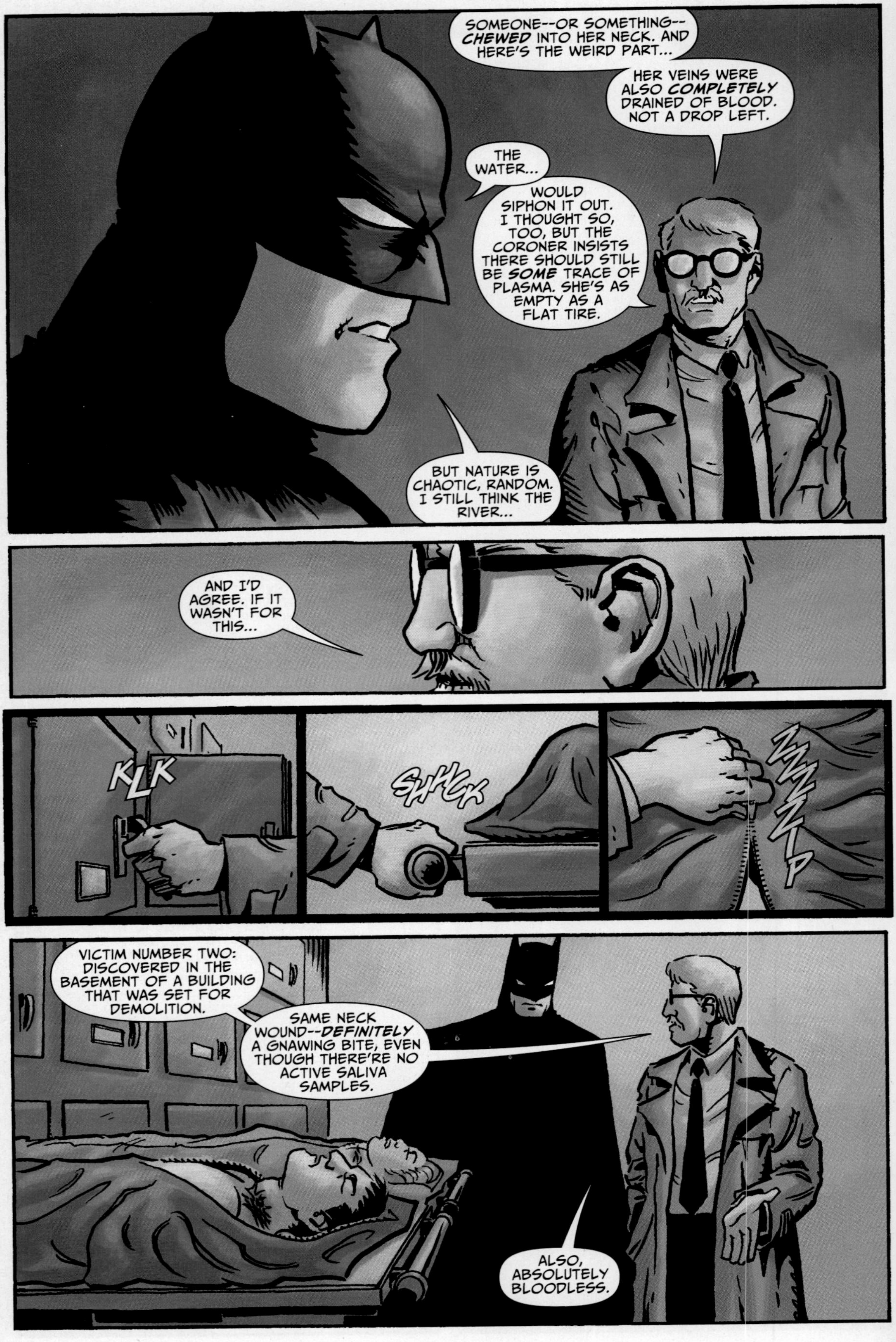
SOMEONE--OR SOMETHING--CHEWED INTO HER NECK. AND HERE'S THE WEIRD PART...
HER VEINS WERE ALSO COMPLETELY DRAINED OF BLOOD. NOT A DROP LEFT.
THE WATER...
WOULD SIPHON IT OUT. I THOUGHT SO, TOO, BUT THE CORONER INSISTS THERE SHOULD STILL BE SOME TRACE OF PLASMA. SHE'S AS EMPTY AS A FLAT TIRE.
BUT NATURE IS CHAOTIC, RANDOM. I STILL THINK THE RIVER...
AND I'D AGREE. IF IT WASN'T FOR THIS...
KLK
SHHCK
ZZZZIP
VICTIM NUMBER TWO: DISCOVERED IN THE BASEMENT OF A BUILDING THAT WAS SET FOR DEMOLITION.
SAME NECK WOUND--DEFINITELY A GNAWING BITE, EVEN THOUGH THERE'RE NO ACTIVE SALIVA SAMPLES.
ALSO, ABSOLUTELY BLOODLESS.

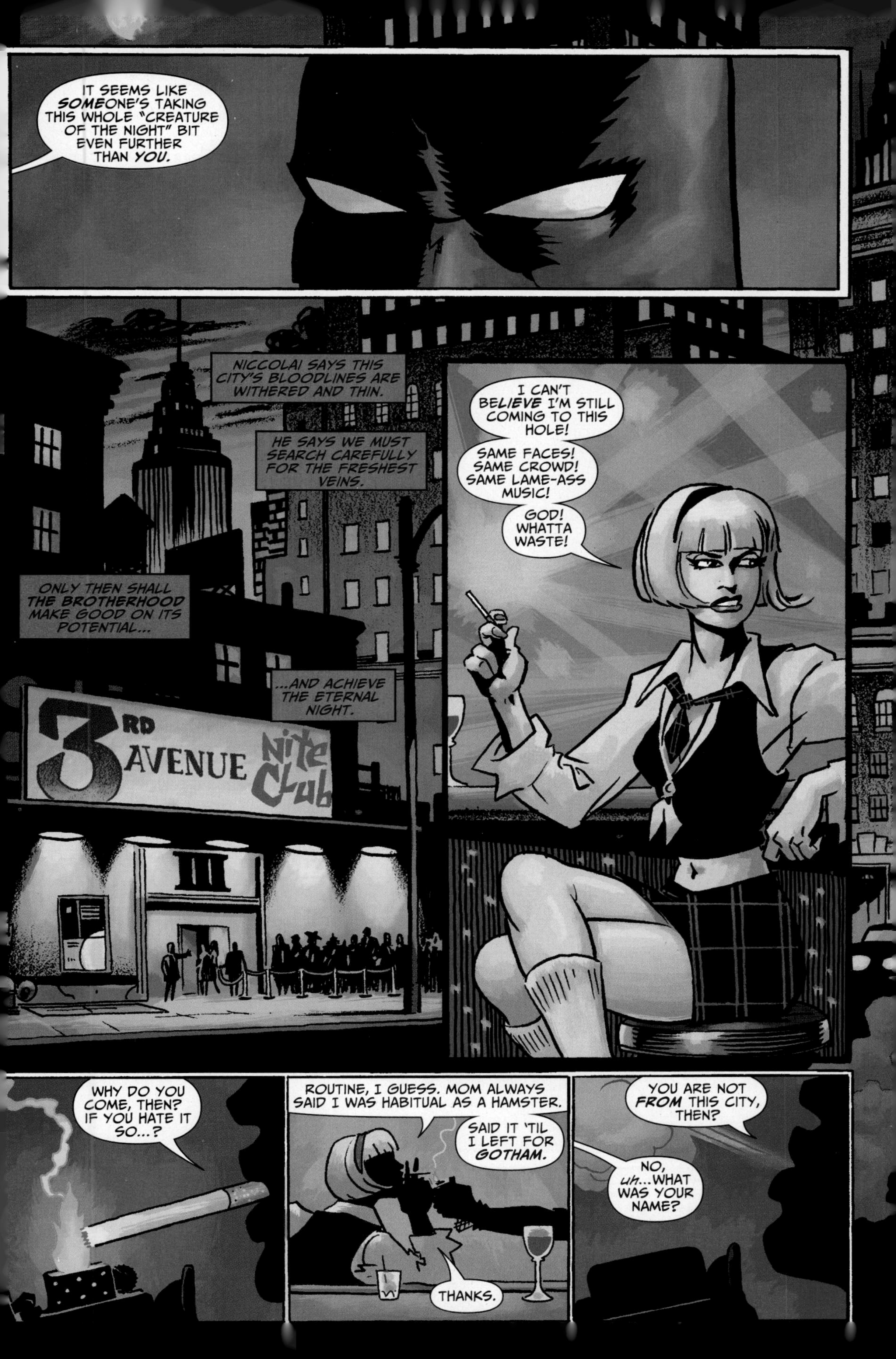

IT SEEMS LIKE SOMEONE'S TAKING THIS WHOLE "CREATURE OF THE NIGHT" BIT EVEN FURTHER THAN YOU.
NICCOLAI SAYS THIS CITY'S BLOODLINES ARE WITHERED AND THIN.
HE SAYS WE MUST SEARCH CAREFULLY FOR THE FRESHEST VEINS.
ONLY THEN SHALL THE BROTHERHOOD MAKE GOOD ON ITS POTENTIAL...
...AND ACHIEVE THE ETERNAL NIGHT.
3RD AVENUE Nite Club
III
I CAN'T BELIEVE I'M STILL COMING TO THIS HOLE!
SAME FACES! SAME CROWD! SAME LAME-ASS MUSIC!
GOD! WHATTA WASTE!
WHY DO YOU COME, THEN? IF YOU HATE IT SO...?
ROUTINE, I GUESS. MOM ALWAYS SAID I WAS HABITUAL AS A HAMSTER.
SAID IT 'TIL I LEFT FOR GOTHAM.
THANKS.
YOU ARE NOT FROM THIS CITY, THEN?
NO, uh...WHAT WAS YOUR NAME?

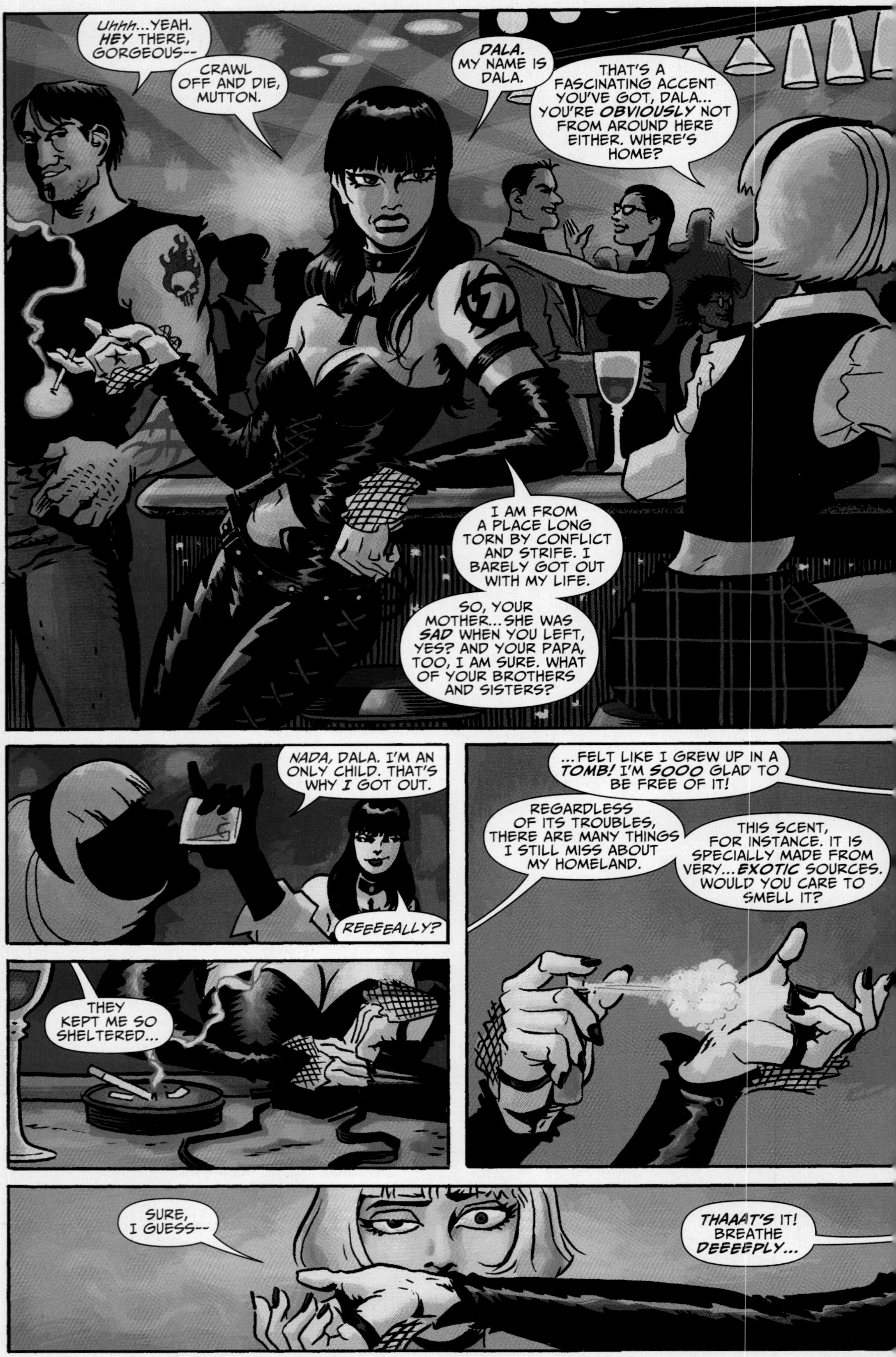
Uhhh...YEAH. HEY THERE, GORGEOUS--
CRAWL OFF AND DIE, MUTTON.
DALA. MY NAME IS DALA.
THAT'S A FASCINATING ACCENT YOU'VE GOT, DALA... YOU'RE OBVIOUSLY NOT FROM AROUND HERE EITHER. WHERE'S HOME?
I AM FROM A PLACE LONG TORN BY CONFLICT AND STRIFE. I BARELY GOT OUT WITH MY LIFE.
SO, YOUR MOTHER...SHE WAS SAD WHEN YOU LEFT, YES? AND YOUR PAPA, TOO, I AM SURE. WHAT OF YOUR BROTHERS AND SISTERS?
NADA, DALA. I'M AN ONLY CHILD. THAT'S WHY I GOT OUT.
REEEEALLY?
THEY KEPT ME SO SHELTERED...
...FELT LIKE I GREW UP IN A TOMB! I'M SOOO GLAD TO BE FREE OF IT!
REGARDLESS OF ITS TROUBLES, THERE ARE MANY THINGS I STILL MISS ABOUT MY HOMELAND.
THIS SCENT, FOR INSTANCE. IT IS SPECIALLY MADE FROM VERY...EXOTIC SOURCES. WOULD YOU CARE TO SMELL IT?
SURE, I GUESS--
THAAAT'S IT! BREATHE DEEEEPLY...

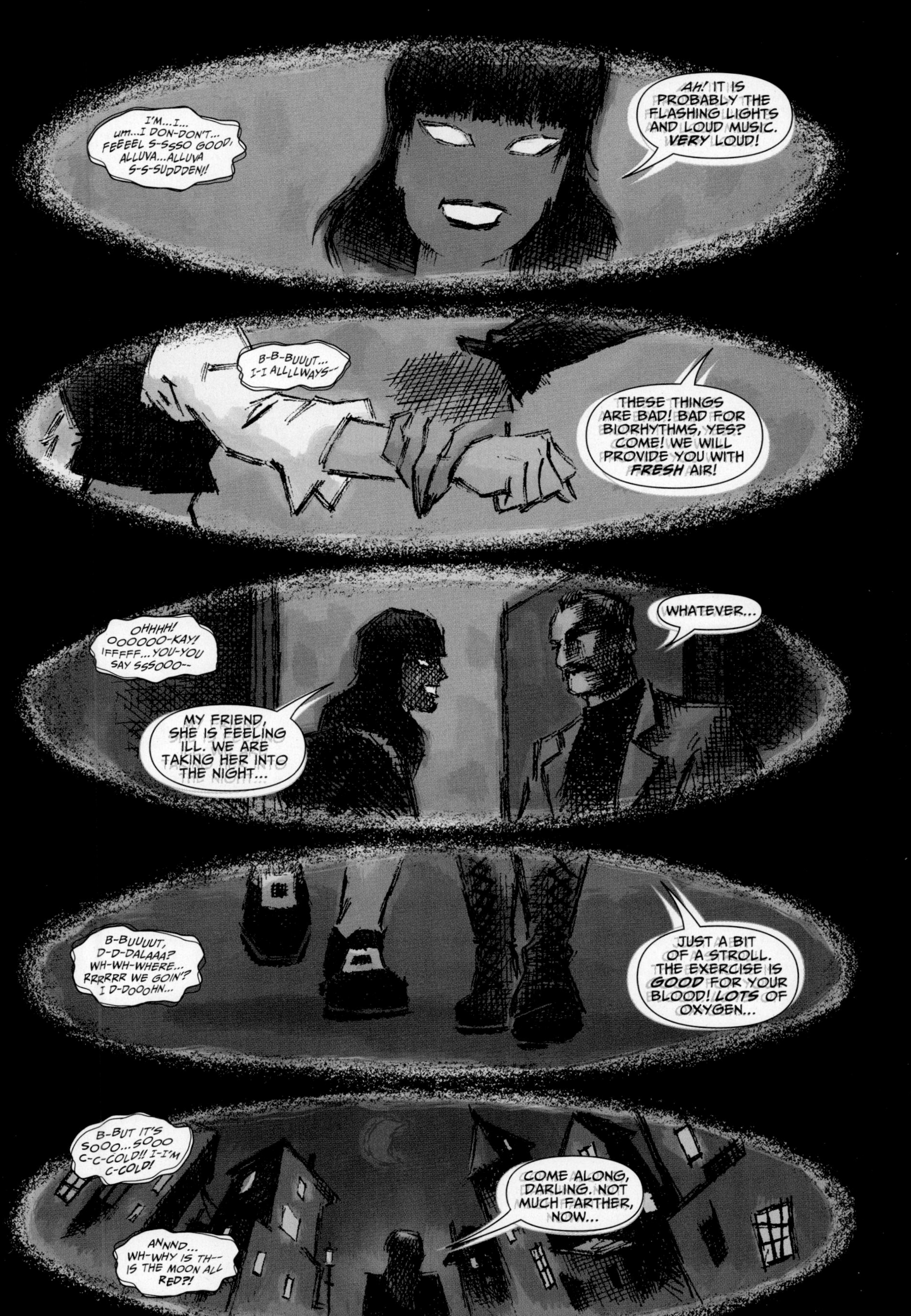
I'M...I... um...I DON-DON'T... FEEEEL S-SSSO GOOD, ALLUVA...ALLUVA S-S-SUDDDEN!!
AH! IT IS PROBABLY THE FLASHING LIGHTS AND LOUD MUSIC. VERY LOUD!
B-B-BUUUT... I-I ALLLLWAYS--
THESE THINGS ARE BAD! BAD FOR BIORHYTHMS, YES? COME! WE WILL PROVIDE YOU WITH FRESH AIR!
OHHHH! OOOOOO-KAY! IFFFFF...YOU-YOU SAY SSSOOO--
MY FRIEND, SHE IS FEELING ILL. WE ARE TAKING HER INTO THE NIGHT...
WHATEVER...
B-BUUUUT, D-D-DALAAA? WH-WH-WHERE... RRRRRR WE GOIN'? I D-DOOOHN...
JUST A BIT OF A STROLL. THE EXERCISE IS GOOD FOR YOUR BLOOD! LOTS OF OXYGEN...
B-BUT IT'S SOOO...SOOO C-C-COLD!! I-I'M C-COLD!
COME ALONG, DARLING. NOT MUCH FARTHER, NOW...
ANNND... WH-WHY IS TH-- IS THE MOON ALL RED?!

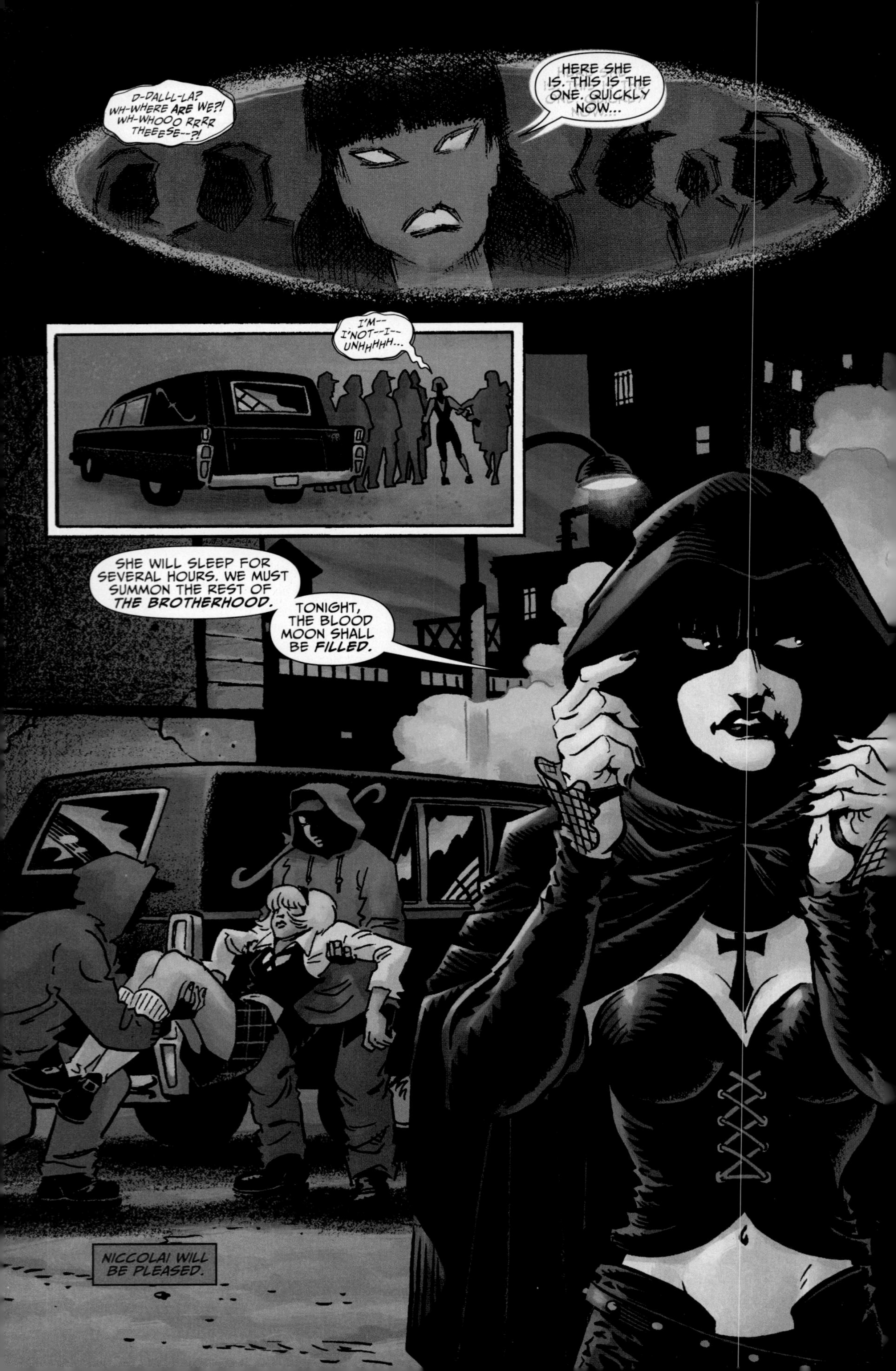
D-DALLL-LA? WH-WHERE ARE WE?! WH-WHOOO RRRR THEEESE--?!
HERE SHE IS. THIS IS THE ONE. QUICKLY NOW...
I'M-- I'NOT--I-- UNHHHHH...
SHE WILL SLEEP FOR SEVERAL HOURS. WE MUST SUMMON THE REST OF THE BROTHERHOOD.
TONIGHT, THE BLOOD MOON SHALL BE FILLED.
NICCOLAI WILL BE PLEASED.

CHAPTER 2

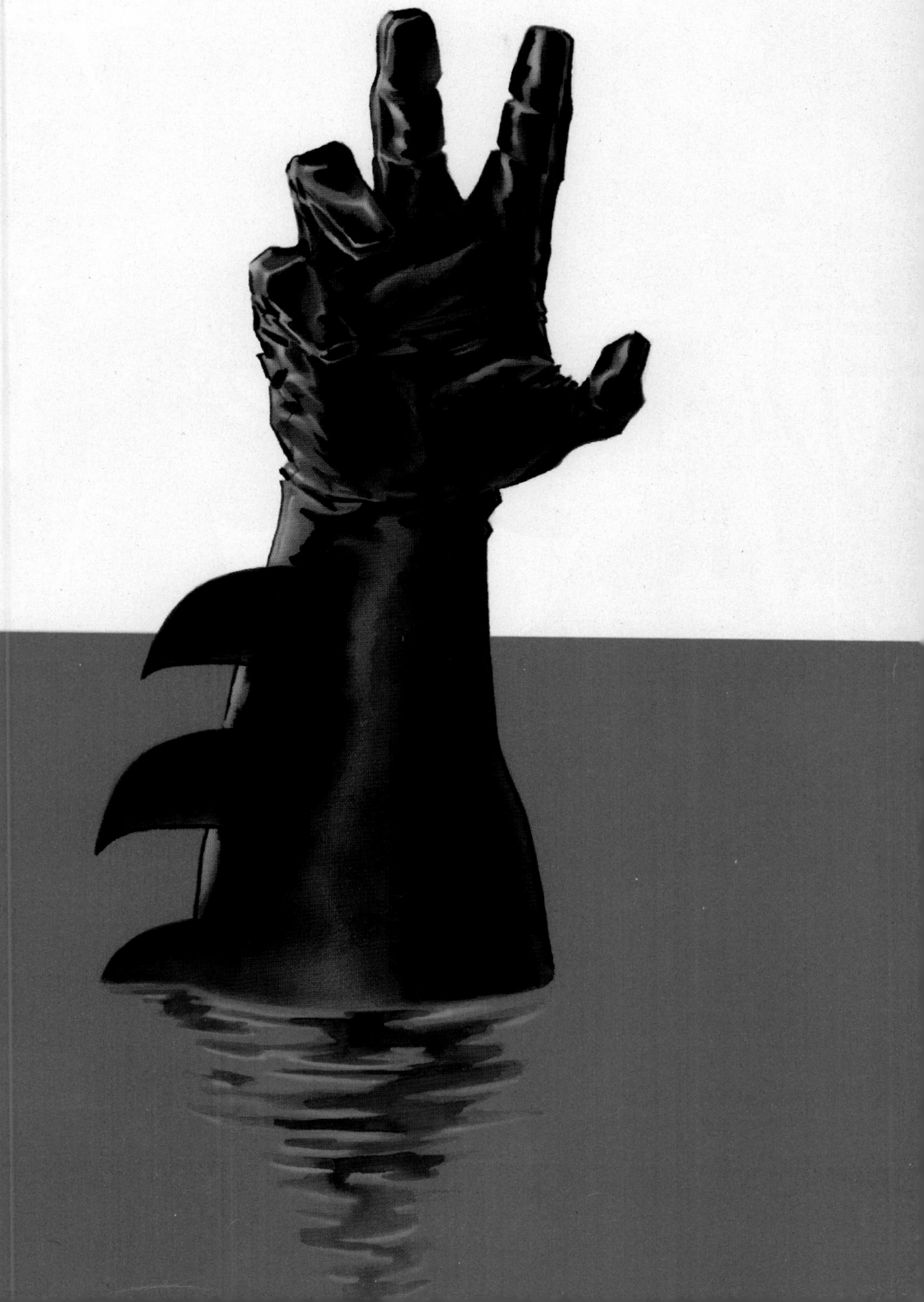

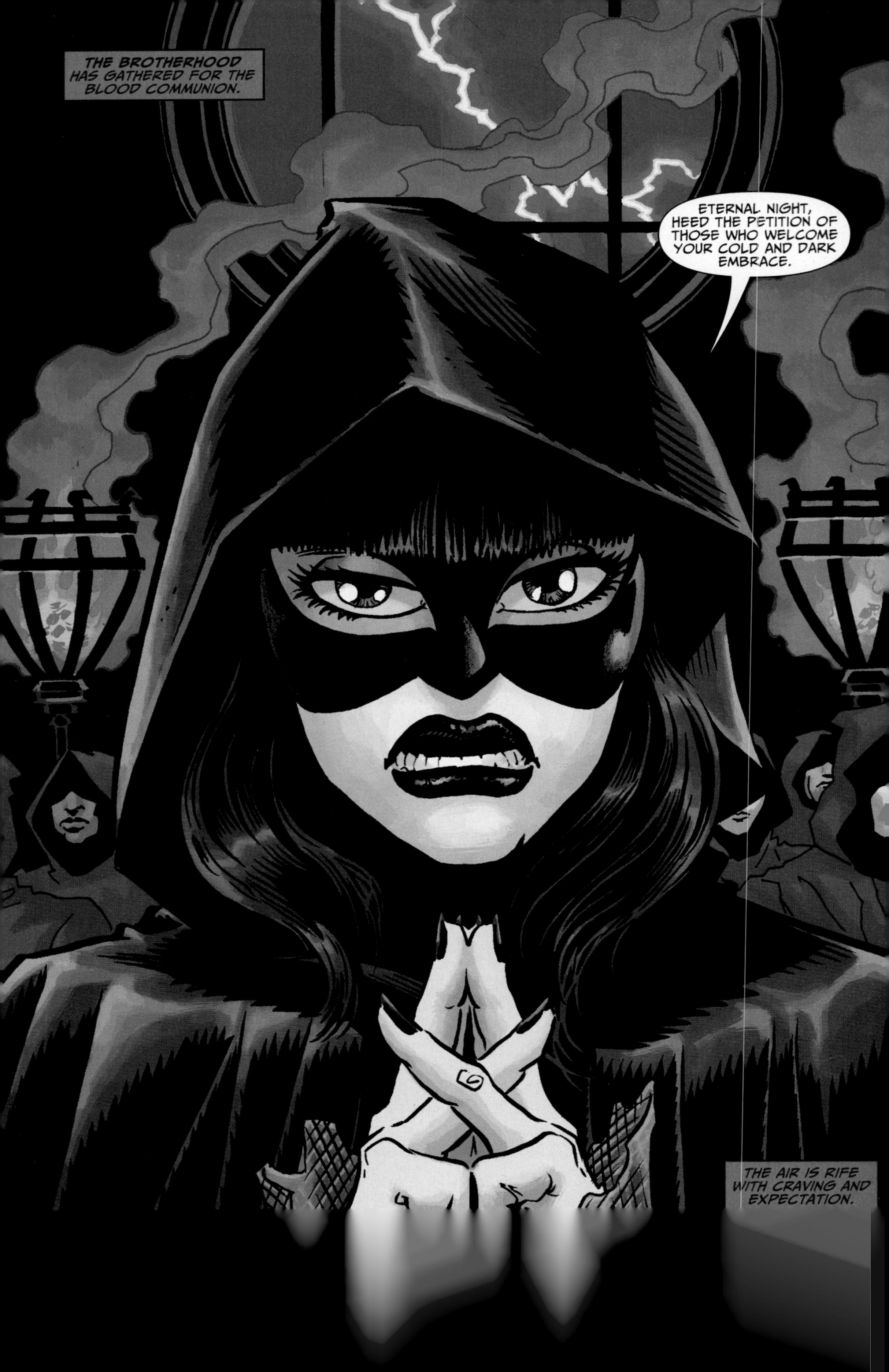
THE BROTHERHOOD HAS GATHERED FOR THE BLOOD COMMUNION.
ETERNAL NIGHT, HEED THE PETITION OF THOSE WHO WELCOME YOUR COLD AND DARK EMBRACE.
THE AIR IS RIFE WITH CRAVING AND EXPECTATION.

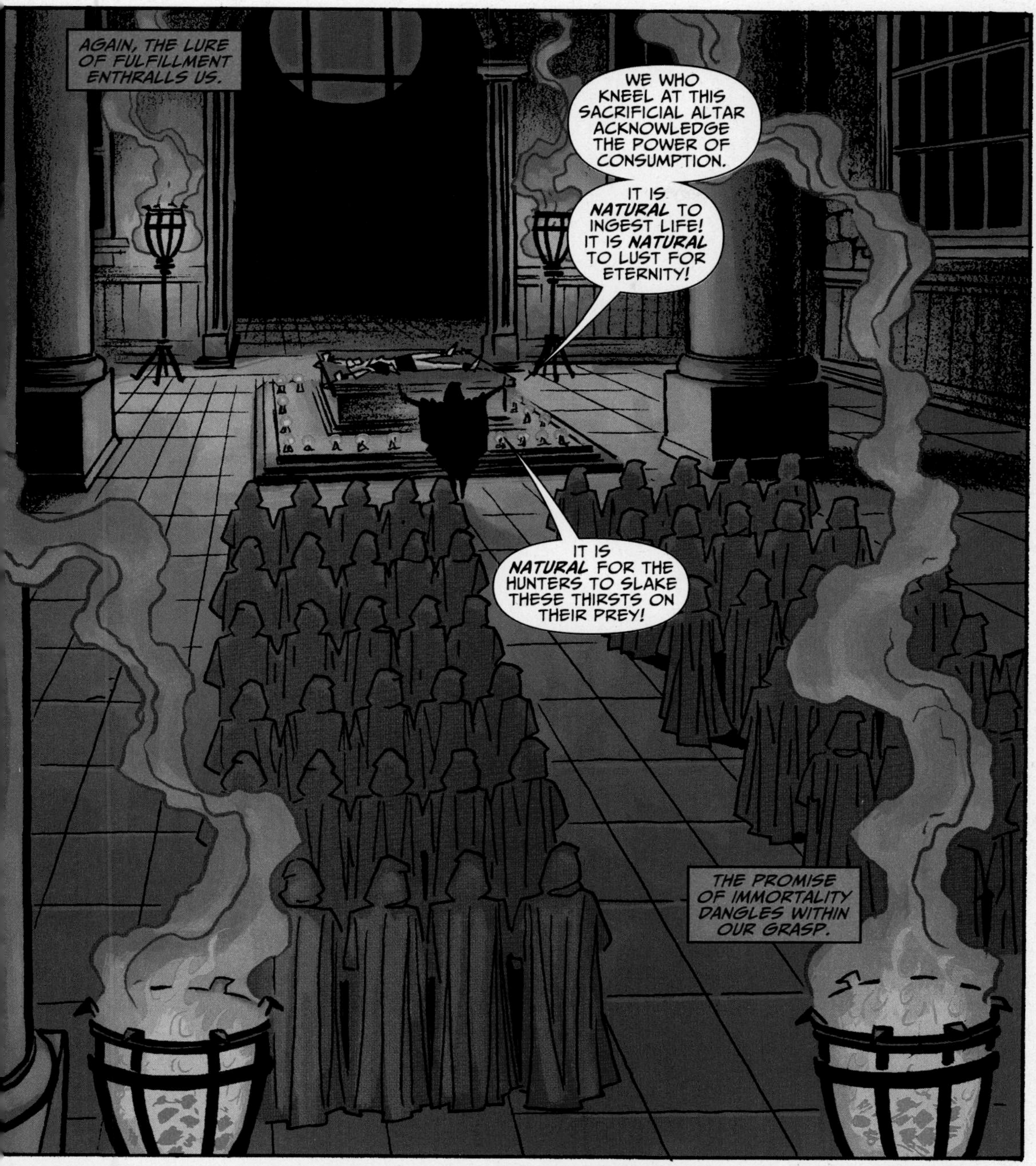
AGAIN, THE LURE OF FULFILLMENT ENTHRALLS US.
WE WHO KNEEL AT THIS SACRIFICIAL ALTAR ACKNOWLEDGE THE POWER OF CONSUMPTION.
IT IS *NATURAL* TO INGEST LIFE! IT IS *NATURAL* TO LUST FOR ETERNITY!
IT IS *NATURAL* FOR THE HUNTERS TO SLAKE THESE THIRSTS ON THEIR PREY!
THE PROMISE OF IMMORTALITY DANGLES WITHIN OUR GRASP.

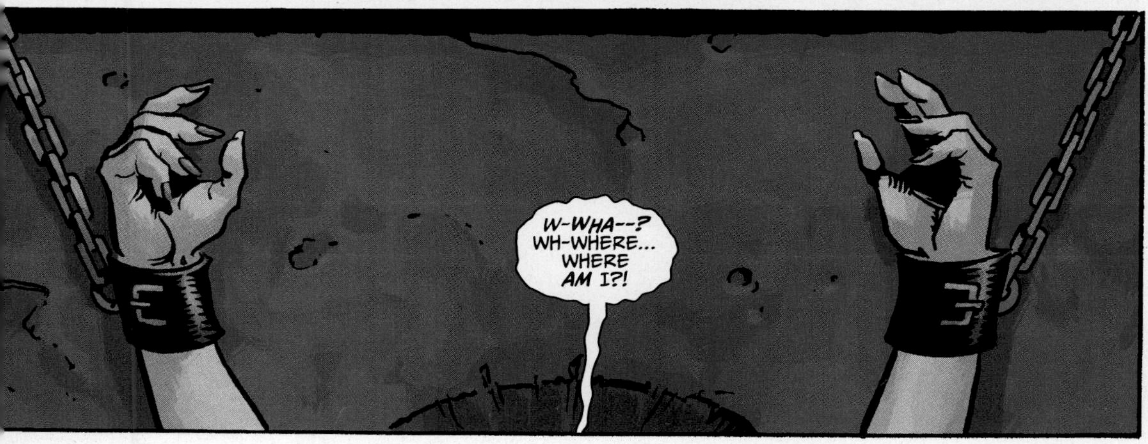
W-WHA--? WH-WHERE... WHERE *AM* I?!

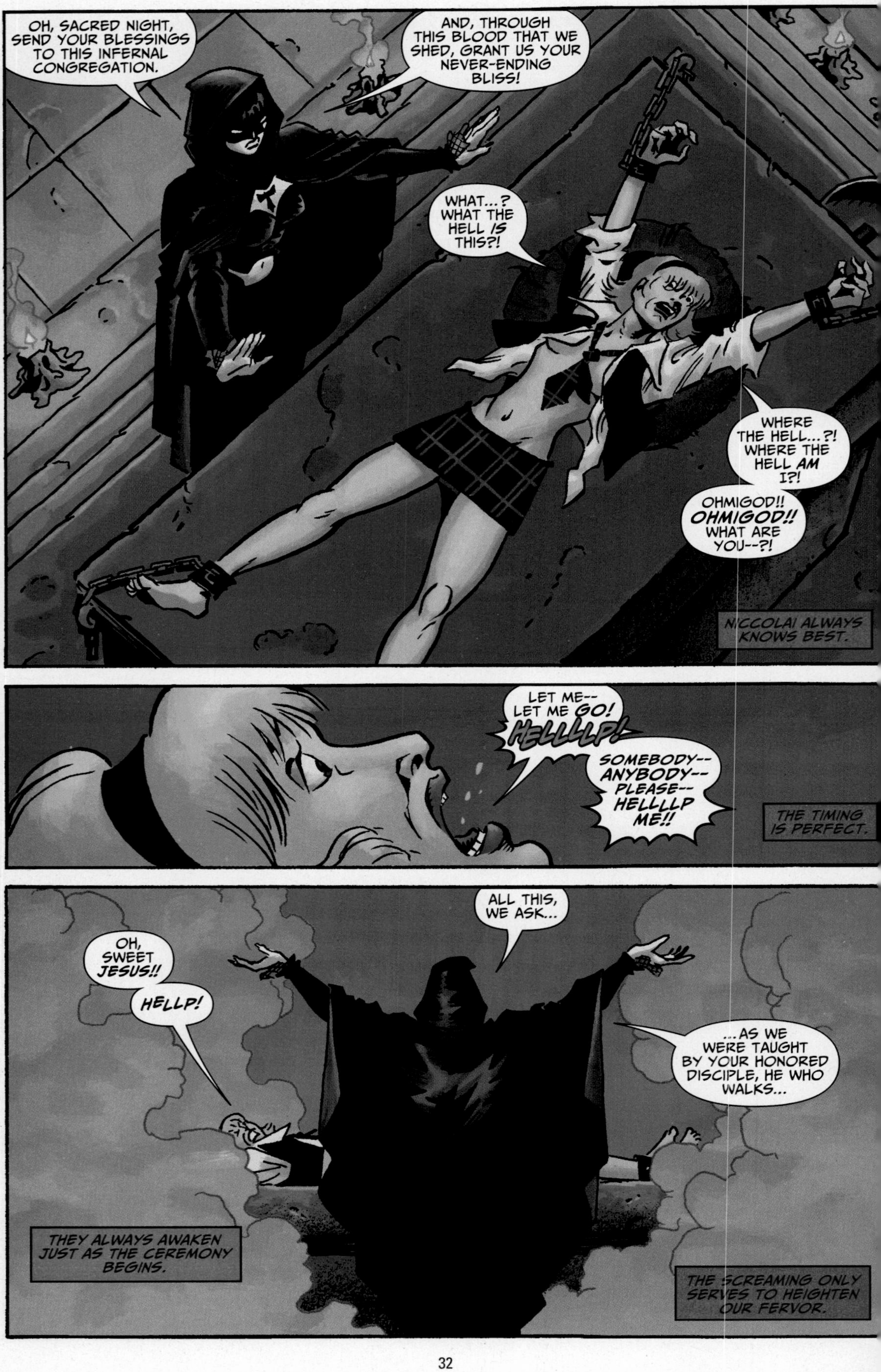
OH, SACRED NIGHT, SEND YOUR BLESSINGS TO THIS INFERNAL CONGREGATION.
AND, THROUGH THIS BLOOD THAT WE SHED, GRANT US YOUR NEVER-ENDING BLISS!
WHAT...? WHAT THE HELL IS THIS?!
WHERE THE HELL...?! WHERE THE HELL AM I?!
OHMIGOD!! OHMIGOD!! WHAT ARE YOU--?!
NICCOLAI ALWAYS KNOWS BEST.
LET ME-- LET ME GO! HELLLLP!
SOMEBODY-- ANYBODY-- PLEASE-- HELLLLP ME!!
THE TIMING IS PERFECT.
ALL THIS, WE ASK...
OH, SWEET JESUS!!
HELLP!
...AS WE WERE TAUGHT BY YOUR HONORED DISCIPLE, HE WHO WALKS...
THEY ALWAYS AWAKEN JUST AS THE CEREMONY BEGINS.
THE SCREAMING ONLY SERVES TO HEIGHTEN OUR FERVOR.

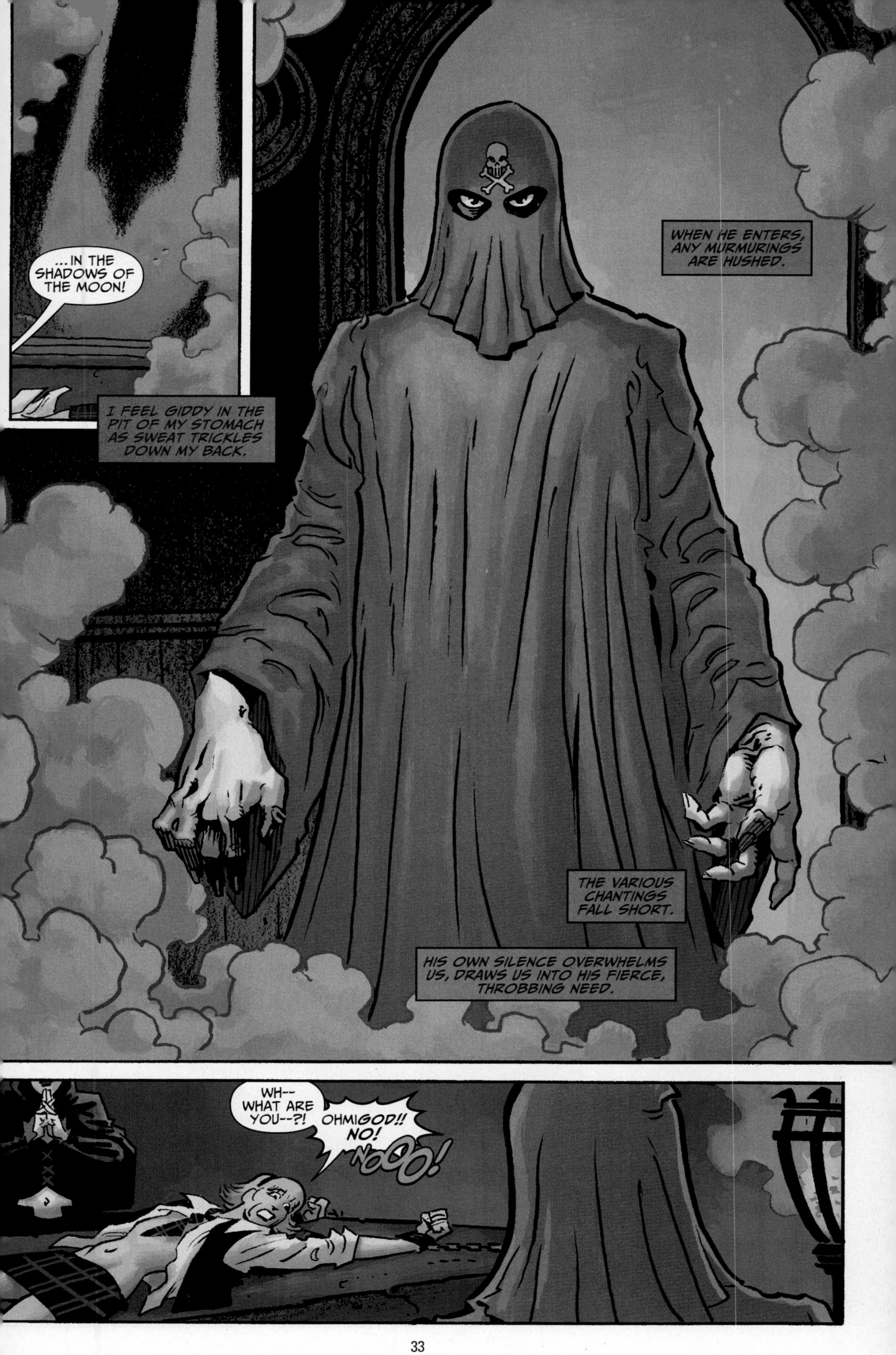

...IN THE SHADOWS OF THE MOON!
I FEEL GIDDY IN THE PIT OF MY STOMACH AS SWEAT TRICKLES DOWN MY BACK.
WHEN HE ENTERS, ANY MURMURINGS ARE HUSHED.
THE VARIOUS CHANTINGS FALL SHORT.
HIS OWN SILENCE OVERWHELMS US, DRAWS US INTO HIS FIERCE, THROBBING NEED.
WH-- WHAT ARE YOU--?!
OHMIGOD!! NO! NOOO!

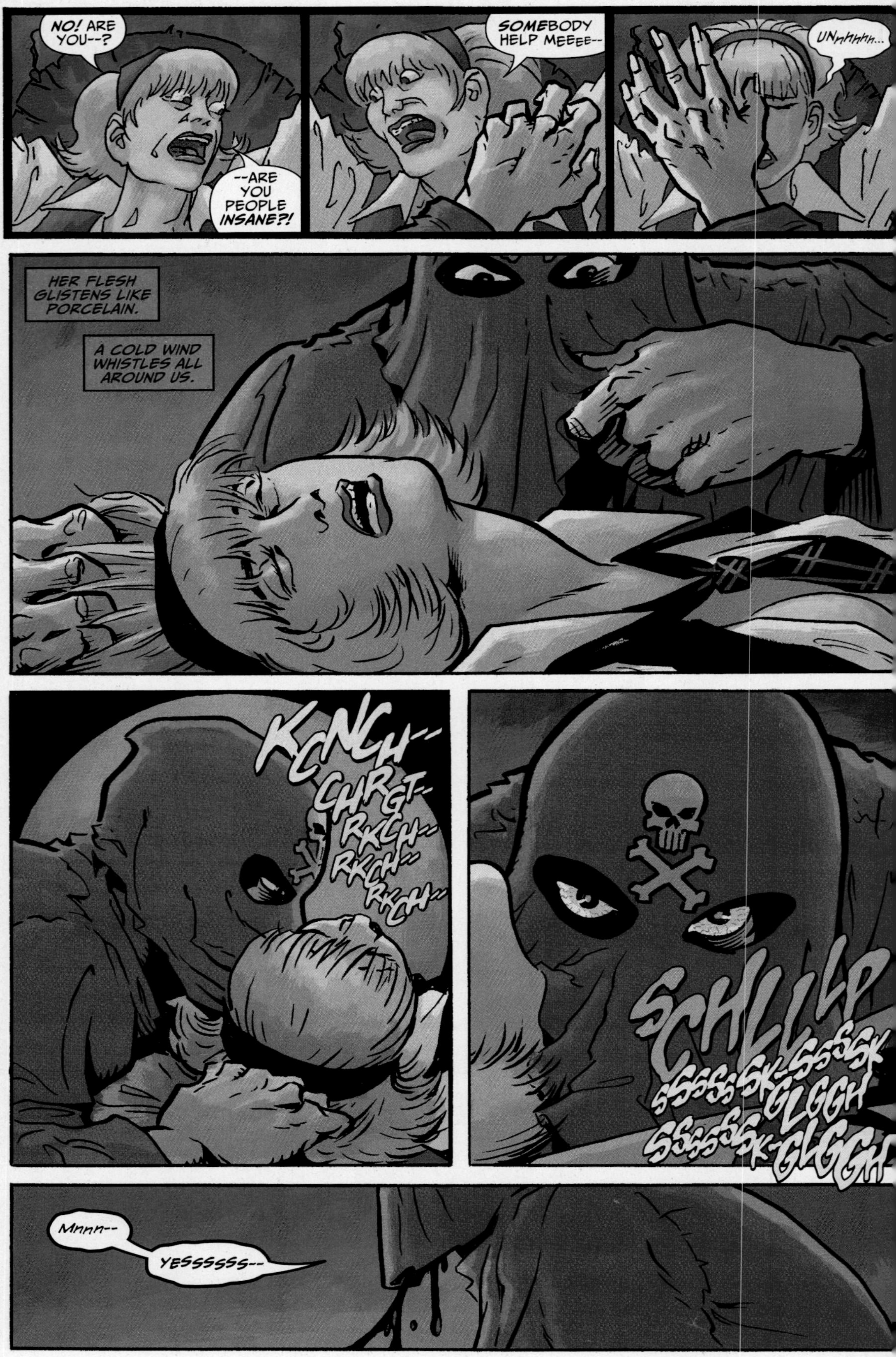
NO! ARE YOU--?
--ARE YOU PEOPLE INSANE?!
SOMEBODY HELP MEEEE--
UNnhhhh...
HER FLESH GLISTENS LIKE PORCELAIN.
A COLD WIND WHISTLES ALL AROUND US.
KCNCH--
CHRGT--
RKCH--
RKCH--
RKCH--
SCHLLP
SSSSSSK-SSSSK
GLGGH
SSSSSSK-GLGGH
Mnnn--
YESSSSSS--

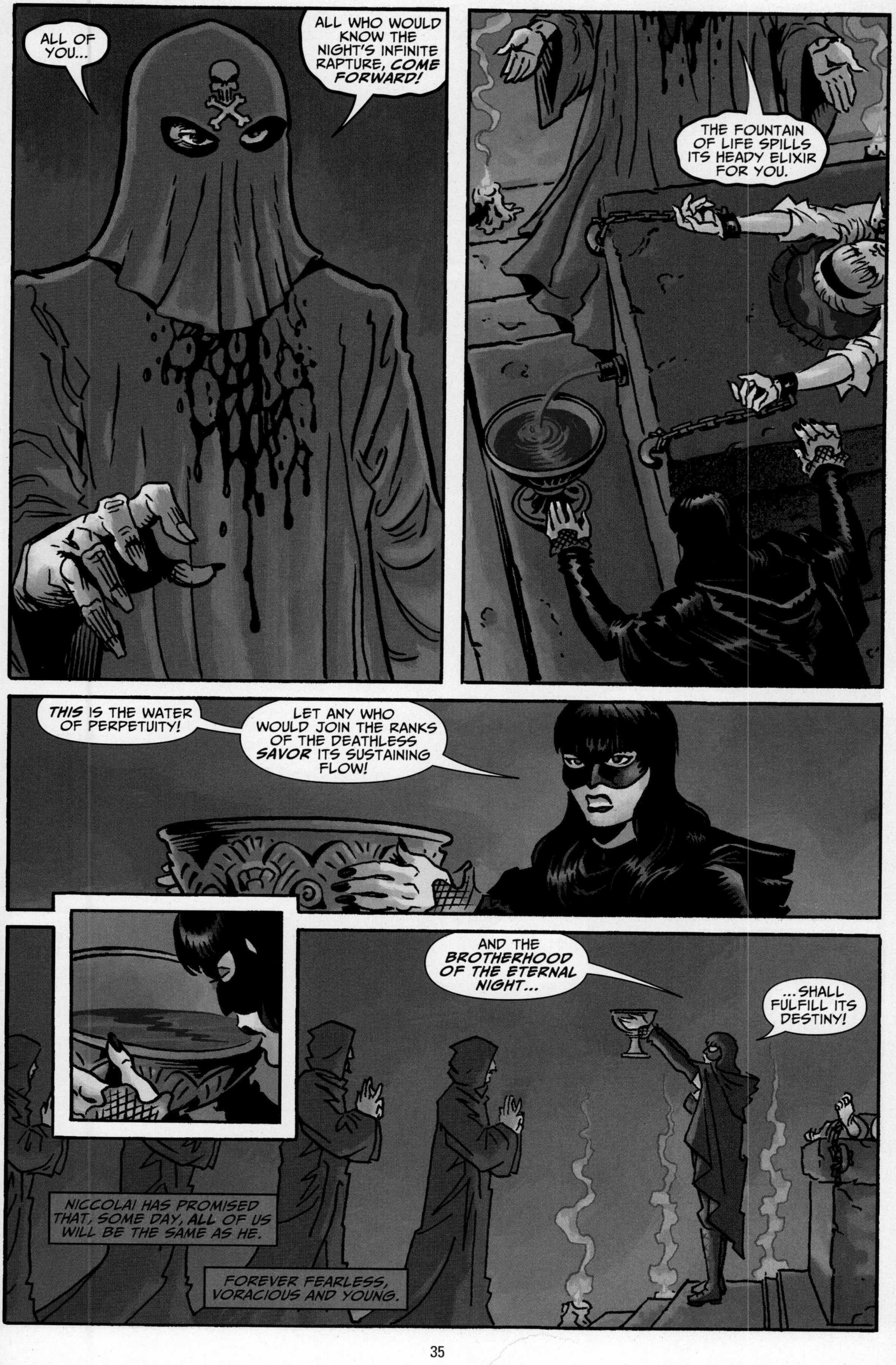
ALL OF YOU...
ALL WHO WOULD KNOW THE NIGHT'S INFINITE RAPTURE, *COME FORWARD!*
THE FOUNTAIN OF LIFE SPILLS ITS HEADY ELIXIR FOR YOU.
THIS IS THE WATER OF PERPETUITY!
LET ANY WHO WOULD JOIN THE RANKS OF THE DEATHLESS *SAVOR* ITS SUSTAINING FLOW!
AND THE *BROTHERHOOD OF THE ETERNAL NIGHT...*
...SHALL FULFILL ITS DESTINY!
NICCOLAI HAS PROMISED THAT, SOME DAY, ALL OF US WILL BE THE SAME AS HE.
FOREVER FEARLESS, VORACIOUS AND YOUNG.

BRUCE... I'M--I'M WORRIED ABOUT MY FATHER...

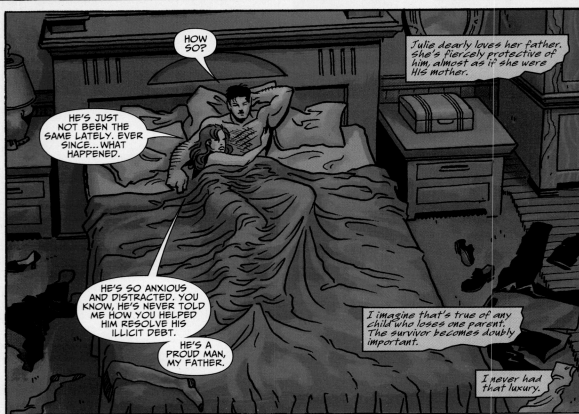

HOW SO?

HE'S JUST NOT BEEN THE SAME LATELY. EVER SINCE...WHAT HAPPENED.

Julie dearly loves her father. She's fiercely protective of him, almost as if she were HIS mother.

HE'S SO ANXIOUS AND DISTRACTED. YOU KNOW, HE'S NEVER TOLD ME HOW YOU HELPED HIM RESOLVE HIS ILLICIT DEBT.

HE'S A PROUD MAN, MY FATHER.

I imagine that's true of any child who loses one parent. The survivor becomes doubly important.

I never had that luxury.

I JUST WISH HE COULD LEARN TO FORGIVE HIMSELF.

LIKE *I* HAVE.

HE MAY JUST NEED MORE TIME...

≷*sigh*≷ PERHAPS. THEY SAY IT *DOES* HEAL ALL WOUNDS.

SPEAKING OF WHICH...

...BRUCE, WHERE'D YOU GET THESE *SCRATCHES* ON YOUR CHEST?

I'LL SAY HIS FOR YOU, MADISON...

YOU ARE ONE *PERSISTENT* PAIN-IN-THE-ASS!

YOU WANTED TO TALK TO ME SO BADLY?

SO *TALK!!*

I HAD... *um--*

I HAD *HOPED* THAT WE COULD HAVE A *PRIVATE* CONFERENCE TO DISCUSS OUR... *OUTSTANDING* BUSINESS, MARONI.

NEVER IN MY WILDEST DREAMS HAD I EVER IMAGINED WALKING INTO THE OFFICES OF A CHEAP THUG LIKE *SAL MARONI.*

BUT THEN...I HAVE DONE *MANY* THINGS I'D HAVE NEVER IMAGINED, OF LATE.

FORGET IT, NORMAN. IN CASE YOU AIN'T NOTICED, WE GOT A *WHOLE* NEW CREW AROUND HERE. *WHOLE* NEW CREW.

YOU WANTED A POWWOW AND YOU GOT IT, BUT ON *MY* TERMS. NOW *STOP* WASTIN' MY TIME!

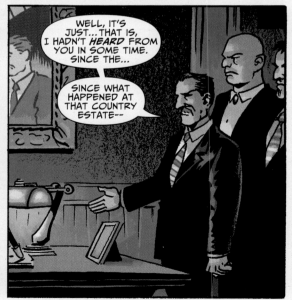

WELL, IT'S JUST... THAT IS, I HADN'T *HEARD* FROM YOU IN SOME TIME. SINCE THE...

SINCE WHAT HAPPENED AT THAT COUNTRY ESTATE--

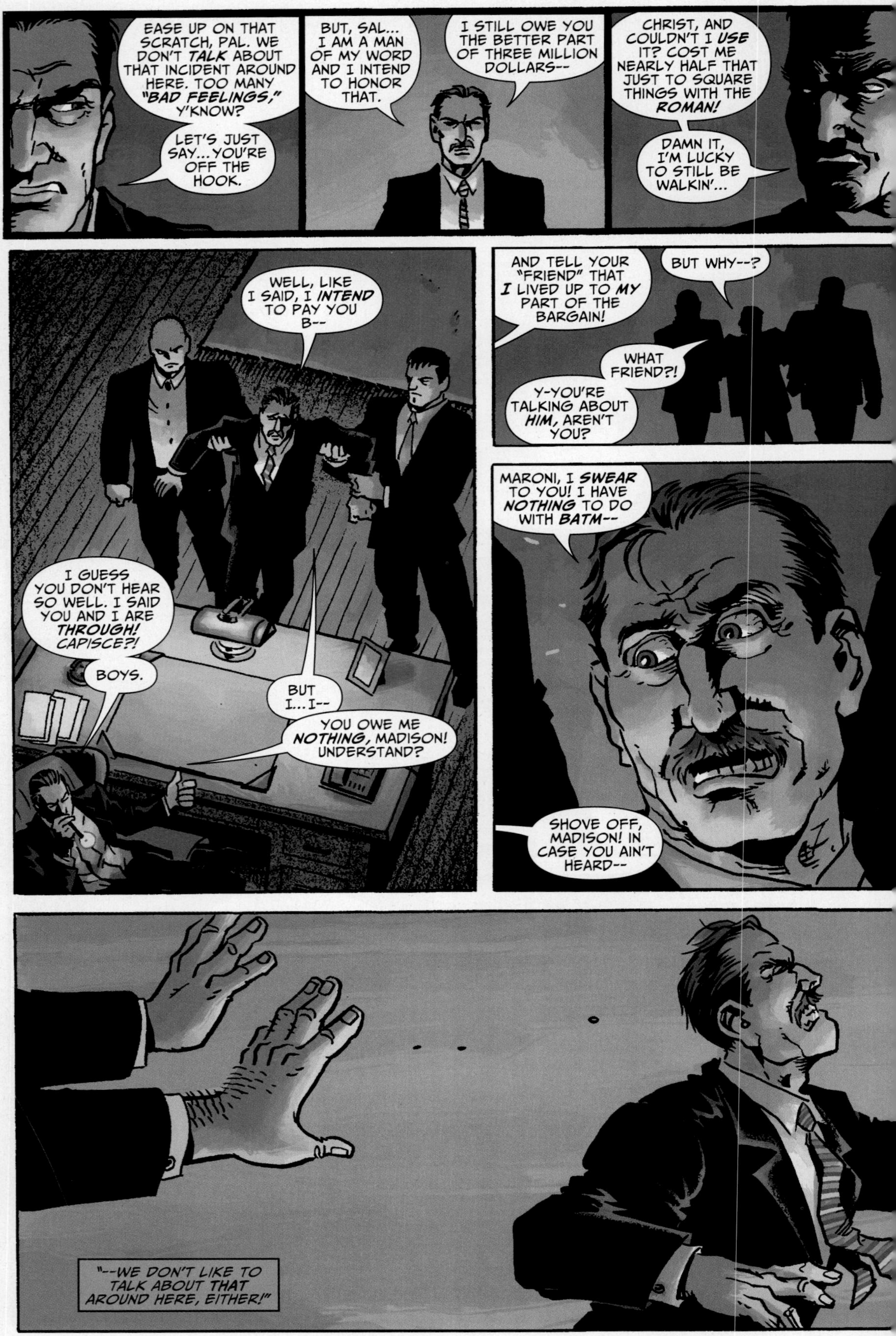
EASE UP ON THAT SCRATCH, PAL. WE DON'T TALK ABOUT THAT INCIDENT AROUND HERE. TOO MANY "BAD FEELINGS," Y'KNOW?
LET'S JUST SAY...YOU'RE OFF THE HOOK.
BUT, SAL... I AM A MAN OF MY WORD AND I INTEND TO HONOR THAT.
I STILL OWE YOU THE BETTER PART OF THREE MILLION DOLLARS--
CHRIST, AND COULDN'T I USE IT? COST ME NEARLY HALF THAT JUST TO SQUARE THINGS WITH THE ROMAN!
DAMN IT, I'M LUCKY TO STILL BE WALKIN'...
WELL, LIKE I SAID, I INTEND TO PAY YOU B--
I GUESS YOU DON'T HEAR SO WELL. I SAID YOU AND I ARE THROUGH! CAPISCE?!
BOYS.
BUT I...I--
YOU OWE ME NOTHING, MADISON! UNDERSTAND?
AND TELL YOUR "FRIEND" THAT I LIVED UP TO MY PART OF THE BARGAIN!
BUT WHY--?
WHAT FRIEND?!
Y-YOU'RE TALKING ABOUT HIM, AREN'T YOU?
MARONI, I SWEAR TO YOU! I HAVE NOTHING TO DO WITH BATM--
SHOVE OFF, MADISON! IN CASE YOU AIN'T HEARD--
"--WE DON'T LIKE TO TALK ABOUT THAT AROUND HERE, EITHER!"

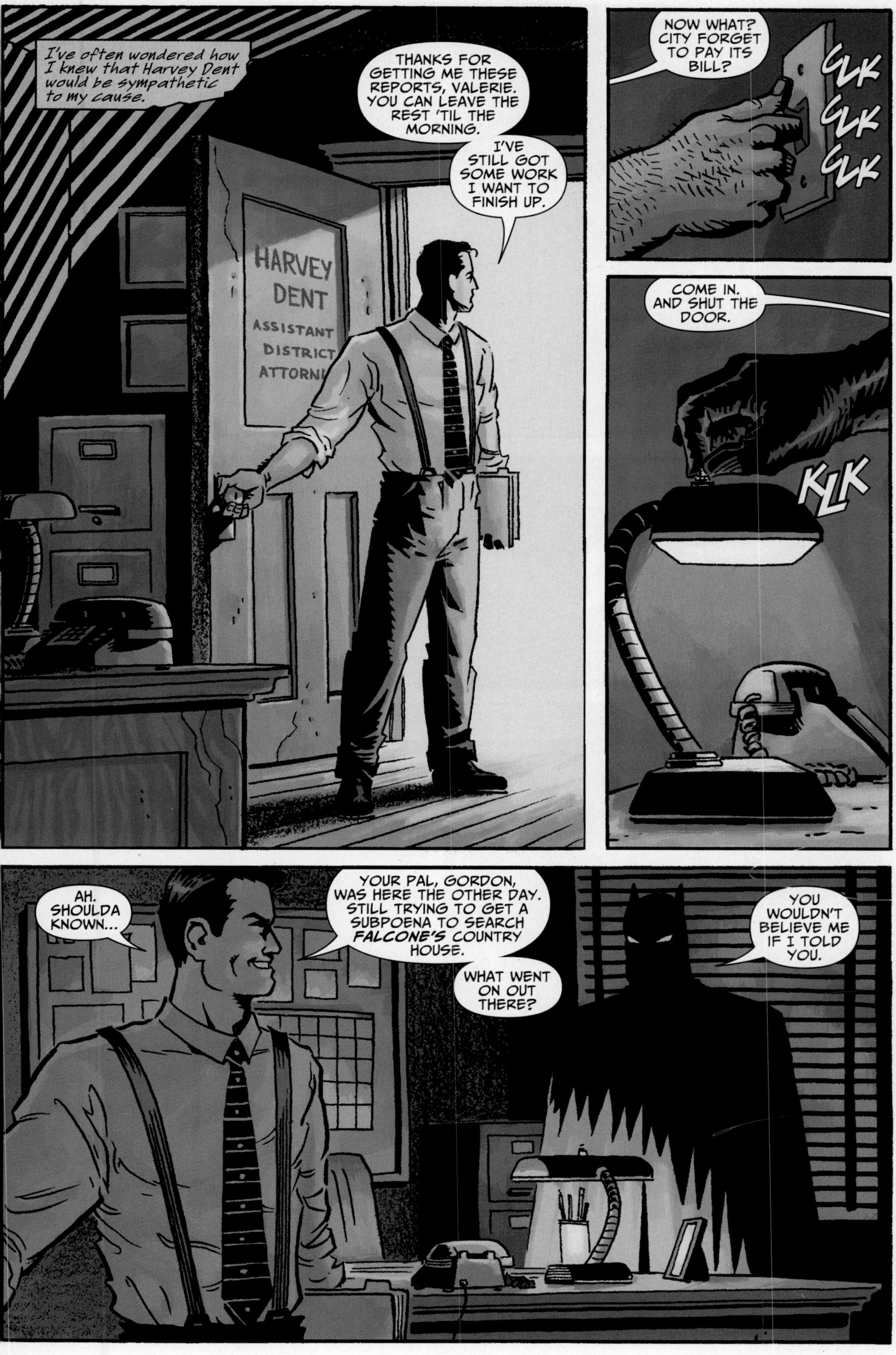
I've often wondered how I knew that Harvey Dent would be sympathetic to my cause.
THANKS FOR GETTING ME THESE REPORTS, VALERIE. YOU CAN LEAVE THE REST 'TIL THE MORNING.
I'VE STILL GOT SOME WORK I WANT TO FINISH UP.
HARVEY DENT ASSISTANT DISTRICT ATTORN
NOW WHAT? CITY FORGET TO PAY ITS BILL?
CLK CLK CLK
COME IN. AND SHUT THE DOOR.
KLK
AH. SHOULDA KNOWN...
YOUR PAL, GORDON, WAS HERE THE OTHER DAY. STILL TRYING TO GET A SUBPOENA TO SEARCH FALCONE'S COUNTRY HOUSE.
WHAT WENT ON OUT THERE?
YOU WOULDN'T BELIEVE ME IF I TOLD YOU.

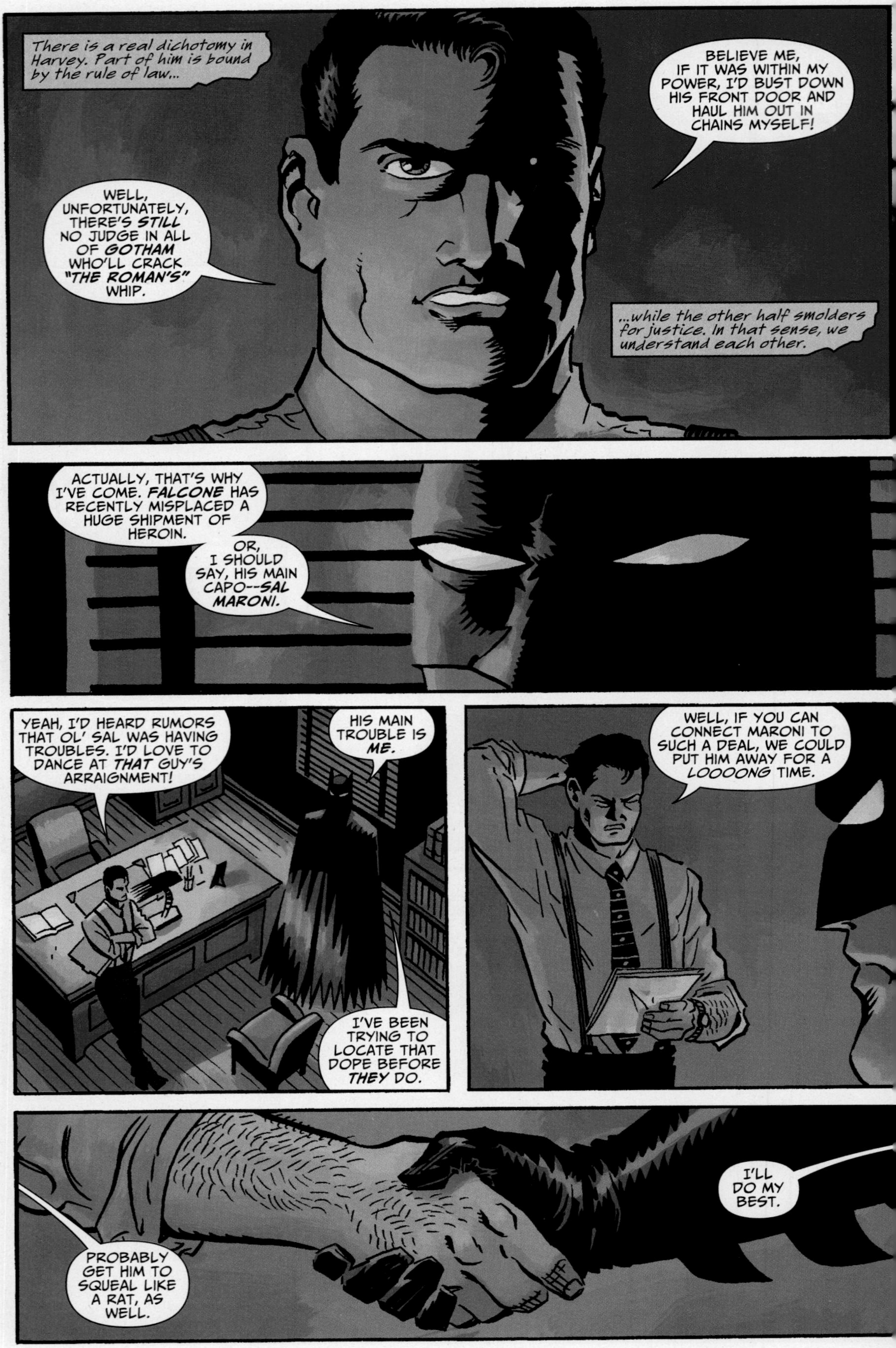
There is a real dichotomy in Harvey. Part of him is bound by the rule of law...
BELIEVE ME, IF IT WAS WITHIN MY POWER, I'D BUST DOWN HIS FRONT DOOR AND HAUL HIM OUT IN CHAINS MYSELF!
WELL, UNFORTUNATELY, THERE'S STILL NO JUDGE IN ALL OF GOTHAM WHO'LL CRACK "THE ROMAN'S" WHIP.
...while the other half smolders for justice. In that sense, we understand each other.
ACTUALLY, THAT'S WHY I'VE COME. FALCONE HAS RECENTLY MISPLACED A HUGE SHIPMENT OF HEROIN.
OR, I SHOULD SAY, HIS MAIN CAPO--SAL MARONI.
YEAH, I'D HEARD RUMORS THAT OL' SAL WAS HAVING TROUBLES. I'D LOVE TO DANCE AT THAT GUY'S ARRAIGNMENT!
HIS MAIN TROUBLE IS ME.
I'VE BEEN TRYING TO LOCATE THAT DOPE BEFORE THEY DO.
WELL, IF YOU CAN CONNECT MARONI TO SUCH A DEAL, WE COULD PUT HIM AWAY FOR A LOOOONG TIME.
I'LL DO MY BEST.
PROBABLY GET HIM TO SQUEAL LIKE A RAT, AS WELL.

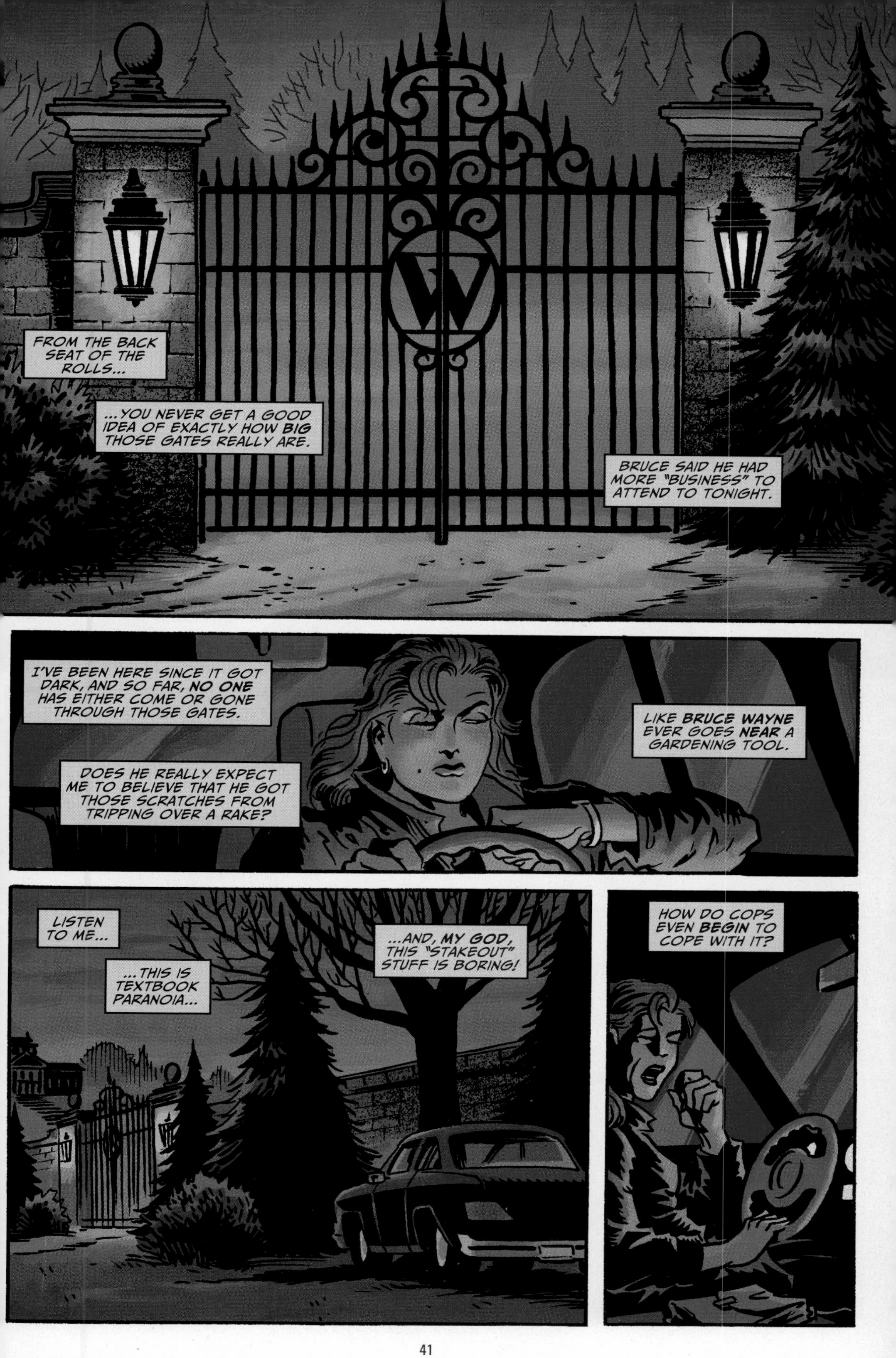
FROM THE BACK SEAT OF THE ROLLS...
...YOU NEVER GET A GOOD IDEA OF EXACTLY HOW BIG THOSE GATES REALLY ARE.
BRUCE SAID HE HAD MORE "BUSINESS" TO ATTEND TO TONIGHT.
I'VE BEEN HERE SINCE IT GOT DARK, AND SO FAR, NO ONE HAS EITHER COME OR GONE THROUGH THOSE GATES.
DOES HE REALLY EXPECT ME TO BELIEVE THAT HE GOT THOSE SCRATCHES FROM TRIPPING OVER A RAKE?
LIKE BRUCE WAYNE EVER GOES NEAR A GARDENING TOOL.
LISTEN TO ME...
...THIS IS TEXTBOOK PARANOIA...
...AND, MY GOD, THIS "STAKEOUT" STUFF IS BORING!
HOW DO COPS EVEN BEGIN TO COPE WITH IT?

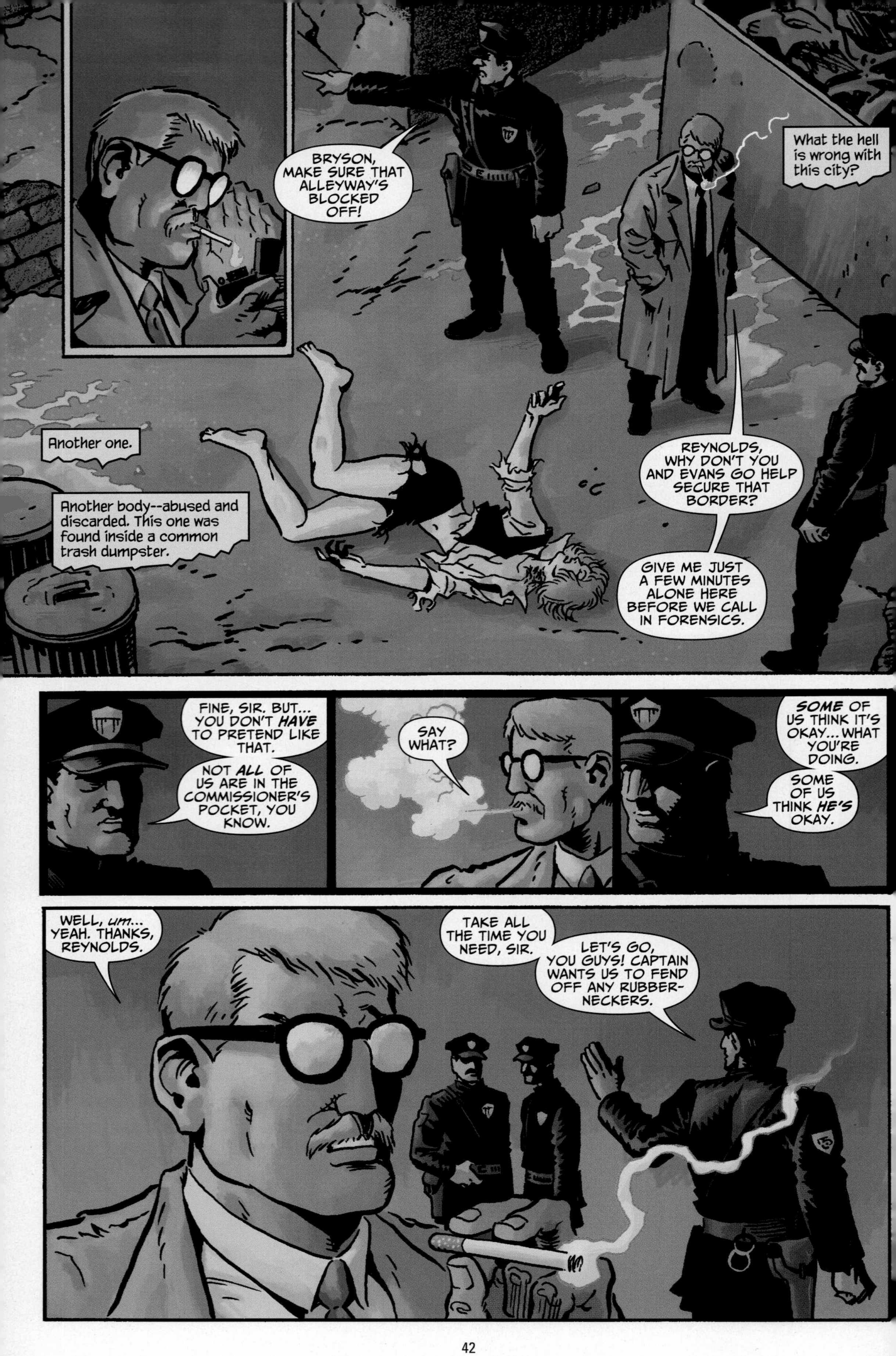
BRYSON, MAKE SURE THAT ALLEYWAY'S BLOCKED OFF!
What the hell is wrong with this city?
Another one.
Another body--abused and discarded. This one was found inside a common trash dumpster.
REYNOLDS, WHY DON'T YOU AND EVANS GO HELP SECURE THAT BORDER?
GIVE ME JUST A FEW MINUTES ALONE HERE BEFORE WE CALL IN FORENSICS.
FINE, SIR. BUT... YOU DON'T HAVE TO PRETEND LIKE THAT.
NOT ALL OF US ARE IN THE COMMISSIONER'S POCKET, YOU KNOW.
SAY WHAT?
SOME OF US THINK IT'S OKAY... WHAT YOU'RE DOING.
SOME OF US THINK HE'S OKAY.
WELL, um... YEAH. THANKS, REYNOLDS.
TAKE ALL THE TIME YOU NEED, SIR.
LET'S GO, YOU GUYS! CAPTAIN WANTS US TO FEND OFF ANY RUBBER-NECKERS.

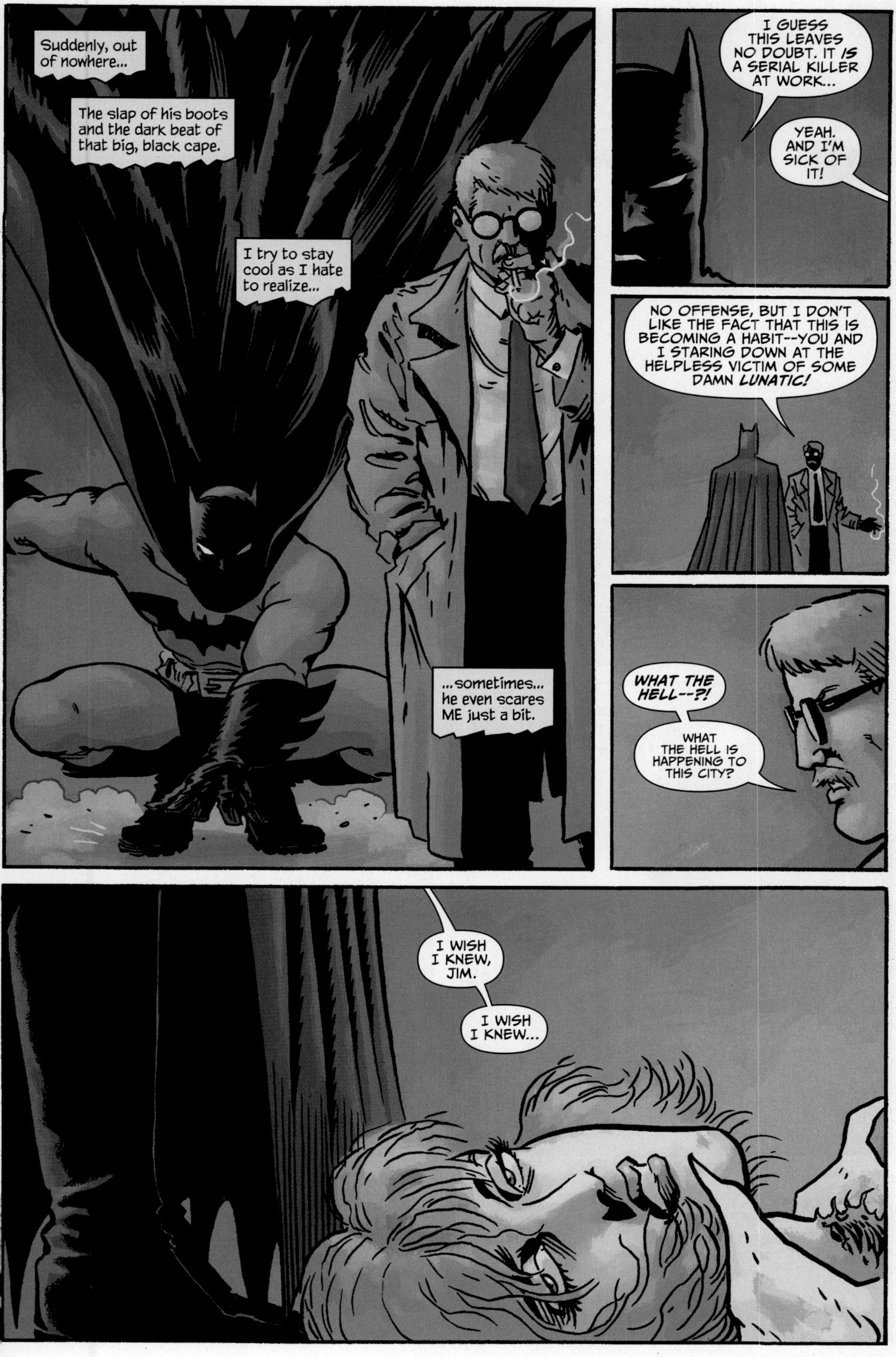
Suddenly, out of nowhere...
The slap of his boots and the dark beat of that big, black cape.
I try to stay cool as I hate to realize...
...sometimes... he even scares ME just a bit.
I GUESS THIS LEAVES NO DOUBT. IT IS A SERIAL KILLER AT WORK...
YEAH. AND I'M SICK OF IT!
NO OFFENSE, BUT I DON'T LIKE THE FACT THAT THIS IS BECOMING A HABIT--YOU AND I STARING DOWN AT THE HELPLESS VICTIM OF SOME DAMN LUNATIC!
WHAT THE HELL--?!
WHAT THE HELL IS HAPPENING TO THIS CITY?
I WISH I KNEW, JIM.
I WISH I KNEW...

KITCHEN WORKER FOUND HER A COUPLE OF HOURS AGO--INSIDE THAT DUMPSTER.

TSHHH

SHE APPEARS TO HAVE BEEN KILLED IN THE SAME MANNER AS THE OTHERS. NECK'S A MESS.

NO BLOOD.

HER WRISTS AND ANKLES WERE BOUND. AND THE LEVEL OF BRUISING WOULD INDICATE THAT SHE STRUGGLED A LOT.

HER HEELS AND KNUCKLES ARE BADLY SCRAPED. SHE MUST HAVE BEEN TIED DOWN ON A HARD, ROUGH SURFACE.

THE FORMER VICTIMS HAD THAT AS WELL...

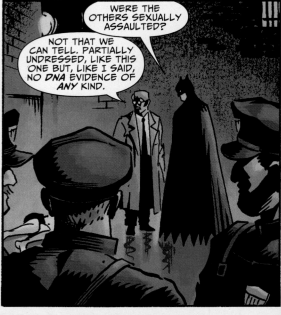

WERE THE OTHERS SEXUALLY ASSAULTED?

NOT THAT WE CAN TELL. PARTIALLY UNDRESSED, LIKE THIS ONE BUT, LIKE I SAID, NO *DNA* EVIDENCE OF *ANY* KIND.

THE REPETITIVE NATURE OF THESE CRIMES...IT'S ALMOST *RITUALISTIC*.

THE TRASH BINS ARE NEARLY FULL, AND THIS ALLEY DOESN'T APPEAR TO GET MUCH TRAFFIC.

THESE TIRE TREADS ARE TOO SMALL FOR A GARBAGE TRUCK. STILL, FAIRLY *WIDE SET* FOR AN ORDINARY CAR.

YOU'RE RIGHT. AND FAIRLY FRESH...

SSSSST

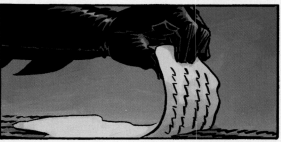

I'LL BE IN TOUCH. THIS *HAS* TO END!

GOOD LUCK.

NICCOLAI?

WHEN CAN *I* BE THE ONE TO HARVEST THE BLOOD FOR OUR NEEDS?

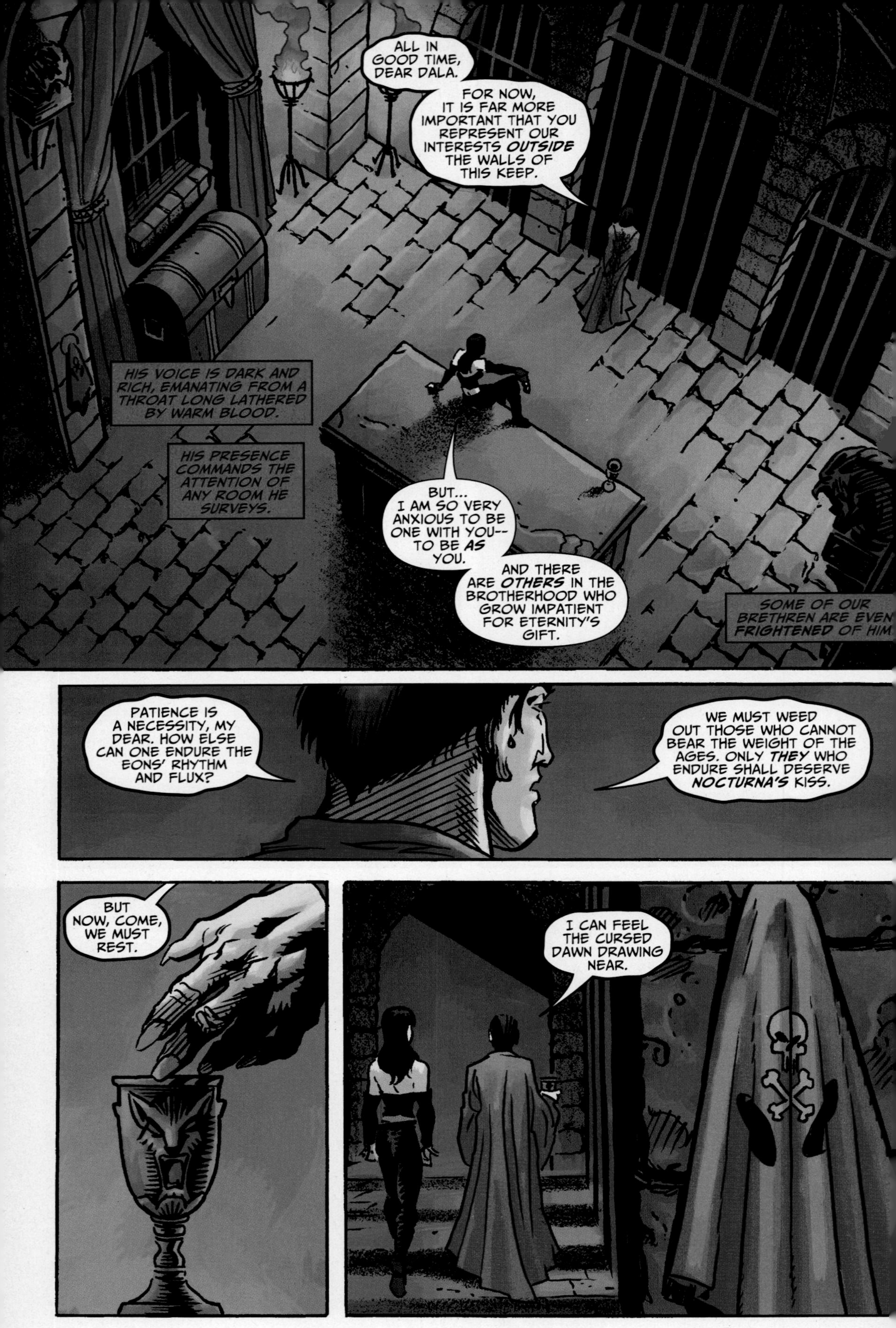
ALL IN GOOD TIME, DEAR DALA.
FOR NOW, IT IS FAR MORE IMPORTANT THAT YOU REPRESENT OUR INTERESTS OUTSIDE THE WALLS OF THIS KEEP.
HIS VOICE IS DARK AND RICH, EMANATING FROM A THROAT LONG LATHERED BY WARM BLOOD.
HIS PRESENCE COMMANDS THE ATTENTION OF ANY ROOM HE SURVEYS.
BUT... I AM SO VERY ANXIOUS TO BE ONE WITH YOU-- TO BE AS YOU.
AND THERE ARE OTHERS IN THE BROTHERHOOD WHO GROW IMPATIENT FOR ETERNITY'S GIFT.
SOME OF OUR BRETHREN ARE EVEN FRIGHTENED OF HIM.
PATIENCE IS A NECESSITY, MY DEAR. HOW ELSE CAN ONE ENDURE THE EONS' RHYTHM AND FLUX?
WE MUST WEED OUT THOSE WHO CANNOT BEAR THE WEIGHT OF THE AGES. ONLY THEY WHO ENDURE SHALL DESERVE NOCTURNA'S KISS.
BUT NOW, COME, WE MUST REST.
I CAN FEEL THE CURSED DAWN DRAWING NEAR.

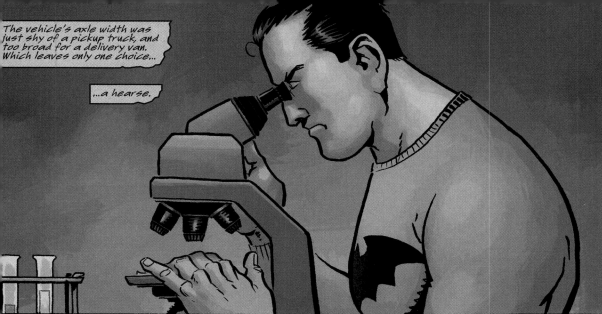

The vehicle's axle width was just shy of a pickup truck, and too broad for a delivery van. Which leaves only one choice...

...a hearse.

And the chemical residues found in the sample I took are a unique combination.

A biochemical compound found mainly in exotic perfumes.

And a neurotoxin used almost exclusively for animal sedatives.

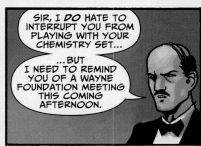

SIR, I *DO* HATE TO INTERRUPT YOU FROM PLAYING WITH YOUR CHEMISTRY SET...

...BUT I NEED TO REMIND YOU OF A WAYNE FOUNDATION MEETING THIS COMING AFTERNOON.

THANKS, ALFRED. I *DO* WANT TO ONLY *APPEAR* TO SLEEP THROUGH THAT SESSION.

AND... ∋yawwn∈... TO DO *THAT*, I AM GOING TO NEED TO GRAB A FEW WINKS BEFOREHAND.

AND, CONVENIENTLY, IT *IS* JUST YOUR BEDTIME, SIR. DAYBREAK IS NIGH.

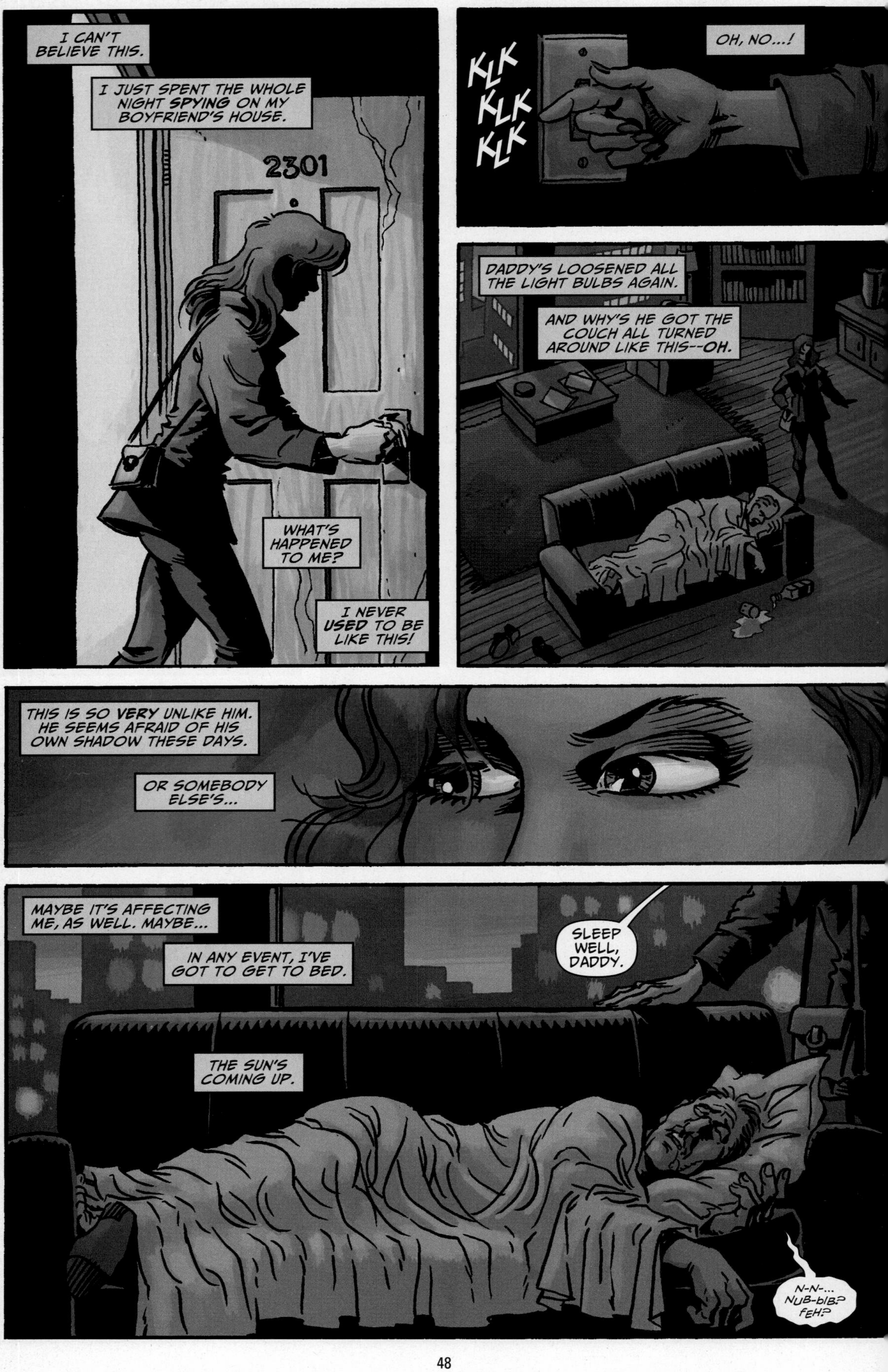
I CAN'T BELIEVE THIS.
I JUST SPENT THE WHOLE NIGHT SPYING ON MY BOYFRIEND'S HOUSE.
2301
WHAT'S HAPPENED TO ME?
I NEVER USED TO BE LIKE THIS!
KLK KLK KLK
OH, NO...!
DADDY'S LOOSENED ALL THE LIGHT BULBS AGAIN.
AND WHY'S HE GOT THE COUCH ALL TURNED AROUND LIKE THIS--OH.
THIS IS SO VERY UNLIKE HIM. HE SEEMS AFRAID OF HIS OWN SHADOW THESE DAYS.
OR SOMEBODY ELSE'S...
MAYBE IT'S AFFECTING ME, AS WELL. MAYBE...
IN ANY EVENT, I'VE GOT TO GET TO BED.
SLEEP WELL, DADDY.
THE SUN'S COMING UP.
N-N-... NUB-blB? fEH?

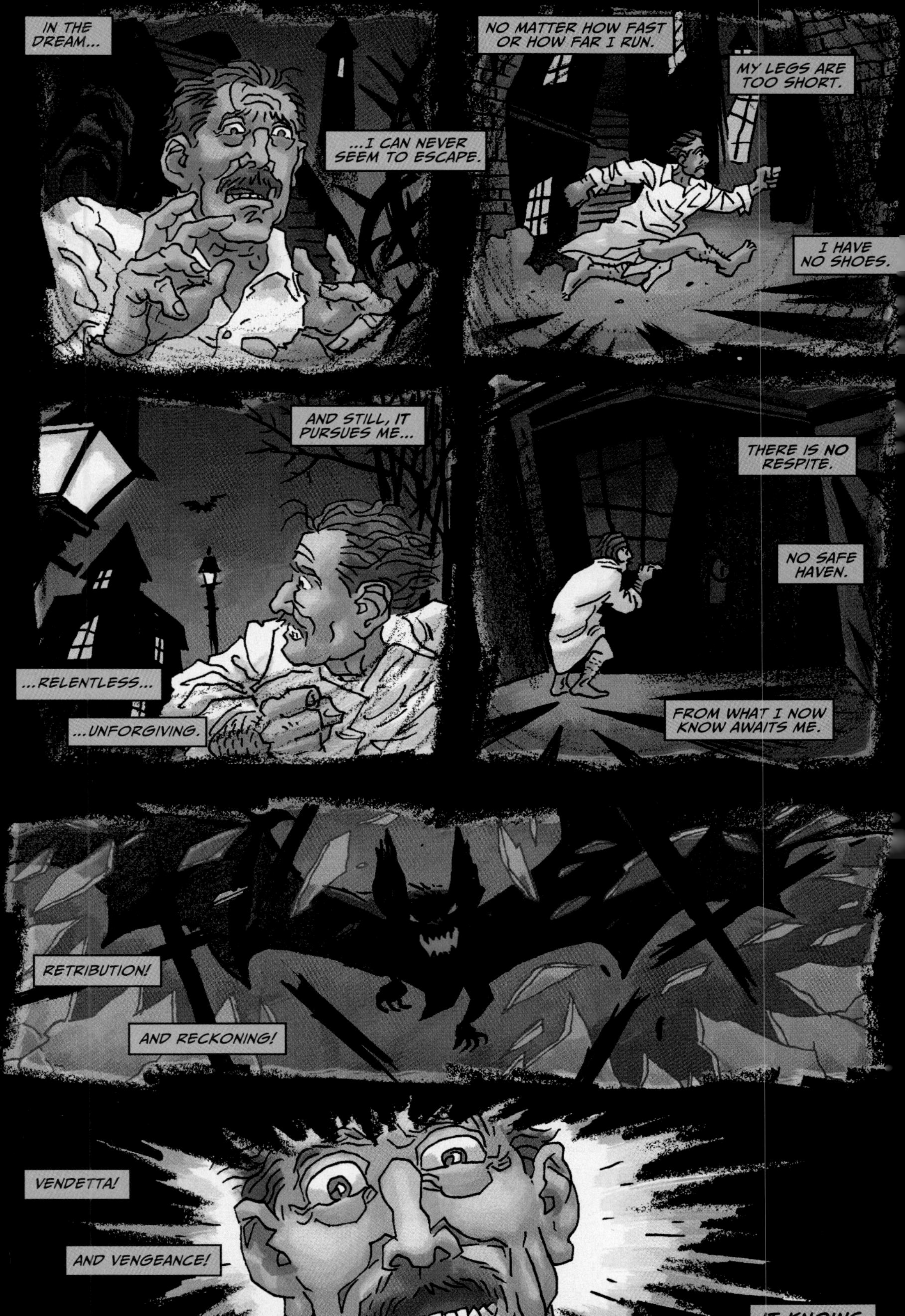
IN THE DREAM...
...I CAN NEVER SEEM TO ESCAPE.
NO MATTER HOW FAST OR HOW FAR I RUN.
MY LEGS ARE TOO SHORT.
I HAVE NO SHOES.
AND STILL, IT PURSUES ME...
...RELENTLESS...
...UNFORGIVING.
THERE IS NO RESPITE.
NO SAFE HAVEN.
FROM WHAT I NOW KNOW AWAITS ME.
RETRIBUTION!
AND RECKONING!
VENDETTA!
AND VENGEANCE!
IT KNOWS MY NAME!!

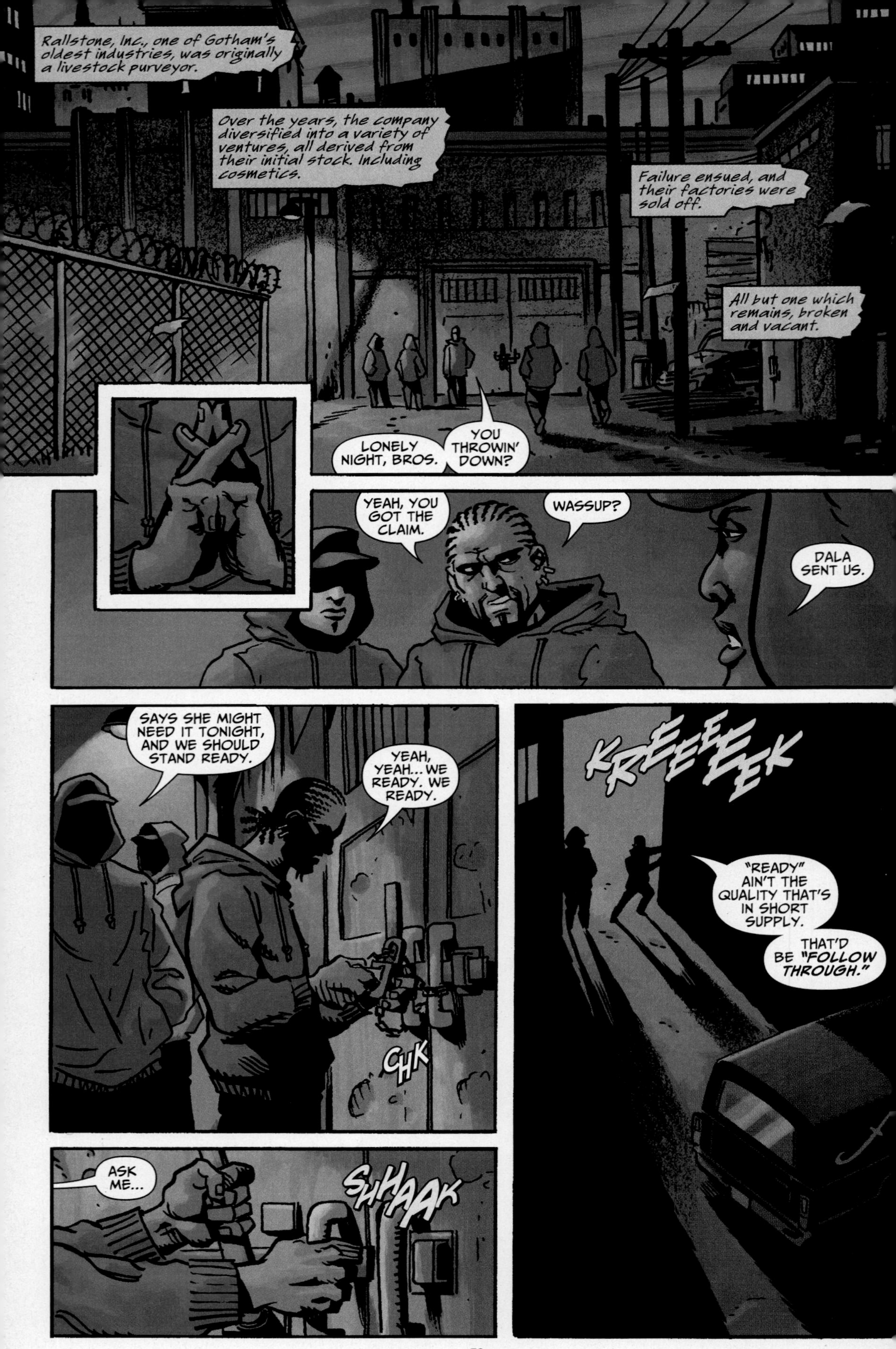

Rallstone, Inc., one of Gotham's oldest industries, was originally a livestock purveyor.
Over the years, the company diversified into a variety of ventures, all derived from their initial stock. Including cosmetics.
Failure ensued, and their factories were sold off.
All but one which remains, broken and vacant.
LONELY NIGHT, BROS.
YOU THROWIN' DOWN?
YEAH, YOU GOT THE CLAIM.
WASSUP?
DALA SENT US.
SAYS SHE MIGHT NEED IT TONIGHT, AND WE SHOULD STAND READY.
YEAH, YEAH... WE READY. WE READY.
CHK
ASK ME...
SHHAAK
KREEEEEK
"READY" AIN'T THE QUALITY THAT'S IN SHORT SUPPLY.
THAT'D BE "FOLLOW THROUGH."

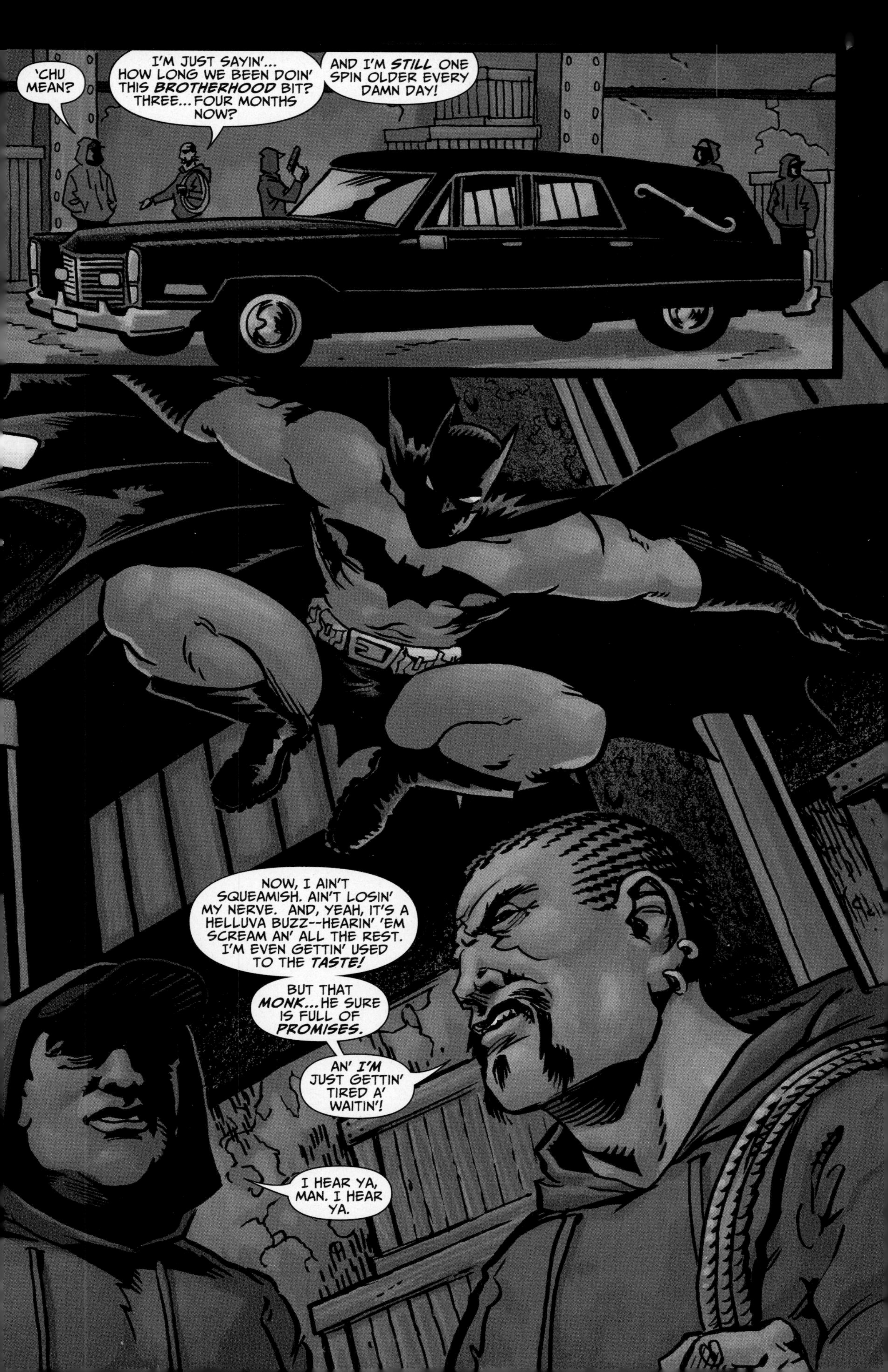
'CHU MEAN?
I'M JUST SAYIN'... HOW LONG WE BEEN DOIN' THIS BROTHERHOOD BIT? THREE... FOUR MONTHS NOW?
AND I'M STILL ONE SPIN OLDER EVERY DAMN DAY!
NOW, I AIN'T SQUEAMISH. AIN'T LOSIN' MY NERVE. AND, YEAH, IT'S A HELLUVA BUZZ--HEARIN' 'EM SCREAM AN' ALL THE REST. I'M EVEN GETTIN' USED TO THE TASTE!
BUT THAT MONK... HE SURE IS FULL OF PROMISES.
AN' I'M JUST GETTIN' TIRED A' WAITIN'!
I HEAR YA, MAN. I HEAR YA.

CHAPTER 3

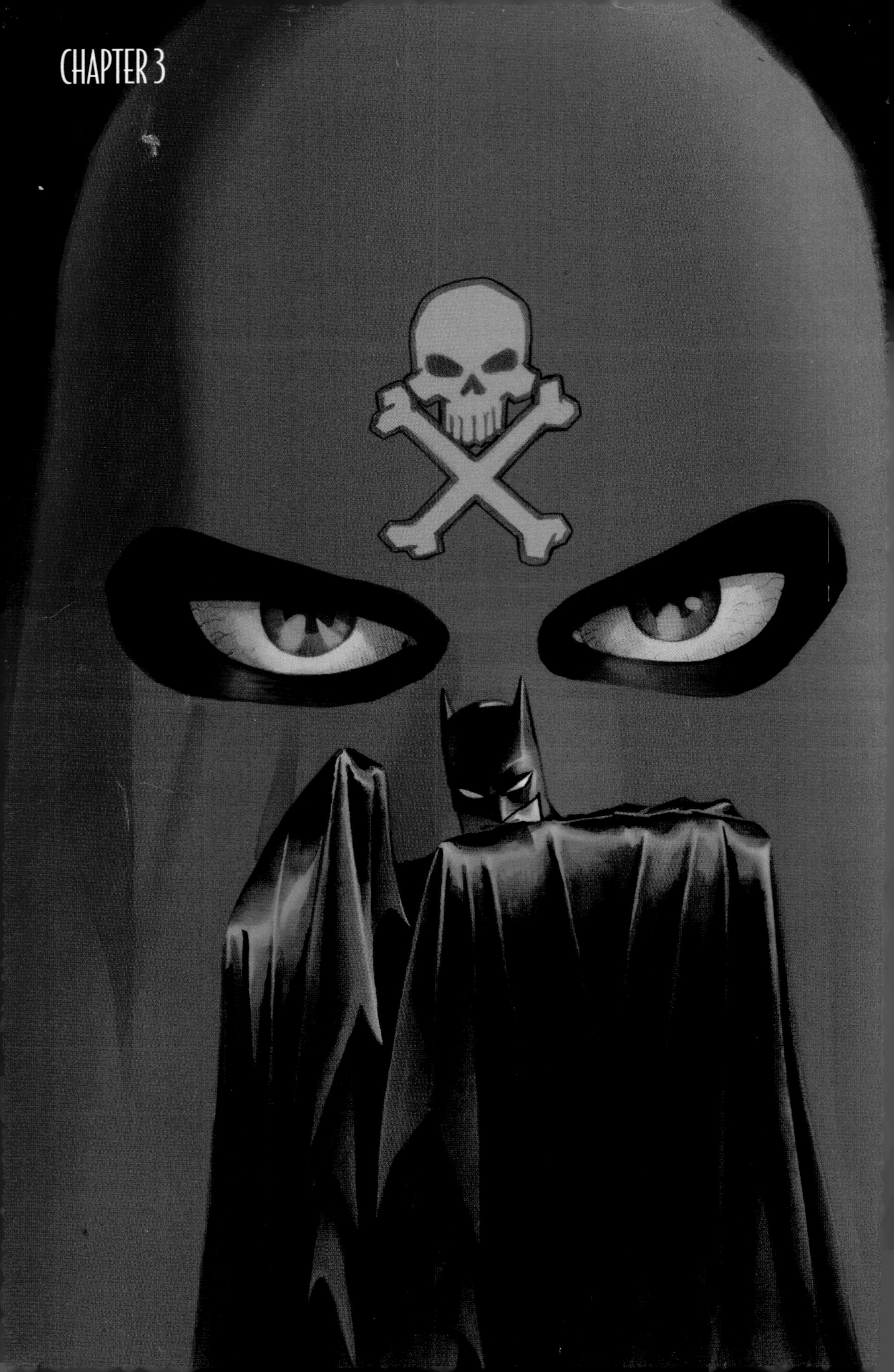

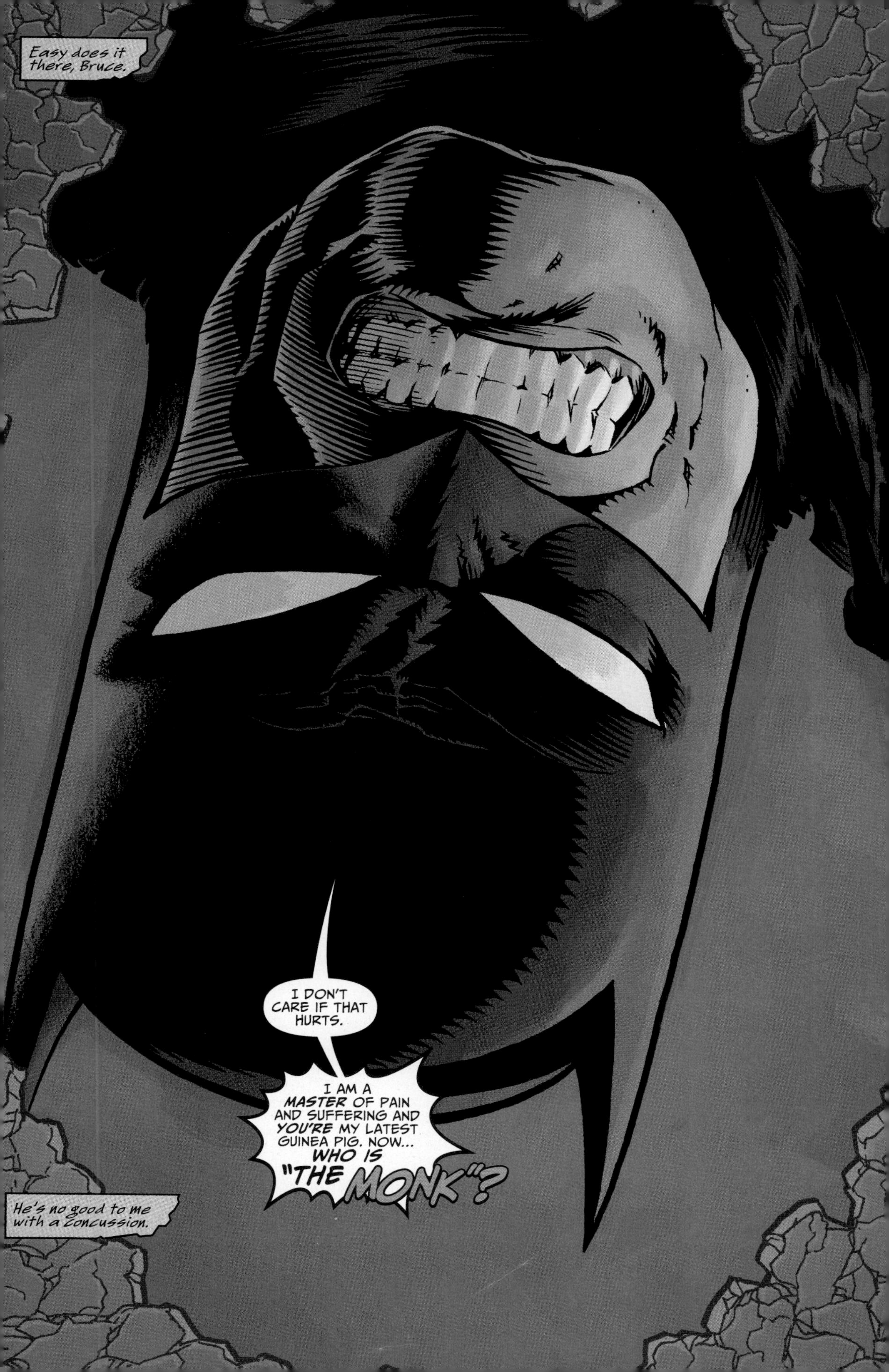
Easy does it there, Bruce.
I DON'T CARE IF THAT HURTS.
I AM A MASTER OF PAIN AND SUFFERING AND YOU'RE MY LATEST GUINEA PIG. NOW... WHO IS "THE MONK"?
He's no good to me with a concussion.

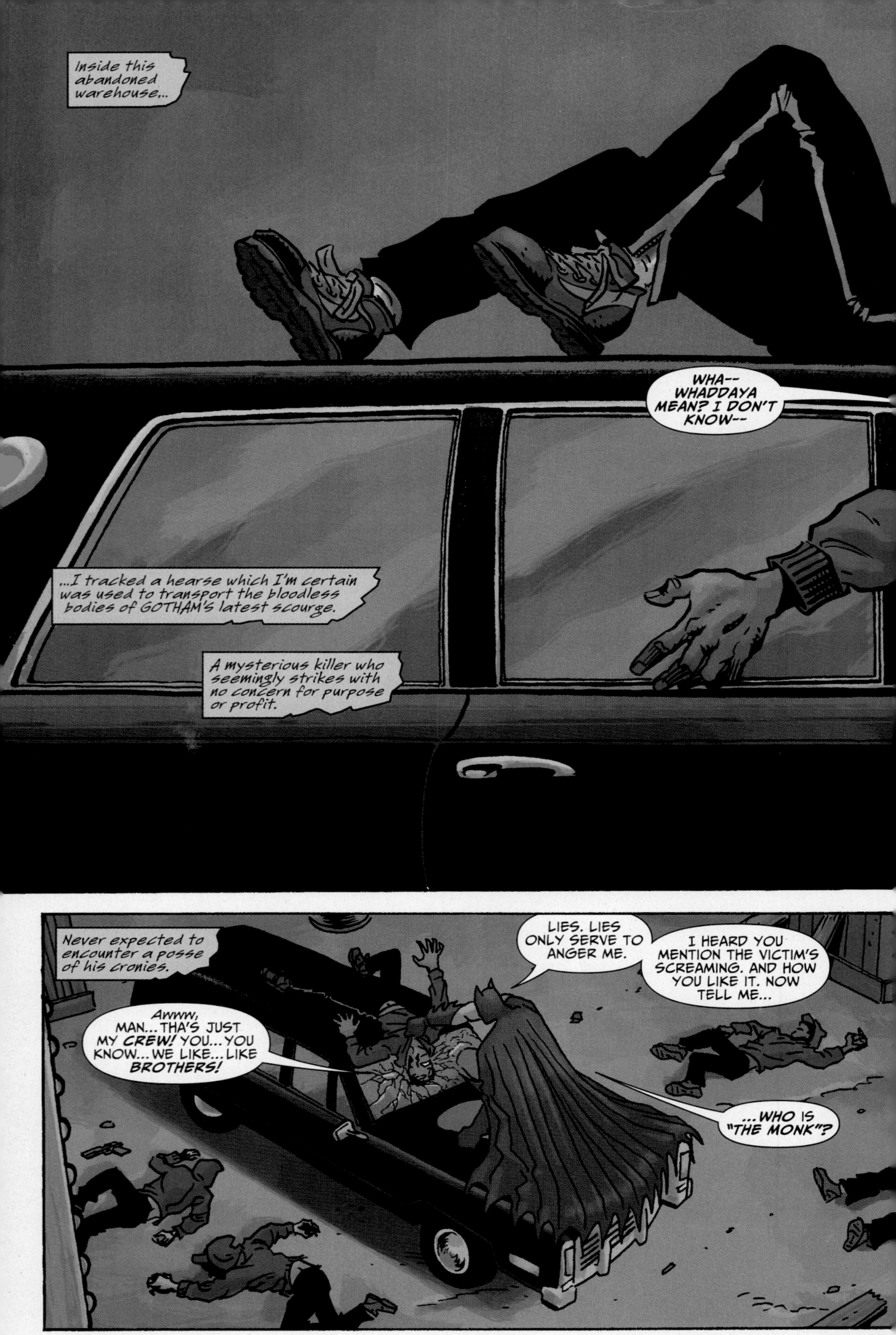
Inside this abandoned warehouse...
WHA-- WHADDAYA MEAN? I DON'T KNOW--
...I tracked a hearse which I'm certain was used to transport the bloodless bodies of GOTHAM'S latest scourge.
A mysterious killer who seemingly strikes with no concern for purpose or profit.
Never expected to encounter a posse of his cronies.
LIES. LIES ONLY SERVE TO ANGER ME.
I HEARD YOU MENTION THE VICTIM'S SCREAMING. AND HOW YOU LIKE IT. NOW TELL ME...
Awww, MAN... THA'S JUST MY CREW! YOU... YOU KNOW... WE LIKE... LIKE BROTHERS!
...WHO IS "THE MONK"?

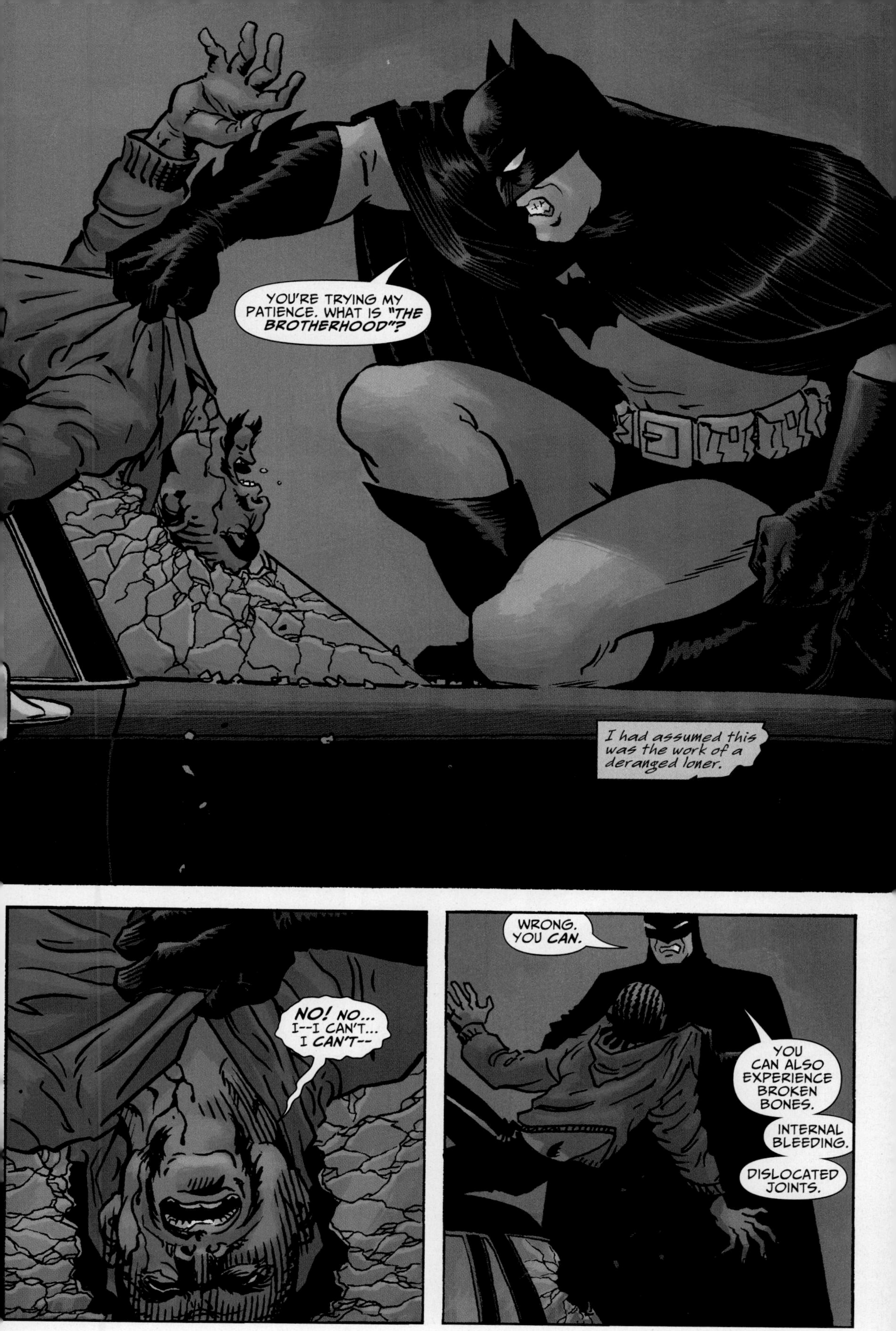
YOU'RE TRYING MY PATIENCE. WHAT IS "THE BROTHERHOOD"?
I had assumed this was the work of a deranged loner.
NO! NO... I--I CAN'T... I CAN'T--
WRONG. YOU CAN.
YOU CAN ALSO EXPERIENCE BROKEN BONES.
INTERNAL BLEEDING.
DISLOCATED JOINTS.

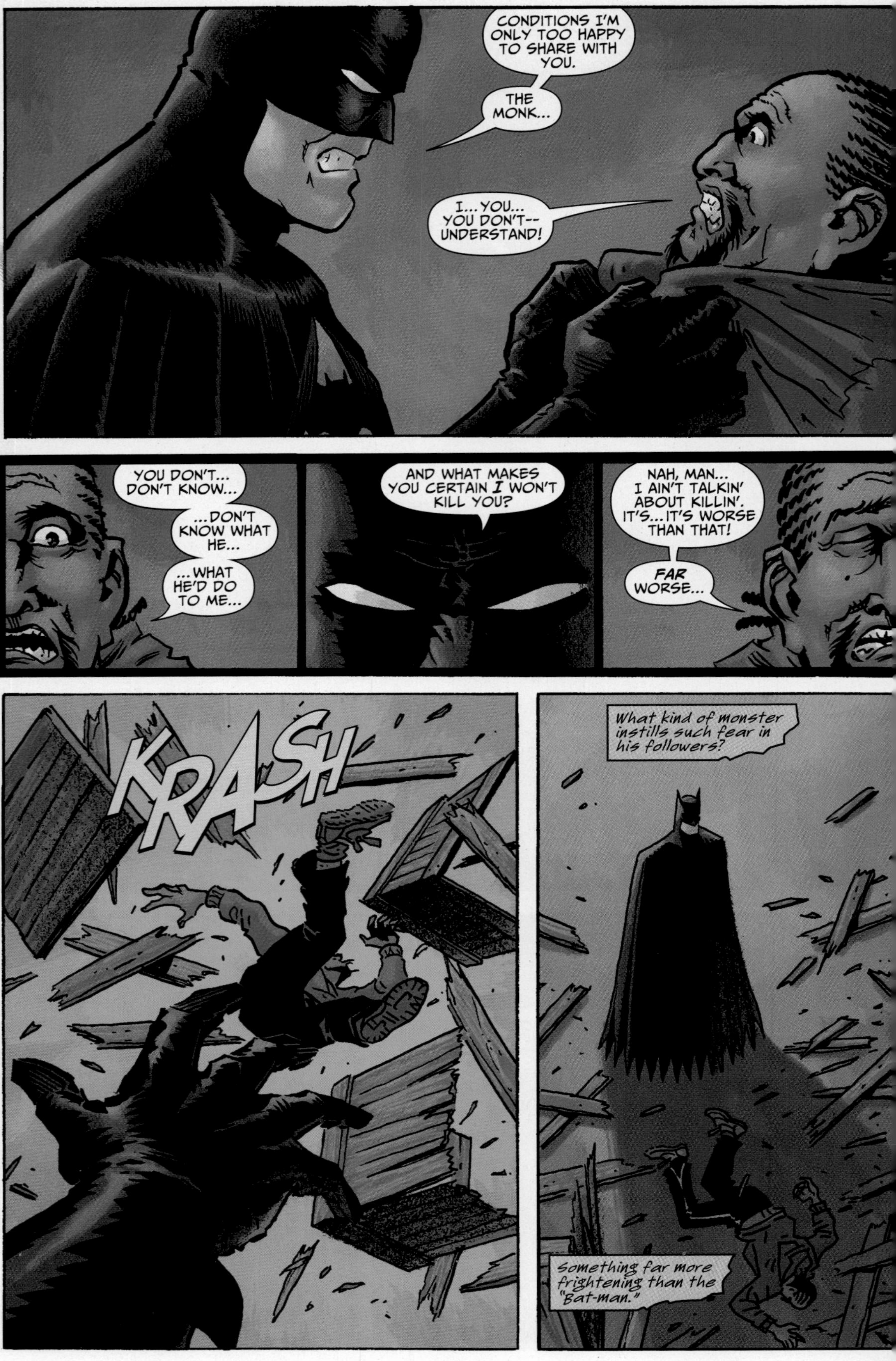
CONDITIONS I'M ONLY TOO HAPPY TO SHARE WITH YOU.
THE MONK...
I... YOU... YOU DON'T-- UNDERSTAND!
YOU DON'T... DON'T KNOW...
...DON'T KNOW WHAT HE...
...WHAT HE'D DO TO ME...
AND WHAT MAKES YOU CERTAIN I WON'T KILL YOU?
NAH, MAN... I AIN'T TALKIN' ABOUT KILLIN'. IT'S...IT'S WORSE THAN THAT!
FAR WORSE...
KRASH
What kind of monster instills such fear in his followers?
Something far more frightening than the "Bat-man."

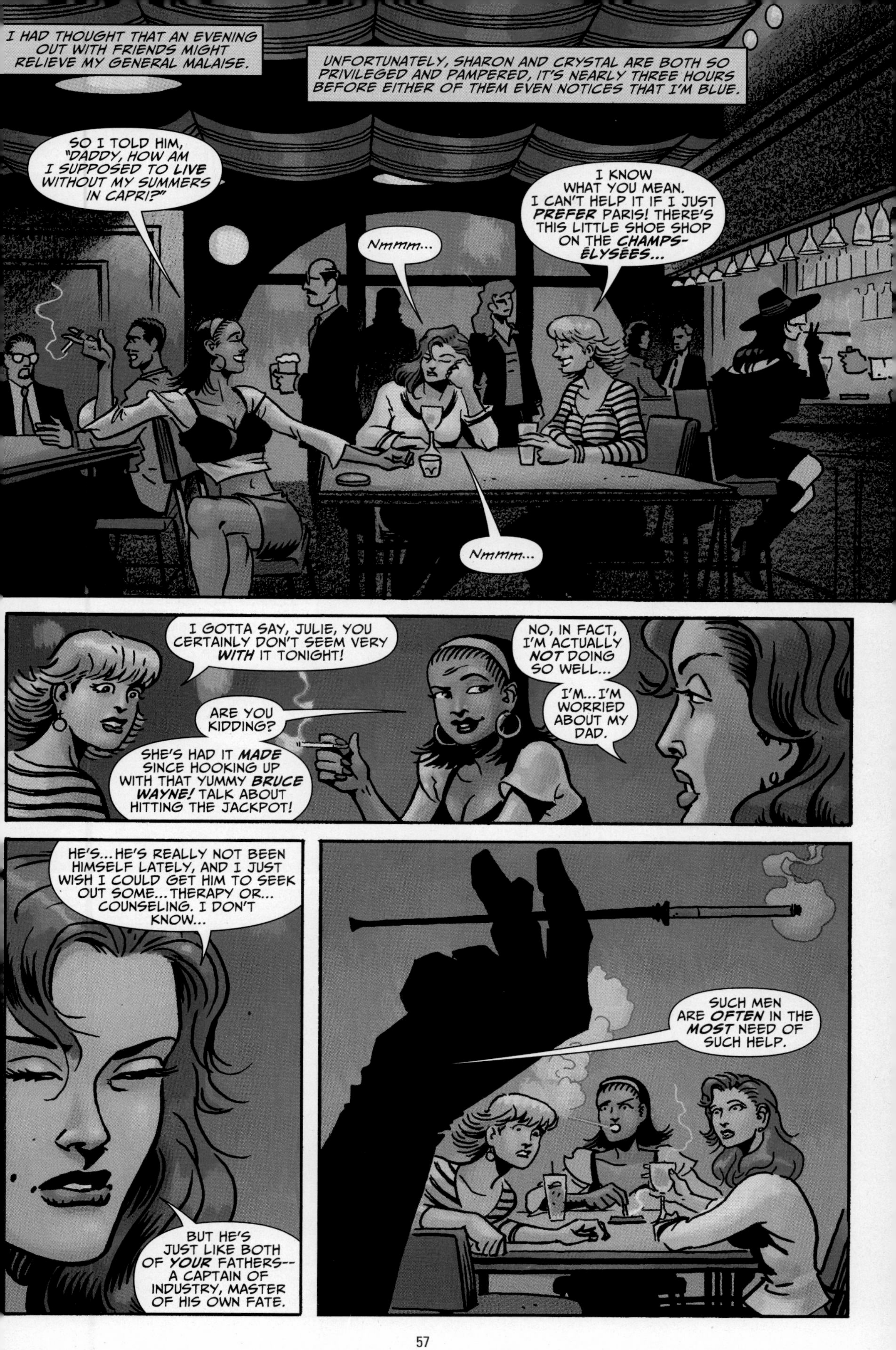
I HAD THOUGHT THAT AN EVENING OUT WITH FRIENDS MIGHT RELIEVE MY GENERAL MALAISE.
UNFORTUNATELY, SHARON AND CRYSTAL ARE BOTH SO PRIVILEGED AND PAMPERED, IT'S NEARLY THREE HOURS BEFORE EITHER OF THEM EVEN NOTICES THAT I'M BLUE.
SO I TOLD HIM, "DADDY, HOW AM I SUPPOSED TO LIVE WITHOUT MY SUMMERS IN CAPRI?"
Nmmm...
I KNOW WHAT YOU MEAN. I CAN'T HELP IT IF I JUST PREFER PARIS! THERE'S THIS LITTLE SHOE SHOP ON THE CHAMPS-ÉLYSÉES...
Nmmm...
I GOTTA SAY, JULIE, YOU CERTAINLY DON'T SEEM VERY WITH IT TONIGHT!
ARE YOU KIDDING?
SHE'S HAD IT MADE SINCE HOOKING UP WITH THAT YUMMY BRUCE WAYNE! TALK ABOUT HITTING THE JACKPOT!
NO, IN FACT, I'M ACTUALLY NOT DOING SO WELL...
I'M... I'M WORRIED ABOUT MY DAD.
HE'S... HE'S REALLY NOT BEEN HIMSELF LATELY, AND I JUST WISH I COULD GET HIM TO SEEK OUT SOME... THERAPY OR... COUNSELING. I DON'T KNOW...
BUT HE'S JUST LIKE BOTH OF YOUR FATHERS-- A CAPTAIN OF INDUSTRY, MASTER OF HIS OWN FATE.
SUCH MEN ARE OFTEN IN THE MOST NEED OF SUCH HELP.

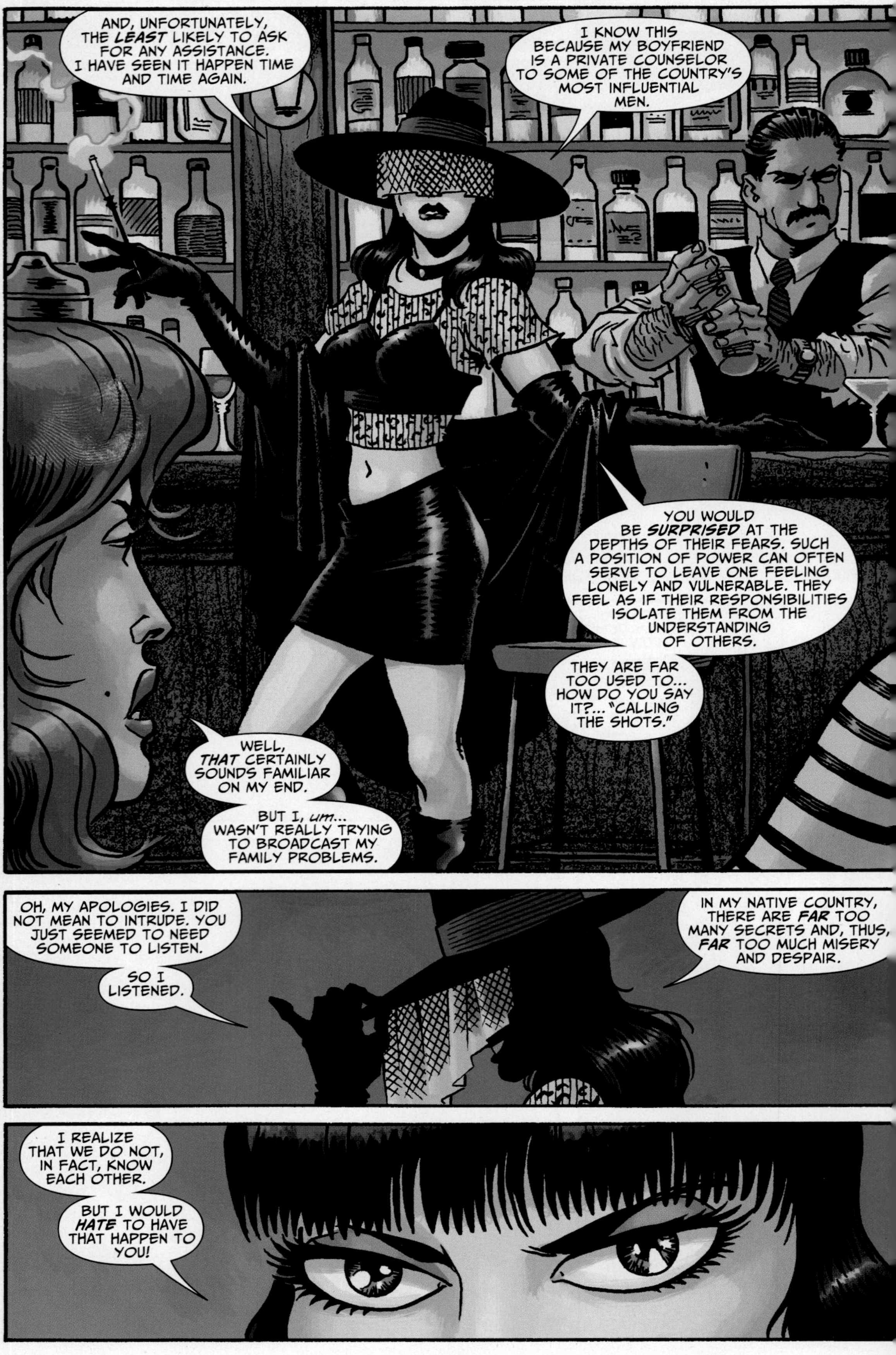

AND, UNFORTUNATELY, THE *LEAST* LIKELY TO ASK FOR ANY ASSISTANCE. I HAVE SEEN IT HAPPEN TIME AND TIME AGAIN.
I KNOW THIS BECAUSE MY BOYFRIEND IS A PRIVATE COUNSELOR TO SOME OF THE COUNTRY'S MOST INFLUENTIAL MEN.
YOU WOULD BE *SURPRISED* AT THE DEPTHS OF THEIR FEARS. SUCH A POSITION OF POWER CAN OFTEN SERVE TO LEAVE ONE FEELING LONELY AND VULNERABLE. THEY FEEL AS IF THEIR RESPONSIBILITIES ISOLATE THEM FROM THE UNDERSTANDING OF OTHERS.
THEY ARE FAR TOO USED TO... HOW DO YOU SAY IT?... "CALLING THE SHOTS."
WELL, *THAT* CERTAINLY SOUNDS FAMILIAR ON MY END.
BUT I, *UM*... WASN'T REALLY TRYING TO BROADCAST MY FAMILY PROBLEMS.
OH, MY APOLOGIES. I DID NOT MEAN TO INTRUDE. YOU JUST SEEMED TO NEED SOMEONE TO LISTEN.
SO I LISTENED.
IN MY NATIVE COUNTRY, THERE ARE *FAR* TOO MANY SECRETS AND, THUS, *FAR* TOO MUCH MISERY AND DESPAIR.
I REALIZE THAT WE DO NOT, IN FACT, KNOW EACH OTHER.
BUT I WOULD *HATE* TO HAVE THAT HAPPEN TO YOU!

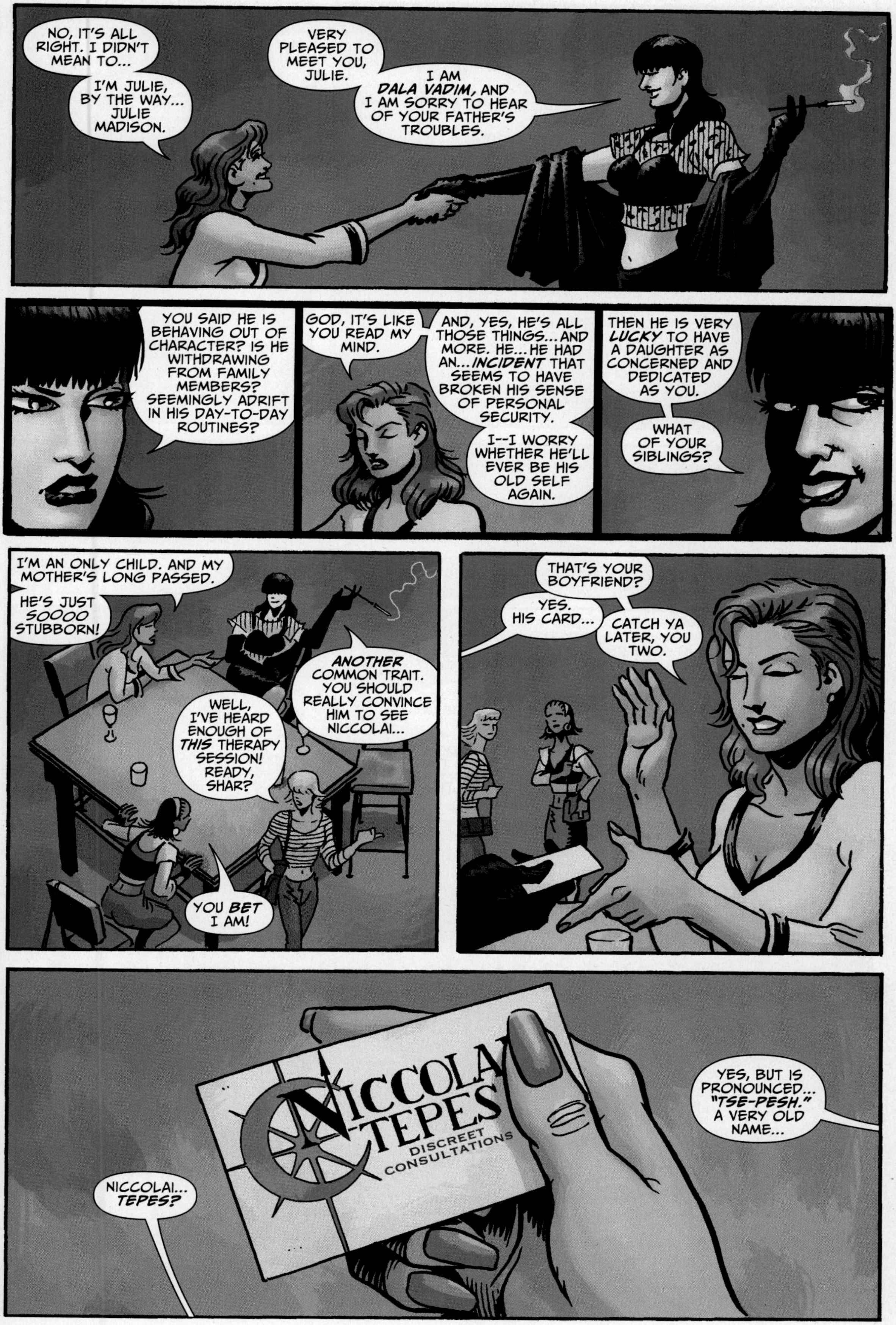

NO, IT'S ALL RIGHT. I DIDN'T MEAN TO...
I'M JULIE, BY THE WAY... JULIE MADISON.
VERY PLEASED TO MEET YOU, JULIE.
I AM DALA VADIM, AND I AM SORRY TO HEAR OF YOUR FATHER'S TROUBLES.
YOU SAID HE IS BEHAVING OUT OF CHARACTER? IS HE WITHDRAWING FROM FAMILY MEMBERS? SEEMINGLY ADRIFT IN HIS DAY-TO-DAY ROUTINES?
GOD, IT'S LIKE YOU READ MY MIND.
AND, YES, HE'S ALL THOSE THINGS... AND MORE. HE... HE HAD AN... INCIDENT THAT SEEMS TO HAVE BROKEN HIS SENSE OF PERSONAL SECURITY.
I--I WORRY WHETHER HE'LL EVER BE HIS OLD SELF AGAIN.
THEN HE IS VERY LUCKY TO HAVE A DAUGHTER AS CONCERNED AND DEDICATED AS YOU.
WHAT OF YOUR SIBLINGS?
I'M AN ONLY CHILD. AND MY MOTHER'S LONG PASSED.
HE'S JUST SOOOO STUBBORN!
ANOTHER COMMON TRAIT. YOU SHOULD REALLY CONVINCE HIM TO SEE NICCOLAI...
WELL, I'VE HEARD ENOUGH OF THIS THERAPY SESSION! READY, SHAR?
YOU BET I AM!
THAT'S YOUR BOYFRIEND?
YES. HIS CARD...
CATCH YA LATER, YOU TWO.
NICCOLAI TEPES
DISCREET CONSULTATIONS
YES, BUT IS PRONOUNCED... "TSE-PESH." A VERY OLD NAME...
NICCOLAI... TEPES?

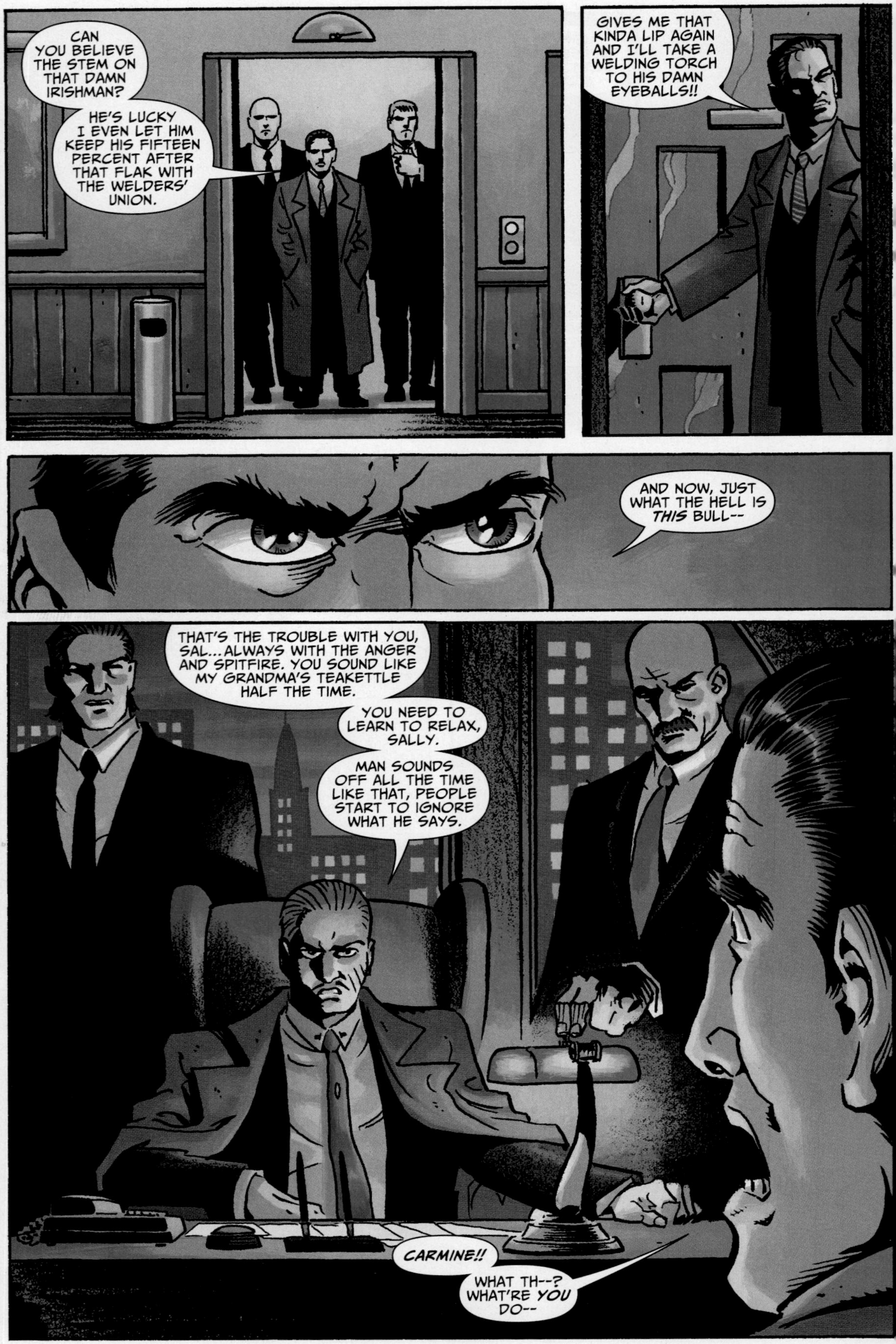
CAN YOU BELIEVE THE STEM ON THAT DAMN IRISHMAN?
HE'S LUCKY I EVEN LET HIM KEEP HIS FIFTEEN PERCENT AFTER THAT FLAK WITH THE WELDERS' UNION.
GIVES ME THAT KINDA LIP AGAIN AND I'LL TAKE A WELDING TORCH TO HIS DAMN EYEBALLS!!
AND NOW, JUST WHAT THE HELL IS *THIS* BULL--
THAT'S THE TROUBLE WITH YOU, SAL... ALWAYS WITH THE ANGER AND SPITFIRE. YOU SOUND LIKE MY GRANDMA'S TEAKETTLE HALF THE TIME.
YOU NEED TO LEARN TO RELAX, SALLY.
MAN SOUNDS OFF ALL THE TIME LIKE THAT, PEOPLE START TO IGNORE WHAT HE SAYS.
CARMINE!!
WHAT TH--? WHAT'RE *YOU* DO--

YOU *KNOW* HOW I LIKE THINGS TO RUN SMOOTHLY, DON'T YOU, SAL?

AND YOU *KNOW* I LIKE MY CAPOS TO LOOK AFTER THEIR OWN DEALINGS.

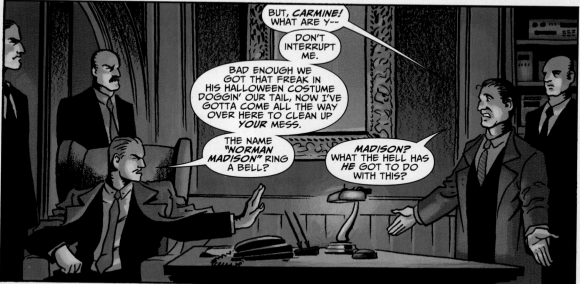

BUT, *CARMINE!* WHAT ARE Y--

DON'T INTERRUPT ME.

BAD ENOUGH WE GOT THAT FREAK IN HIS HALLOWEEN COSTUME DOGGIN' OUR TAIL, NOW I'VE GOTTA COME ALL THE WAY OVER HERE TO CLEAN UP *YOUR* MESS.

THE NAME *"NORMAN MADISON"* RING A BELL?

MADISON? WHAT THE HELL HAS *HE* GOT TO DO WITH THIS?

AS YOU KNOW, HE'S A BIG PLAYER IN THE BUSINESS COMMUNITY. SO WHEN HE CALLS AND ASKS TO MEET WITH ME, I SEE THAT AS "OPPORTUNITY."

THEN HE SHOWS UP AND TRIES TO PAY ME BACK MONEY HE SAYS HE OWES TO *YOU!*

THAT HE--?

YOU *GOTTA* BE FREAKIN' KIDDIN' ME!?

DO I *LOOK* LIKE I'M TELLIN' SOME SORTA *JOKE* OVER HERE?

I DON'T NEED TO KNOW WHAT THE DEAL IS BETWEEN YOU TWO, BUT I *DON'T* WANT IT TO CROSS MY PATH AGAIN.

THEN I WON'T HAVE TO COME ALL THE WAY OVER HERE TO VISIT YOU AGAIN, SALLY. WE CLEAR ON THAT?

YEAH, CARMINE. WE'RE CLEAR.

CONSIDER IT *DONE.*

GOOD GOD...DADDY WOULD HAVE A FIT IF HE KNEW I SPENT THE EVENING DISCUSSING HIS PROBLEMS WITH A VIRTUAL STRANGER.

STILL, IT WAS *SO* NICE TO HAVE SOMEONE TO CONFIDE IN.

I MEAN, BRUCE LISTENS. BUT HE SEEMS *TOO* DISTRACTED HALF THE TIME.

DAMN IT! WHY WON'T THIS OPEN--?

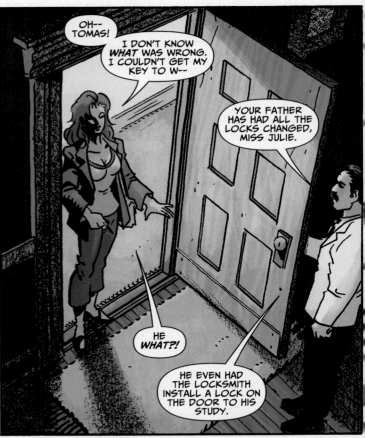

OH-- TOMAS!

I DON'T KNOW *WHAT* WAS WRONG. I COULDN'T GET MY KEY TO W--

YOUR FATHER HAS HAD ALL THE LOCKS CHANGED, MISS JULIE.

HE *WHAT?!*

HE EVEN HAD THE LOCKSMITH INSTALL A LOCK ON THE DOOR TO HIS STUDY.

HE SEEMS *VERY* NERVOUS...

THANK YOU, TOMAS. I...

DADDY?

DADDY, IT'S *ME!* PLEASE OPEN THE DOOR?

KNOCK KNOCK

JULIE! WH-WHAT IS IT? ARE YOU ALL RIGHT?!

OF COURSE. I JUST...I JUST WANTED TO CHECK ON YOU.

I'M FINE, DARLING! I'M FINE! JUST... *BUSY,* THAT'S ALL!

I, *uhh...*I'M AFRAID I CAN'T COME OUT RIGHT NOW!

BUT *DADDY...!* YOU--

SLAM

HE NEEDS HELP. EVEN IF HE WON'T ASK FOR IT HIMSELF.

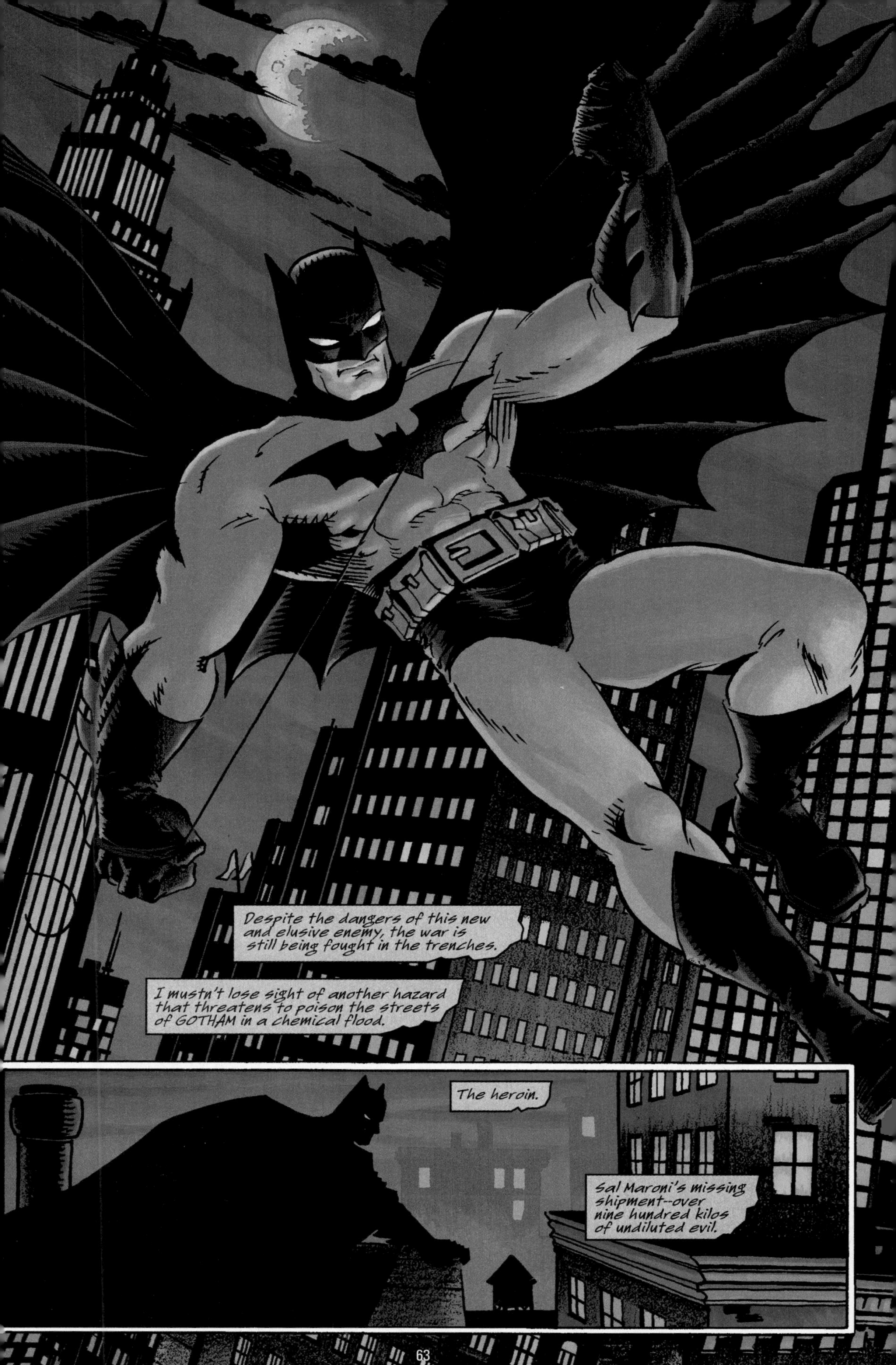
Despite the dangers of this new and elusive enemy, the war is still being fought in the trenches.
I mustn't lose sight of another hazard that threatens to poison the streets of GOTHAM in a chemical flood.
The heroin.
Sal Maroni's missing shipment--over nine hundred kilos of undiluted evil.

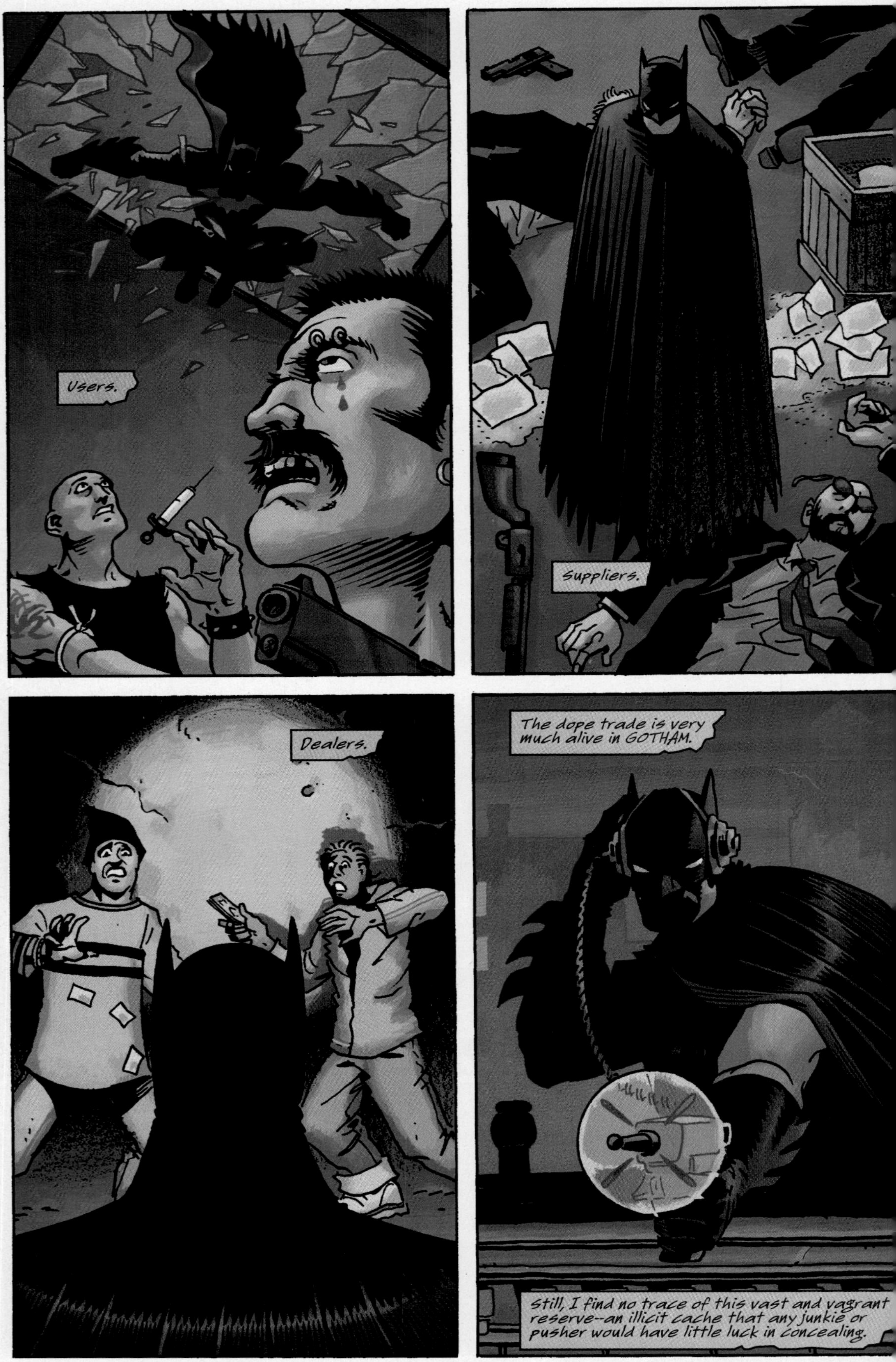
Users.
Suppliers.
Dealers.
The dope trade is very much alive in GOTHAM.
Still, I find no trace of this vast and vagrant reserve--an illicit cache that any junkie or pusher would have little luck in concealing.

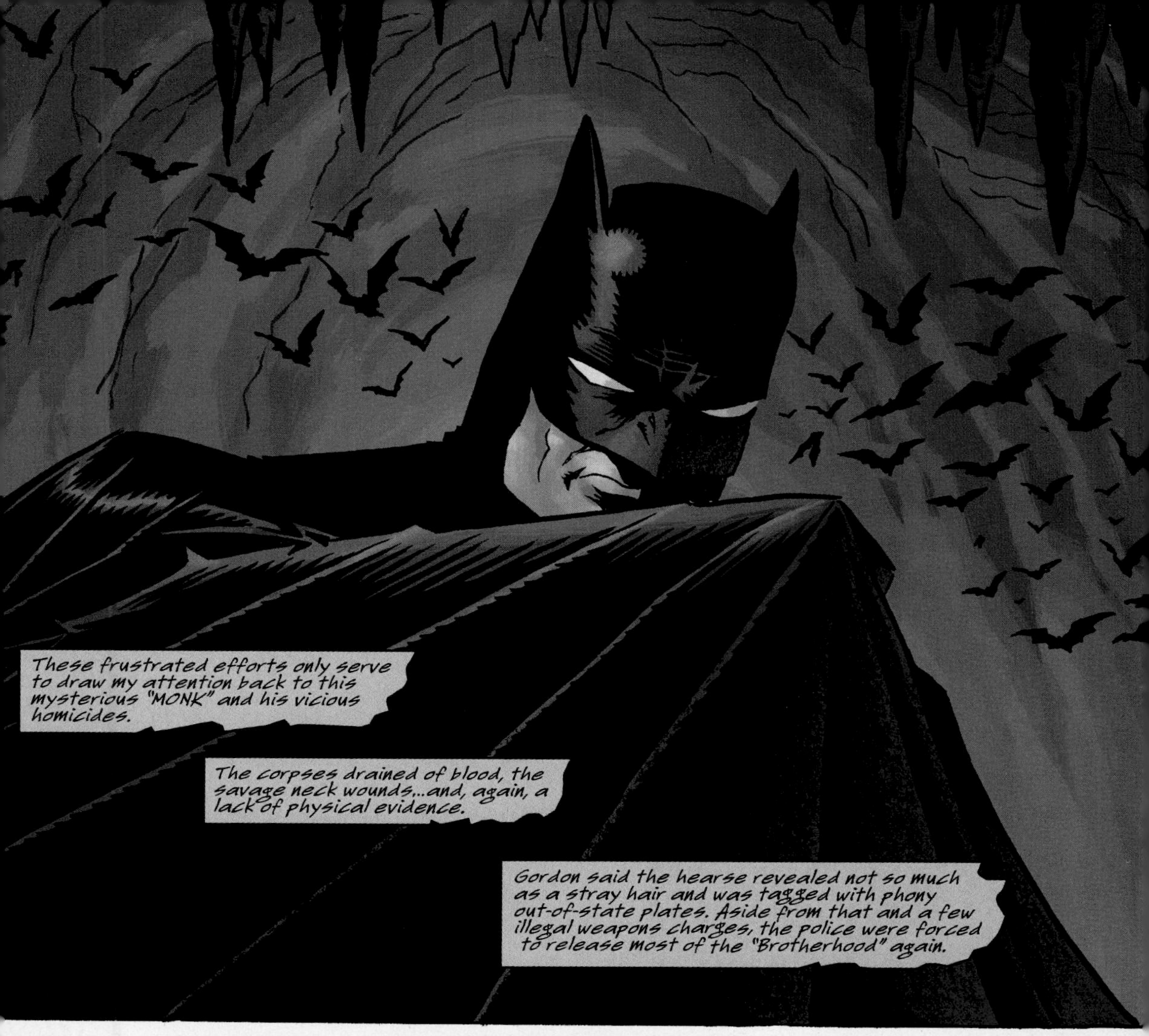
These frustrated efforts only serve to draw my attention back to this mysterious "MONK" and his vicious homicides.
The corpses drained of blood, the savage neck wounds...and, again, a lack of physical evidence.
Gordon said the hearse revealed not so much as a stray hair and was tagged with phony out-of-state plates. Aside from that and a few illegal weapons charges, the police were forced to release most of the "Brotherhood" again.

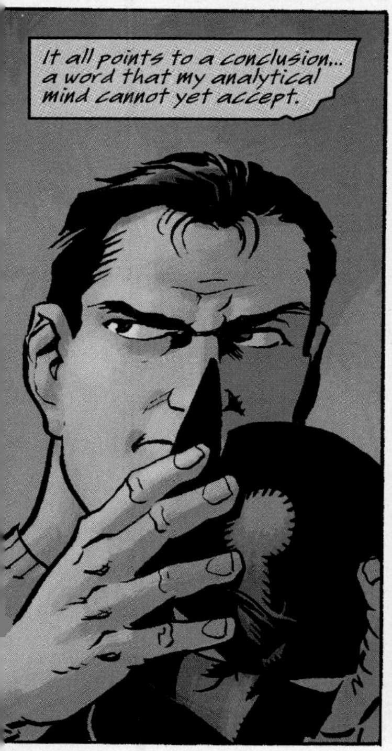
It all points to a conclusion... a word that my analytical mind cannot yet accept.

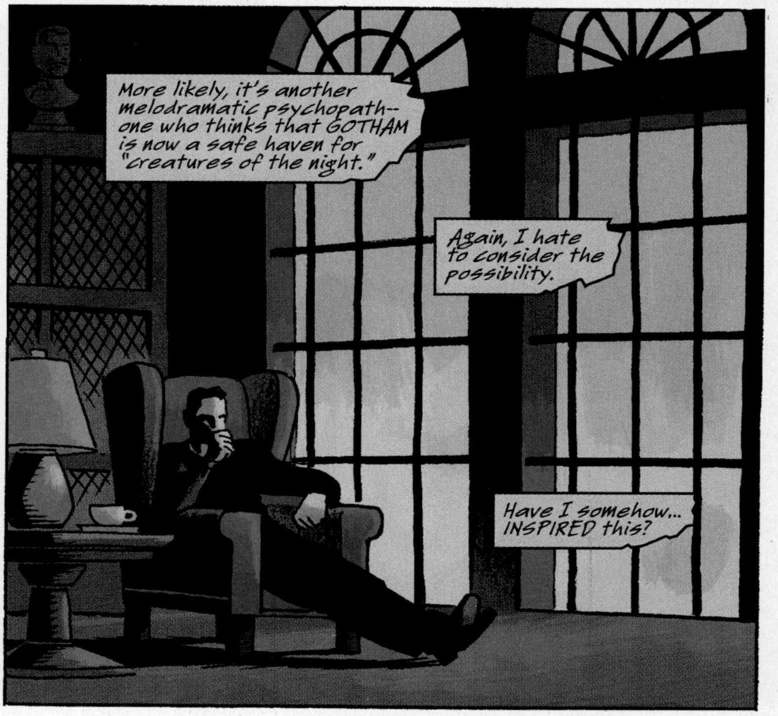
More likely, it's another melodramatic psychopath-- one who thinks that GOTHAM is now a safe haven for "creatures of the night."
Again, I hate to consider the possibility.
Have I somehow... INSPIRED this?

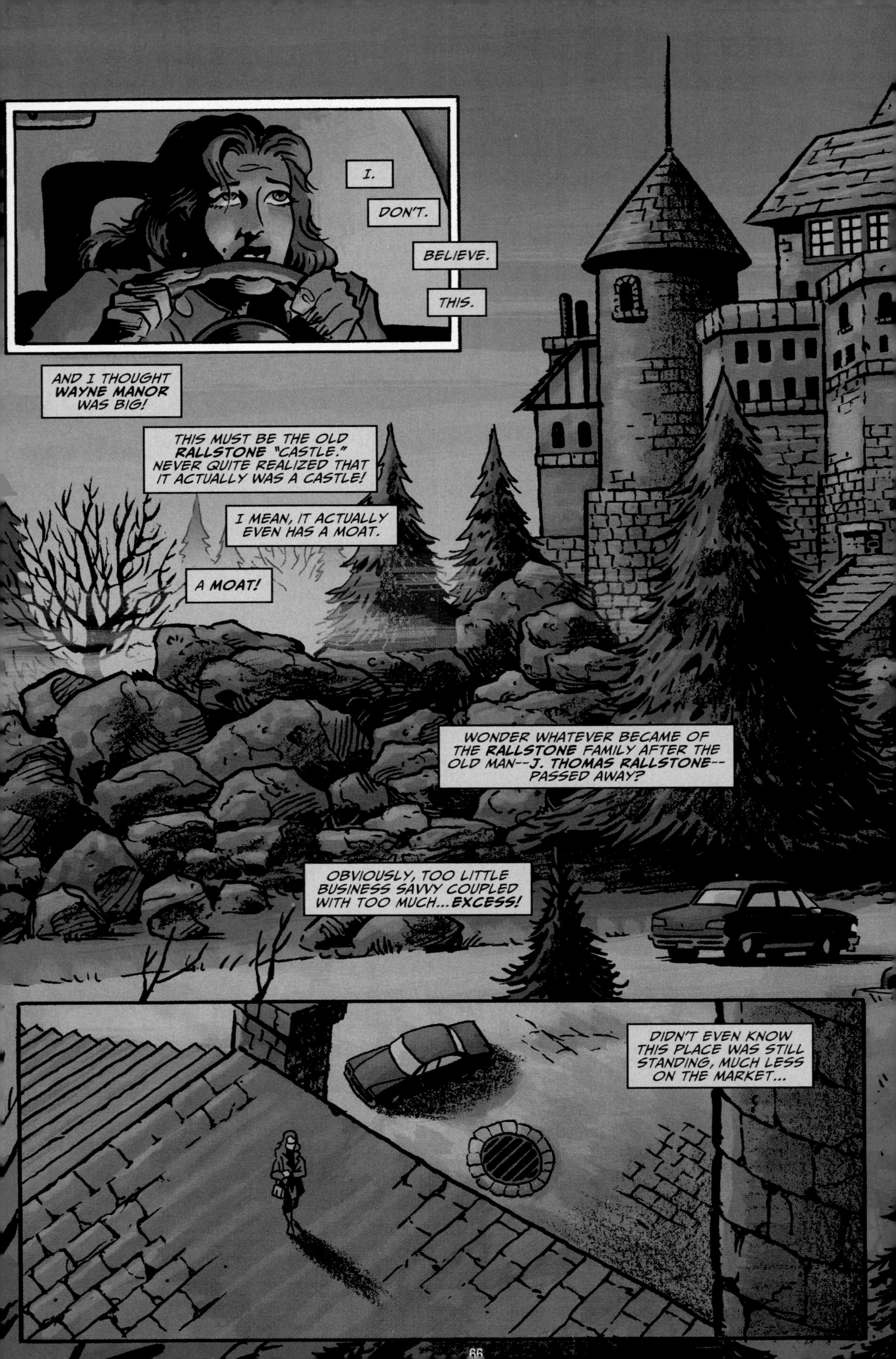
I.
DON'T.
BELIEVE.
THIS.
AND I THOUGHT WAYNE MANOR WAS BIG!
THIS MUST BE THE OLD RALLSTONE "CASTLE." NEVER QUITE REALIZED THAT IT ACTUALLY WAS A CASTLE!
I MEAN, IT ACTUALLY EVEN HAS A MOAT.
A MOAT!
WONDER WHATEVER BECAME OF THE RALLSTONE FAMILY AFTER THE OLD MAN--J. THOMAS RALLSTONE--PASSED AWAY?
OBVIOUSLY, TOO LITTLE BUSINESS SAVVY COUPLED WITH TOO MUCH...EXCESS!
DIDN'T EVEN KNOW THIS PLACE WAS STILL STANDING, MUCH LESS ON THE MARKET...

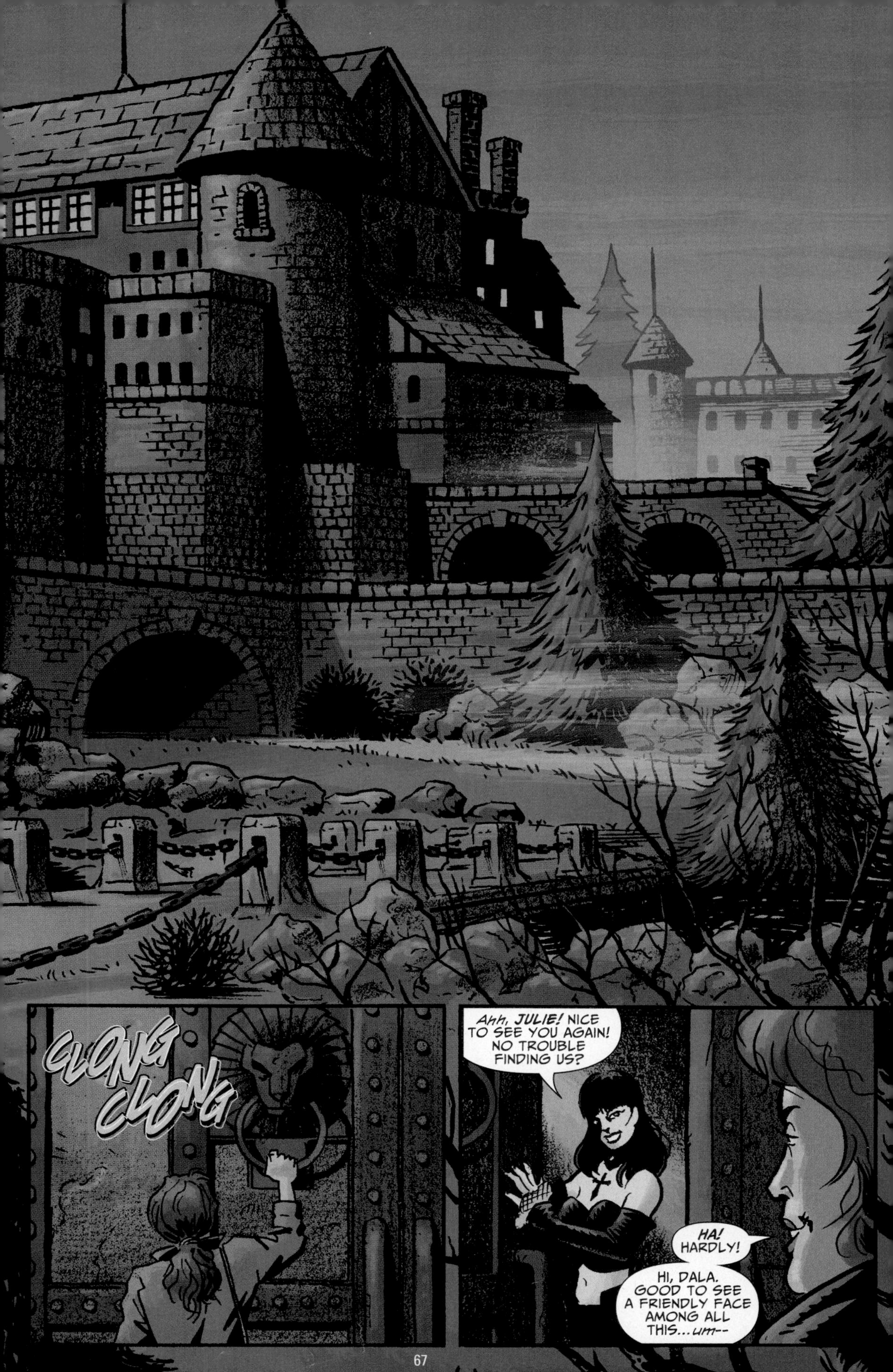
CLONG CLONG
Ahh, JULIE! NICE TO SEE YOU AGAIN! NO TROUBLE FINDING US?
HA! HARDLY!
HI, DALA. GOOD TO SEE A FRIENDLY FACE AMONG ALL THIS... um--

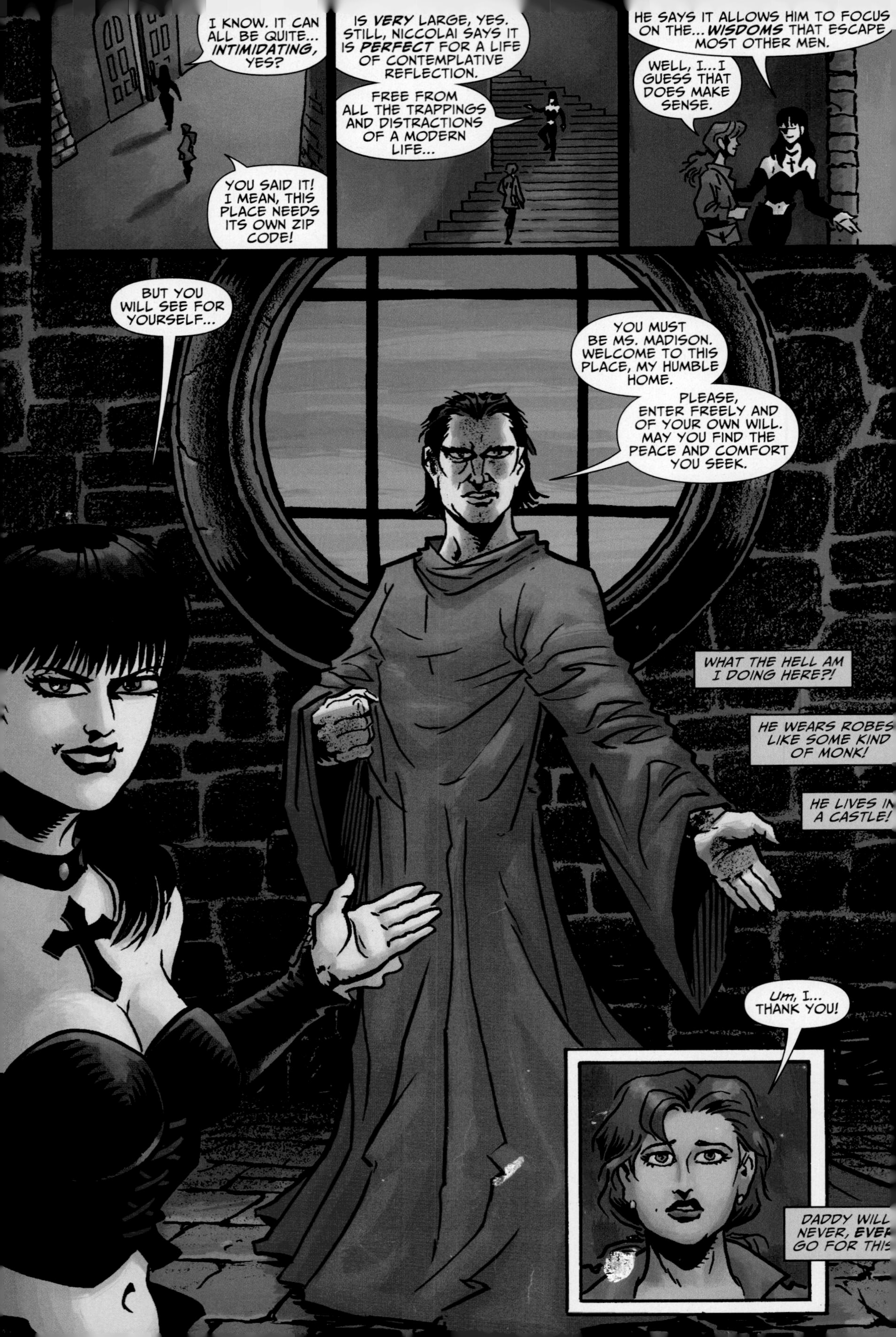

I KNOW. IT CAN ALL BE QUITE... INTIMIDATING, YES?
YOU SAID IT! I MEAN, THIS PLACE NEEDS ITS OWN ZIP CODE!
IS VERY LARGE, YES. STILL, NICCOLAI SAYS IT IS PERFECT FOR A LIFE OF CONTEMPLATIVE REFLECTION.
FREE FROM ALL THE TRAPPINGS AND DISTRACTIONS OF A MODERN LIFE...
HE SAYS IT ALLOWS HIM TO FOCUS ON THE... WISDOMS THAT ESCAPE MOST OTHER MEN.
WELL, I...I GUESS THAT DOES MAKE SENSE.
BUT YOU WILL SEE FOR YOURSELF...
YOU MUST BE MS. MADISON. WELCOME TO THIS PLACE, MY HUMBLE HOME.
PLEASE, ENTER FREELY AND OF YOUR OWN WILL. MAY YOU FIND THE PEACE AND COMFORT YOU SEEK.
WHAT THE HELL AM I DOING HERE?!
HE WEARS ROBES LIKE SOME KIND OF MONK!
HE LIVES IN A CASTLE!
Um, I... THANK YOU!
DADDY WILL NEVER, EVER GO FOR THIS

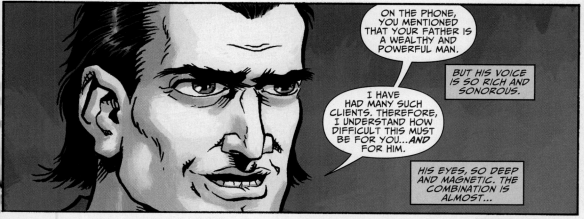

ON THE PHONE, YOU MENTIONED THAT YOUR FATHER IS A WEALTHY AND POWERFUL MAN.

BUT HIS VOICE IS SO RICH AND SONOROUS.

I HAVE HAD MANY SUCH CLIENTS. THEREFORE, I UNDERSTAND HOW DIFFICULT THIS MUST BE FOR YOU...*AND* FOR HIM.

HIS EYES, SO DEEP AND MAGNETIC. THE COMBINATION IS ALMOST...

...HYPNOTIC...

COME.

WE HAD AGREED THAT THIS WOULD BE A GETTING-TO-KNOW-YOU SESSION. SO LET'S SIT AND HAVE IT.

YOU SEEM TO NEED AN EAR, AND I SHALL LOVE TO LISTEN.

MAYBE HE *CAN* HELP DADDY AFTER ALL.

DALA, WE'LL HAVE SOME TEA, IF YOU PLEASE.

WELL, I...I JUST HOPE THIS ISN'T...I JUST DON'T WANT THIS TO ALL BE A WASTE OF YOUR TIME. I HAVE NO IDEA WHETHER I CAN CONVINCE MY FATHER TO COME SEE YOU OR NOT.

YOU SAID HE HAS GROWN RECLUSIVE?

OH, LORD, HE PRACTICALLY BARRICADES HIMSELF IN HIS STUDY. SURELY *THAT* CAN'T BE HEALTHY.

THAT ALL DEPENDS. I, MYSELF, HAVE NOT LEFT THE CONFINES OF THESE STONE WALLS IN NEARLY SEVEN YEARS.

BUT IF YOUR FATHER IS SEEKING REFUGE OUT OF *FEAR* OR DESPERATION, THEN YOU HAVE JUST CAUSE TO WORRY.

HOW LONG HAS HE BEEN LIKE THIS?

FOR SEVERAL MONTHS. AND IT'S BEEN GETTING PROGRESSIVELY WORSE.

HE...HE RECENTLY HAD A *LEGAL* PROBLEM, WHICH HE CONFIDED IN ME, BUT THAT'S ALL OVER NOW.

IT JUST SEEMED TO FRACTURE HIM, THOUGH. I MEAN, I *FORGAVE* HIM, RIGHT FROM THE START.

BUT HE... JUST CAN'T SEEM TO GET OVER IT.

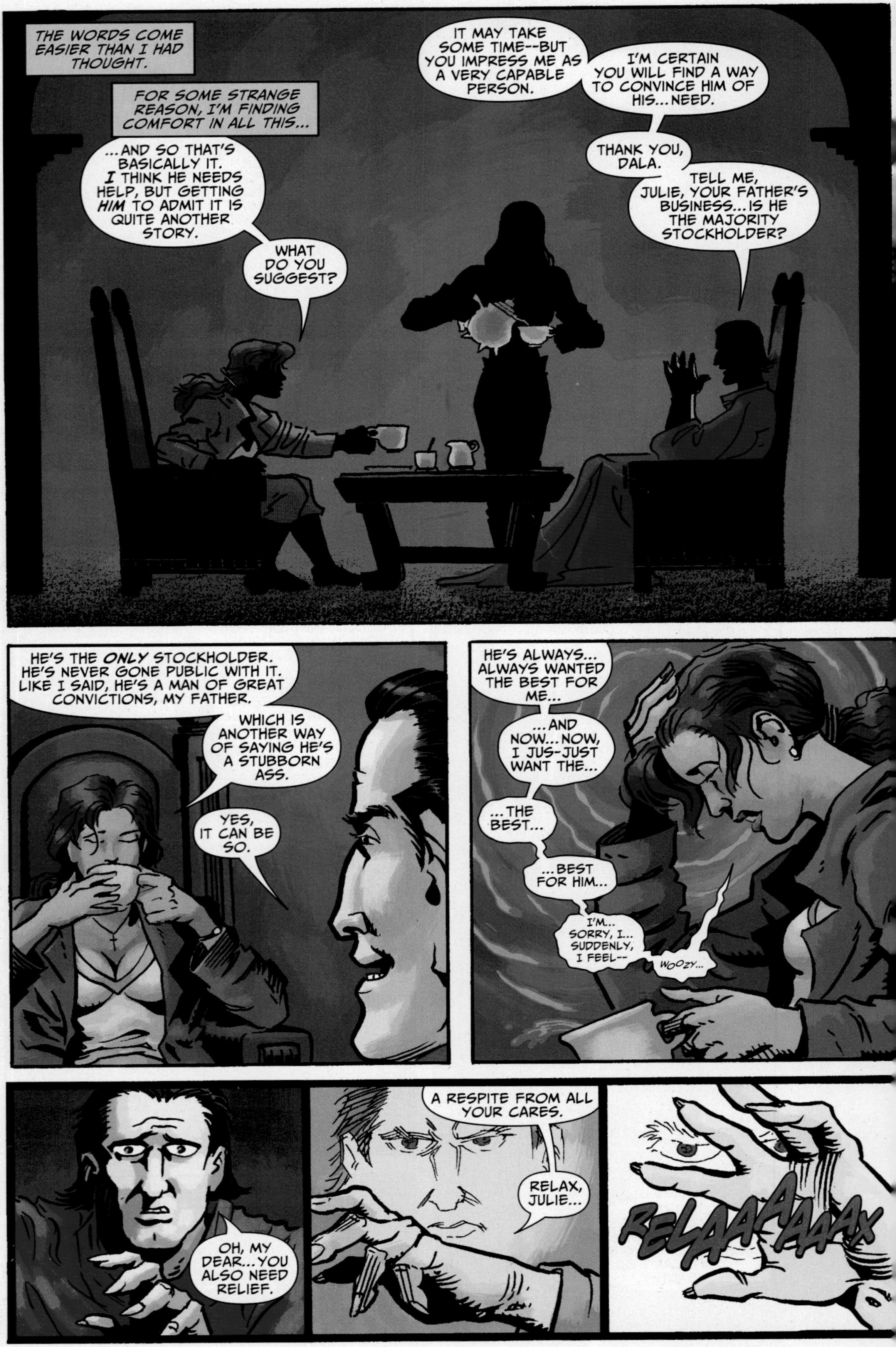
THE WORDS COME EASIER THAN I HAD THOUGHT.
FOR SOME STRANGE REASON, I'M FINDING COMFORT IN ALL THIS...
...AND SO THAT'S BASICALLY IT. I THINK HE NEEDS HELP, BUT GETTING HIM TO ADMIT IT IS QUITE ANOTHER STORY.
WHAT DO YOU SUGGEST?
IT MAY TAKE SOME TIME--BUT YOU IMPRESS ME AS A VERY CAPABLE PERSON.
I'M CERTAIN YOU WILL FIND A WAY TO CONVINCE HIM OF HIS...NEED.
THANK YOU, DALA.
TELL ME, JULIE, YOUR FATHER'S BUSINESS...IS HE THE MAJORITY STOCKHOLDER?
HE'S THE ONLY STOCKHOLDER. HE'S NEVER GONE PUBLIC WITH IT. LIKE I SAID, HE'S A MAN OF GREAT CONVICTIONS, MY FATHER.
WHICH IS ANOTHER WAY OF SAYING HE'S A STUBBORN ASS.
YES, IT CAN BE SO.
HE'S ALWAYS... ALWAYS WANTED THE BEST FOR ME...
...AND NOW...NOW, I JUS-JUST WANT THE...
...THE BEST...
...BEST FOR HIM...
I'M... SORRY, I... SUDDENLY, I FEEL--
WOOZY...
OH, MY DEAR...YOU ALSO NEED RELIEF.
A RESPITE FROM ALL YOUR CARES.
RELAX, JULIE...
RELAAAAAAAX

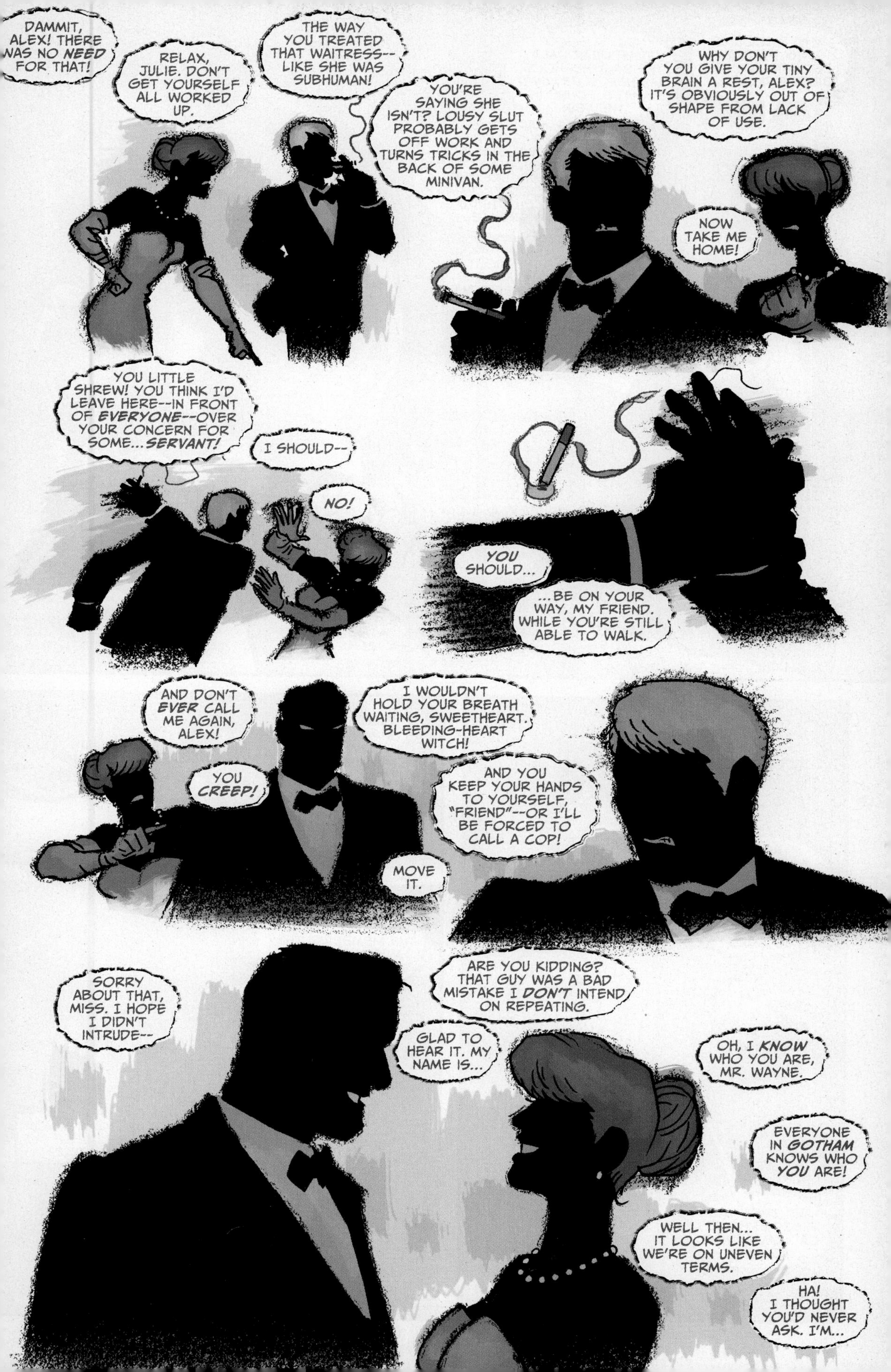
DAMMIT, ALEX! THERE WAS NO NEED FOR THAT!
RELAX, JULIE. DON'T GET YOURSELF ALL WORKED UP.
THE WAY YOU TREATED THAT WAITRESS-- LIKE SHE WAS SUBHUMAN!
YOU'RE SAYING SHE ISN'T? LOUSY SLUT PROBABLY GETS OFF WORK AND TURNS TRICKS IN THE BACK OF SOME MINIVAN.
WHY DON'T YOU GIVE YOUR TINY BRAIN A REST, ALEX? IT'S OBVIOUSLY OUT OF SHAPE FROM LACK OF USE.
NOW TAKE ME HOME!
YOU LITTLE SHREW! YOU THINK I'D LEAVE HERE--IN FRONT OF EVERYONE--OVER YOUR CONCERN FOR SOME... SERVANT!
I SHOULD--
NO!
YOU SHOULD...
...BE ON YOUR WAY, MY FRIEND. WHILE YOU'RE STILL ABLE TO WALK.
AND DON'T EVER CALL ME AGAIN, ALEX!
YOU CREEP!
I WOULDN'T HOLD YOUR BREATH WAITING, SWEETHEART. BLEEDING-HEART WITCH!
AND YOU KEEP YOUR HANDS TO YOURSELF, "FRIEND"--OR I'LL BE FORCED TO CALL A COP!
MOVE IT.
SORRY ABOUT THAT, MISS. I HOPE I DIDN'T INTRUDE--
ARE YOU KIDDING? THAT GUY WAS A BAD MISTAKE I DON'T INTEND ON REPEATING.
GLAD TO HEAR IT. MY NAME IS...
OH, I KNOW WHO YOU ARE, MR. WAYNE.
EVERYONE IN GOTHAM KNOWS WHO YOU ARE!
WELL THEN... IT LOOKS LIKE WE'RE ON UNEVEN TERMS.
HA! I THOUGHT YOU'D NEVER ASK. I'M...

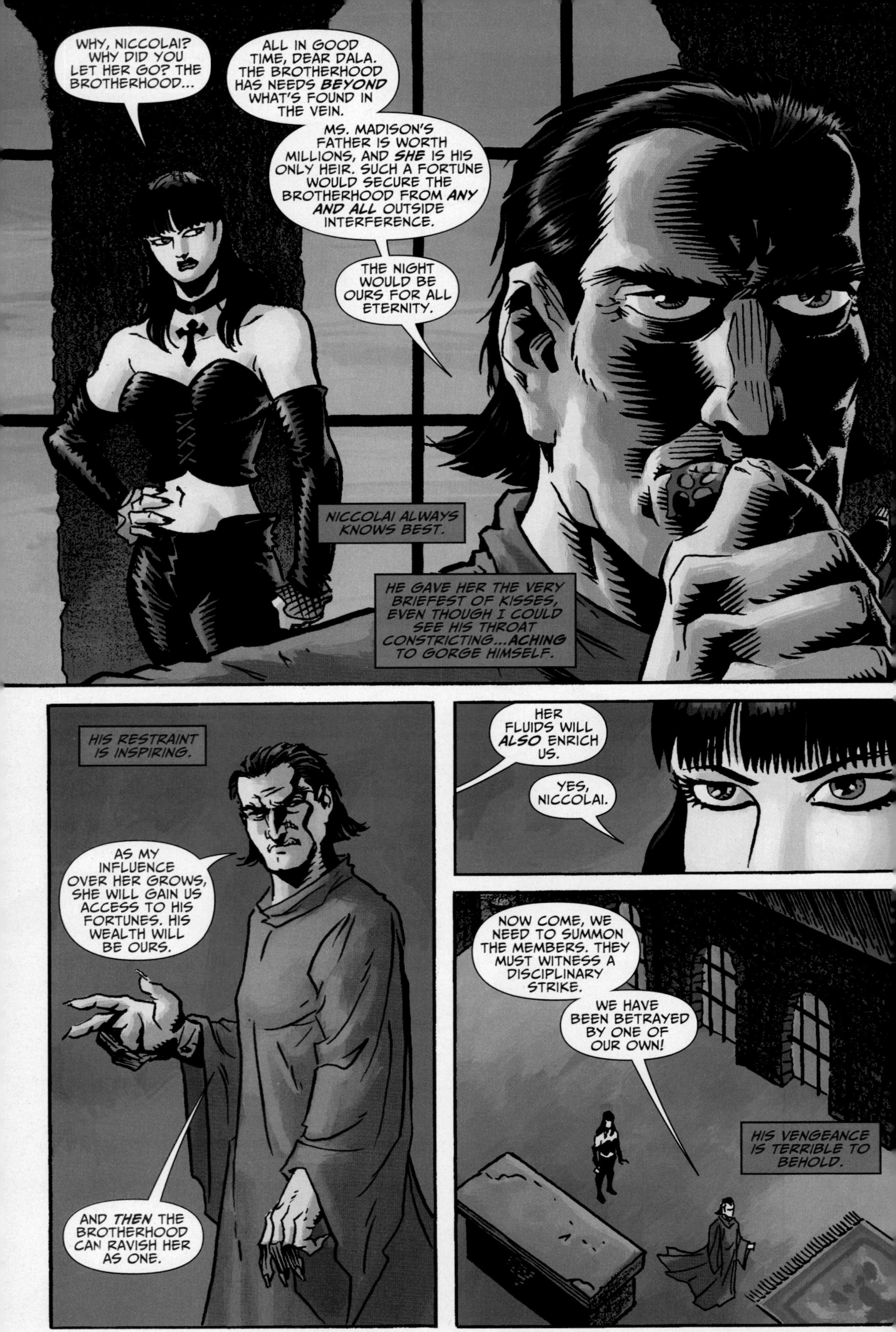
WHY, NICCOLAI? WHY DID YOU LET HER GO? THE BROTHERHOOD...
ALL IN GOOD TIME, DEAR DALA. THE BROTHERHOOD HAS NEEDS *BEYOND* WHAT'S FOUND IN THE VEIN.
MS. MADISON'S FATHER IS WORTH MILLIONS, AND *SHE* IS HIS ONLY HEIR. SUCH A FORTUNE WOULD SECURE THE BROTHERHOOD FROM *ANY AND ALL* OUTSIDE INTERFERENCE.
THE NIGHT WOULD BE OURS FOR ALL ETERNITY.
NICCOLAI ALWAYS KNOWS BEST.
HE GAVE HER THE VERY BRIEFEST OF KISSES, EVEN THOUGH I COULD SEE HIS THROAT CONSTRICTING...*ACHING* TO GORGE HIMSELF.
HIS RESTRAINT IS INSPIRING.
AS MY INFLUENCE OVER HER GROWS, SHE WILL GAIN US ACCESS TO HIS FORTUNES. HIS WEALTH WILL BE OURS.
AND *THEN* THE BROTHERHOOD CAN RAVISH HER AS ONE.
HER FLUIDS WILL *ALSO* ENRICH US.
YES, NICCOLAI.
NOW COME, WE NEED TO SUMMON THE MEMBERS. THEY MUST WITNESS A DISCIPLINARY STRIKE.
WE HAVE BEEN BETRAYED BY ONE OF OUR OWN!
HIS VENGEANCE IS TERRIBLE TO BEHOLD.

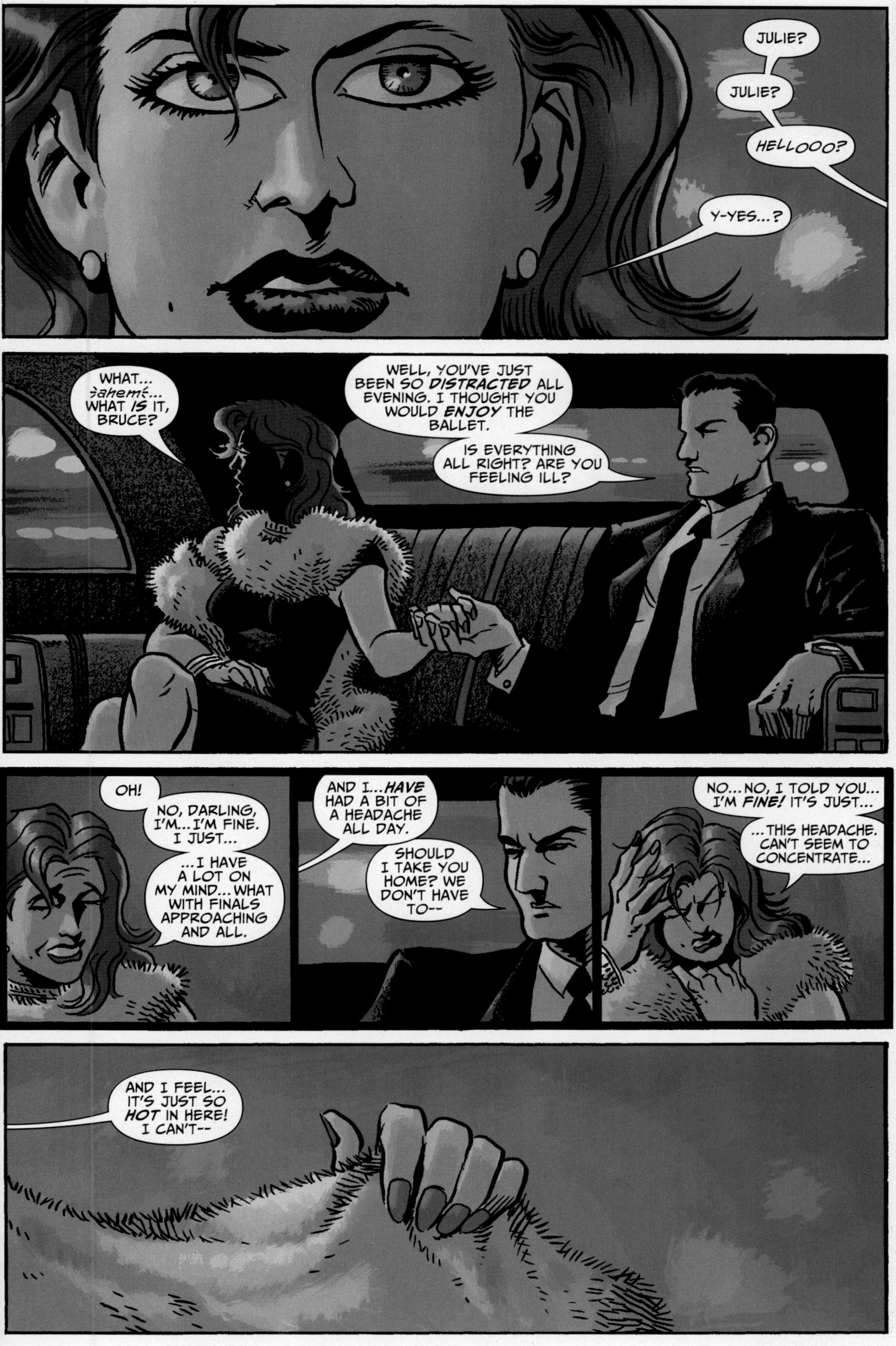
JULIE?
JULIE?
HELLOOO?
Y-YES...?
WHAT... ahem... WHAT IS IT, BRUCE?
WELL, YOU'VE JUST BEEN SO DISTRACTED ALL EVENING. I THOUGHT YOU WOULD ENJOY THE BALLET.
IS EVERYTHING ALL RIGHT? ARE YOU FEELING ILL?
OH!
NO, DARLING, I'M...I'M FINE. I JUST...
...I HAVE A LOT ON MY MIND...WHAT WITH FINALS APPROACHING AND ALL.
AND I...HAVE HAD A BIT OF A HEADACHE ALL DAY.
SHOULD I TAKE YOU HOME? WE DON'T HAVE TO--
NO...NO, I TOLD YOU... I'M FINE! IT'S JUST...
...THIS HEADACHE. CAN'T SEEM TO CONCENTRATE...
AND I FEEL... IT'S JUST SO HOT IN HERE! I CAN'T--

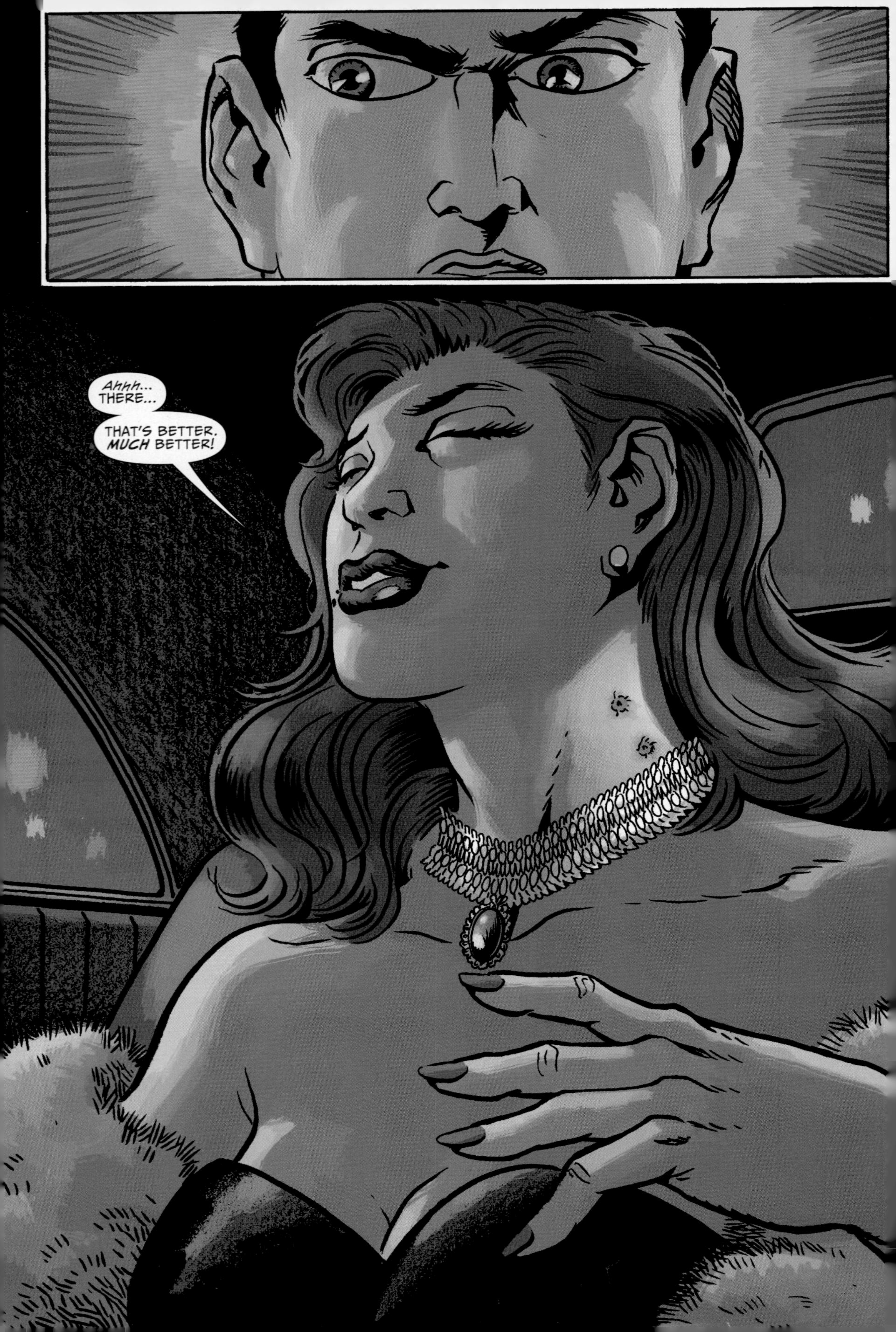
Ahhh... THERE...
THAT'S BETTER. MUCH BETTER!

CHAPTER 4

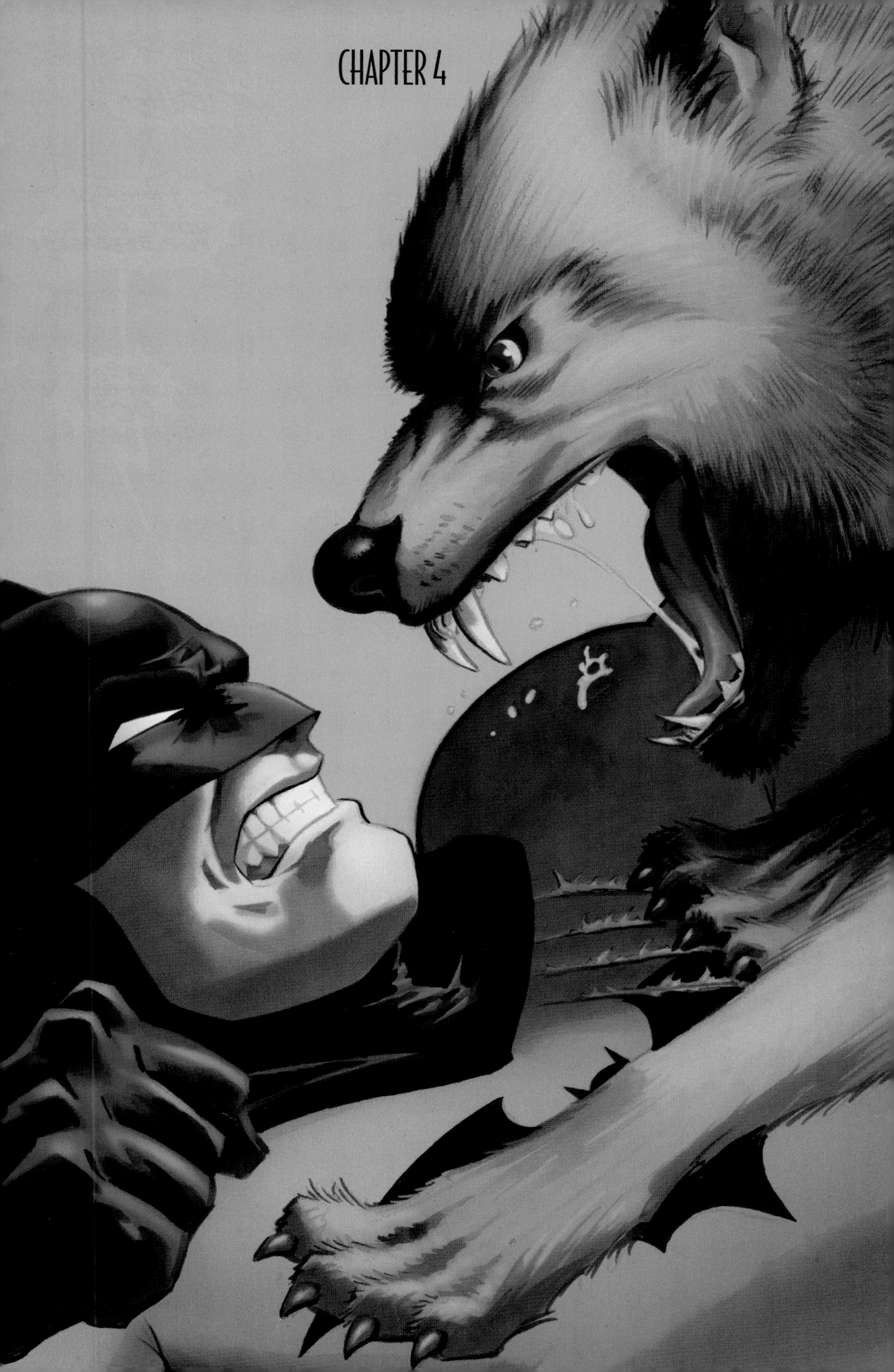

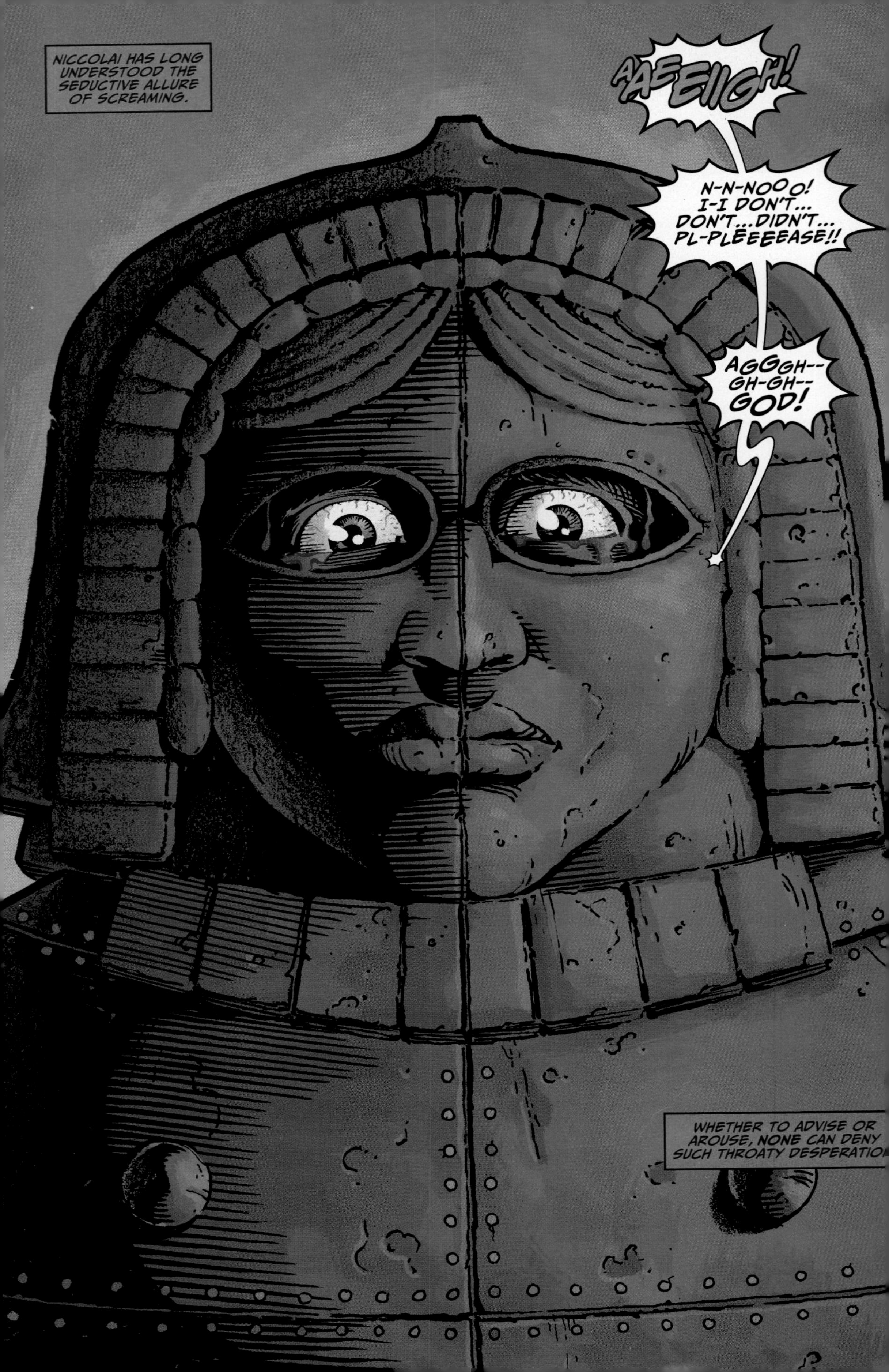
NICCOLAI HAS LONG UNDERSTOOD THE SEDUCTIVE ALLURE OF SCREAMING.
AAEEIIGH!
N-N-NOOO! I-I DON'T... DON'T...DIDN'T... PL-PLEEEEASE!!
AGGGH-- GH-GH-- GOD!
WHETHER TO ADVISE OR AROUSE, NONE CAN DENY SUCH THROATY DESPERATIO

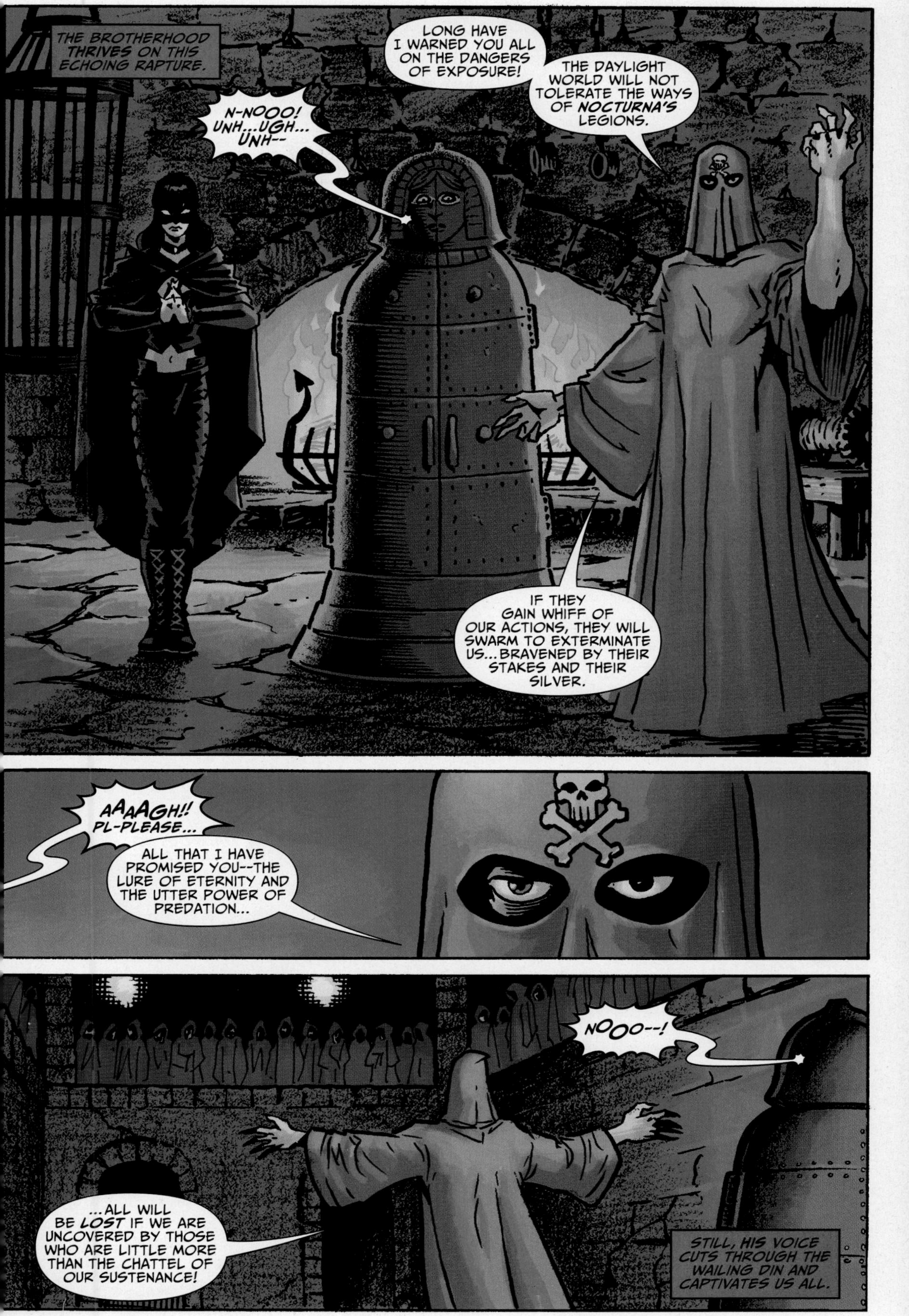

THE BROTHERHOOD THRIVES ON THIS ECHOING RAPTURE.
LONG HAVE I WARNED YOU ALL ON THE DANGERS OF EXPOSURE!
THE DAYLIGHT WORLD WILL NOT TOLERATE THE WAYS OF NOCTURNA'S LEGIONS.
N-NOOO! UNH...UGH... UNH--
IF THEY GAIN WHIFF OF OUR ACTIONS, THEY WILL SWARM TO EXTERMINATE US...BRAVENED BY THEIR STAKES AND THEIR SILVER.
AAAAGH!! PL-PLEASE...
ALL THAT I HAVE PROMISED YOU--THE LURE OF ETERNITY AND THE UTTER POWER OF PREDATION...
NOOO--!
...ALL WILL BE LOST IF WE ARE UNCOVERED BY THOSE WHO ARE LITTLE MORE THAN THE CHATTEL OF OUR SUSTENANCE!
STILL, HIS VOICE CUTS THROUGH THE WAILING DIN AND CAPTIVATES US ALL.

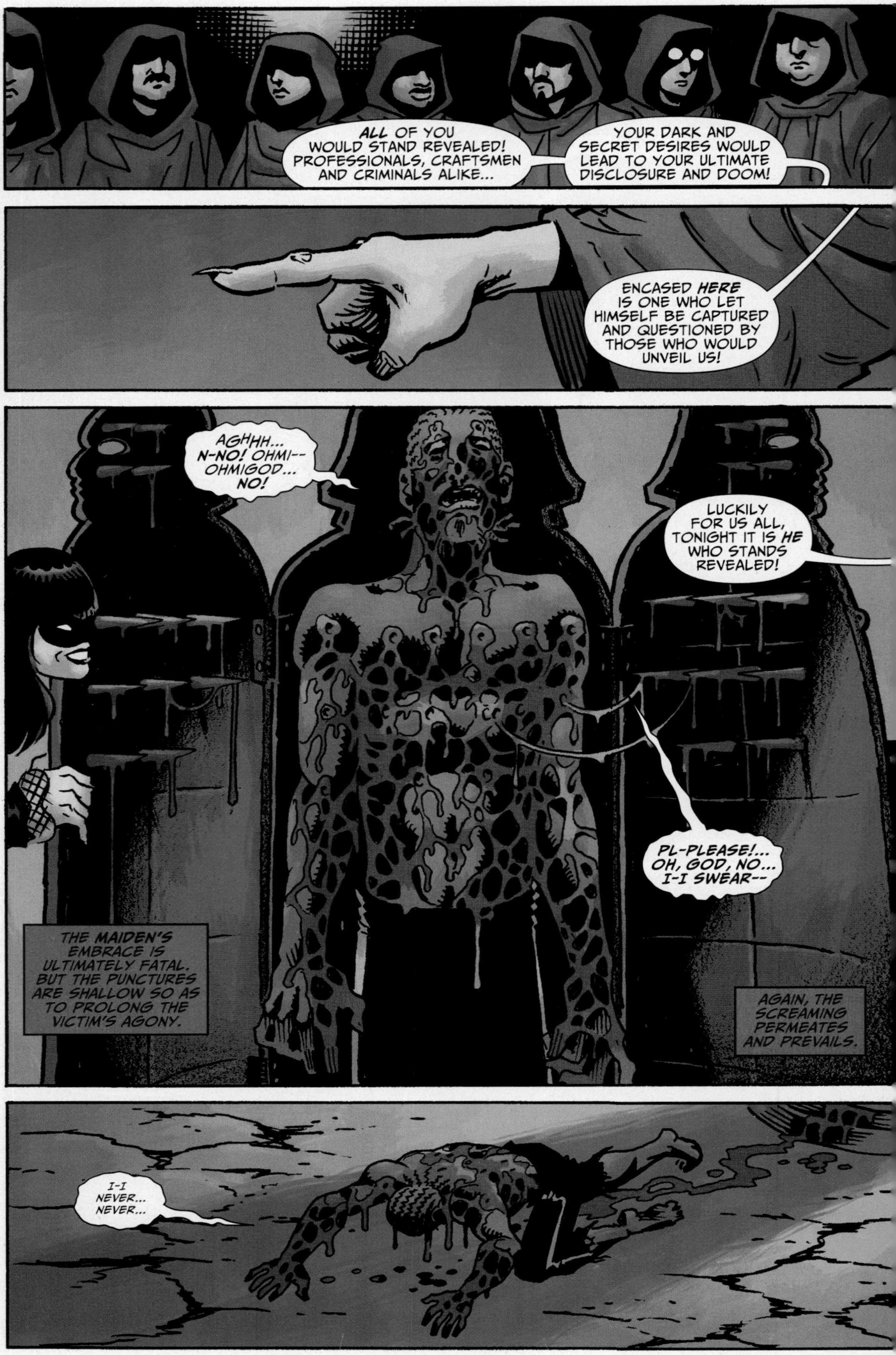
ALL OF YOU WOULD STAND REVEALED! PROFESSIONALS, CRAFTSMEN AND CRIMINALS ALIKE...
YOUR DARK AND SECRET DESIRES WOULD LEAD TO YOUR ULTIMATE DISCLOSURE AND DOOM!
ENCASED HERE IS ONE WHO LET HIMSELF BE CAPTURED AND QUESTIONED BY THOSE WHO WOULD UNVEIL US!
AGHHH... N-NO! OHMI-- OHMIGOD... NO!
LUCKILY FOR US ALL, TONIGHT IT IS HE WHO STANDS REVEALED!
PL-PLEASE!... OH, GOD, NO... I-I SWEAR--
THE MAIDEN'S EMBRACE IS ULTIMATELY FATAL. BUT THE PUNCTURES ARE SHALLOW SO AS TO PROLONG THE VICTIM'S AGONY.
AGAIN, THE SCREAMING PERMEATES AND PREVAILS.
I-I NEVER... NEVER...

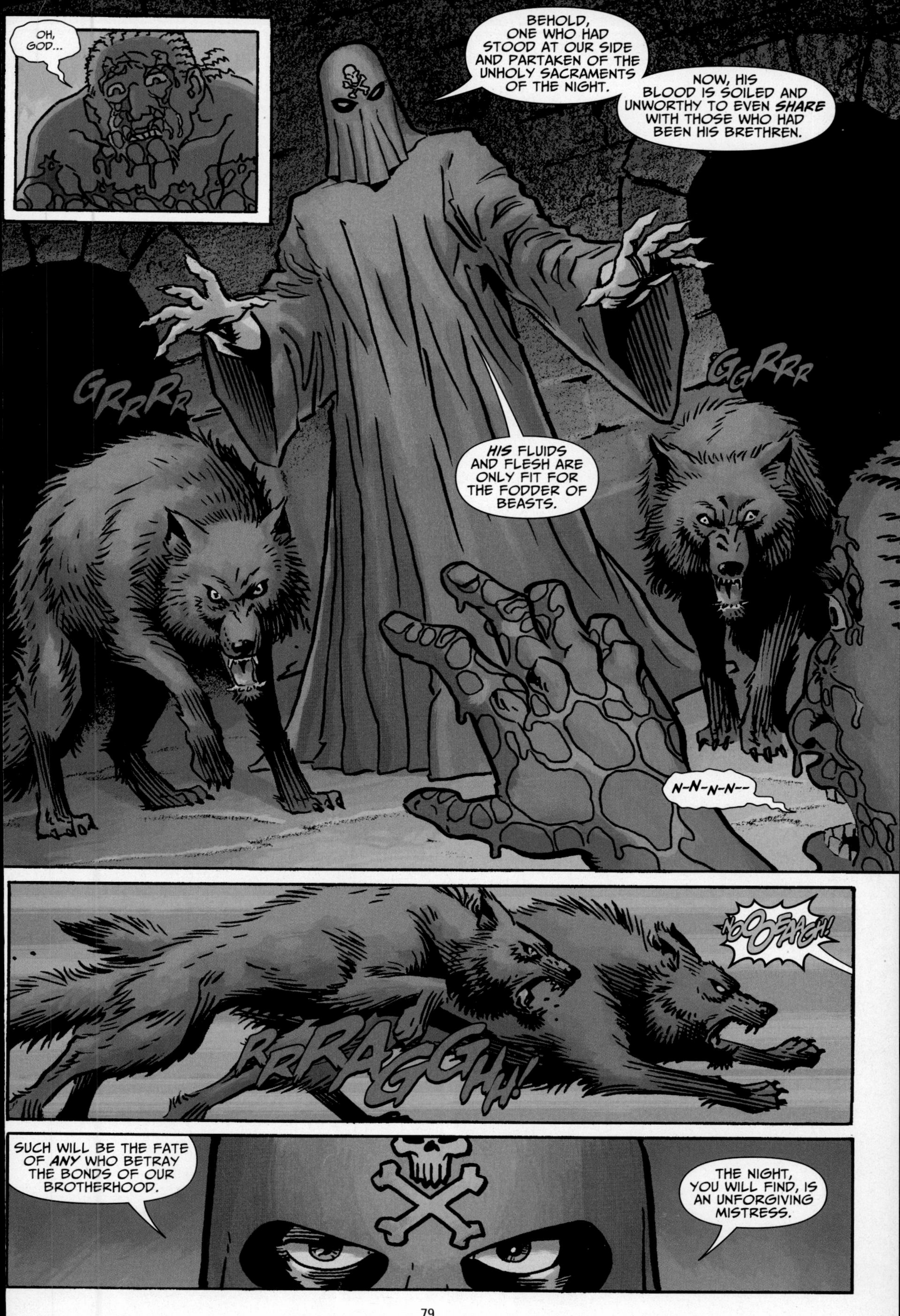
OH, GOD...
BEHOLD, ONE WHO HAD STOOD AT OUR SIDE AND PARTAKEN OF THE UNHOLY SACRAMENTS OF THE NIGHT.
NOW, HIS BLOOD IS SOILED AND UNWORTHY TO EVEN SHARE WITH THOSE WHO HAD BEEN HIS BRETHREN.
GRRRRR
GGRRRR
HIS FLUIDS AND FLESH ARE ONLY FIT FOR THE FODDER OF BEASTS.
N-N-N-N--
NOOOFAAGH!
RRRAGGH!
SUCH WILL BE THE FATE OF ANY WHO BETRAY THE BONDS OF OUR BROTHERHOOD.
THE NIGHT, YOU WILL FIND, IS AN UNFORGIVING MISTRESS.

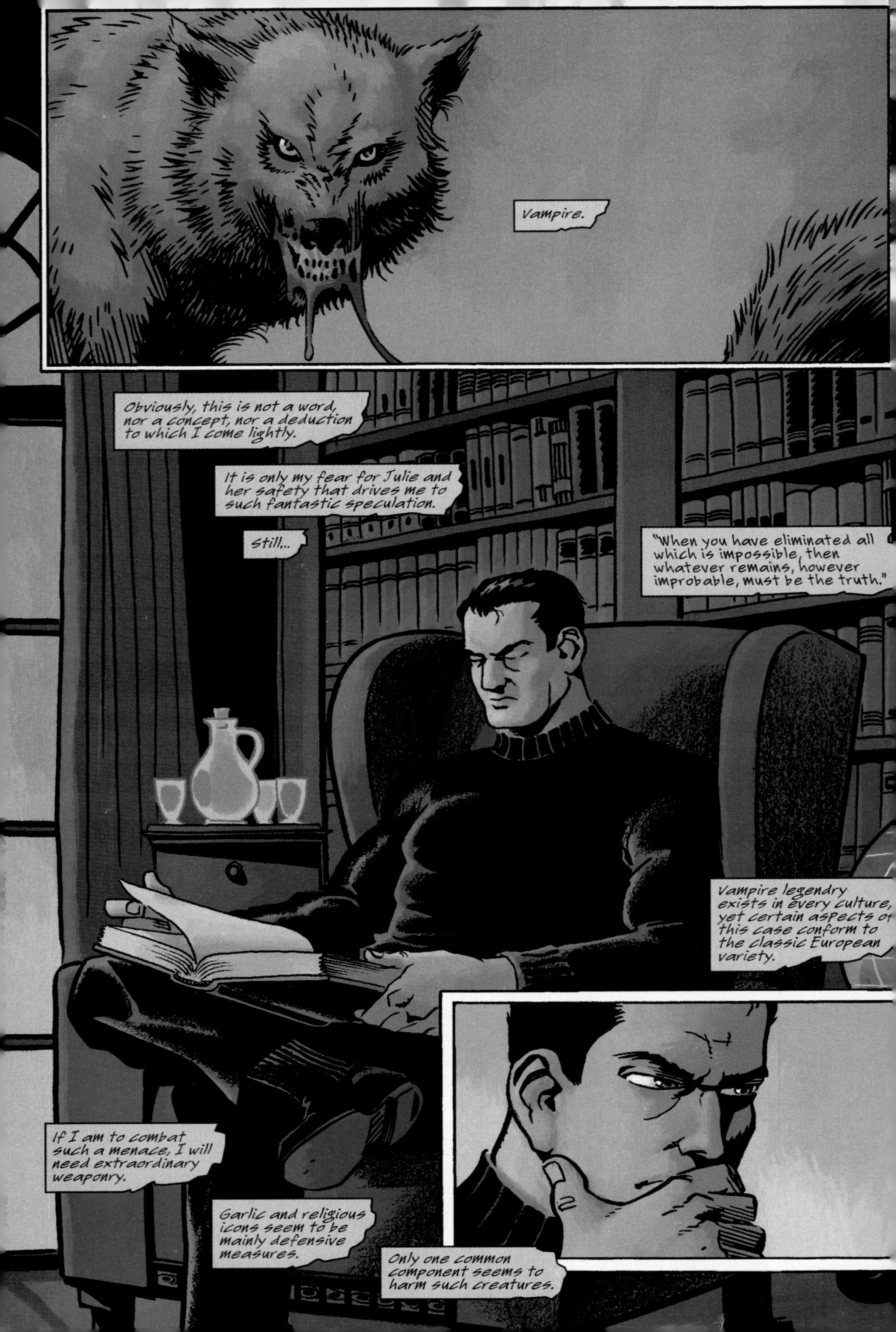
Vampire.
Obviously, this is not a word, nor a concept, nor a deduction to which I come lightly.
It is only my fear for Julie and her safety that drives me to such fantastic speculation.
Still...
"When you have eliminated all which is impossible, then whatever remains, however improbable, must be the truth."
Vampire legendry exists in every culture, yet certain aspects of this case conform to the classic European variety.
If I am to combat such a menace, I will need extraordinary weaponry.
Garlic and religious icons seem to be mainly defensive measures.
Only one common component seems to harm such creatures.

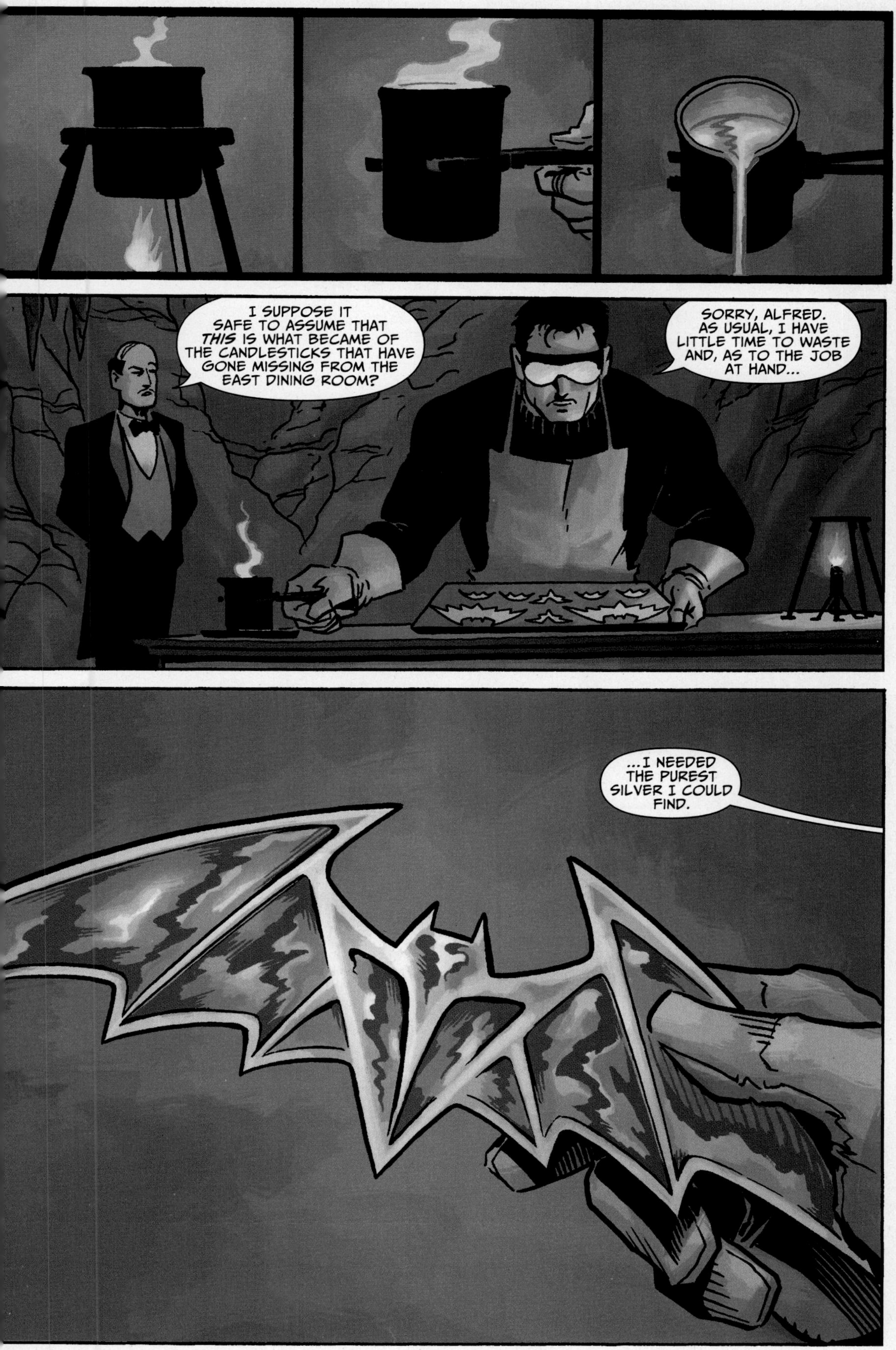
I SUPPOSE IT SAFE TO ASSUME THAT THIS IS WHAT BECAME OF THE CANDLESTICKS THAT HAVE GONE MISSING FROM THE EAST DINING ROOM?
SORRY, ALFRED. AS USUAL, I HAVE LITTLE TIME TO WASTE AND, AS TO THE JOB AT HAND...
...I NEEDED THE PUREST SILVER I COULD FIND.

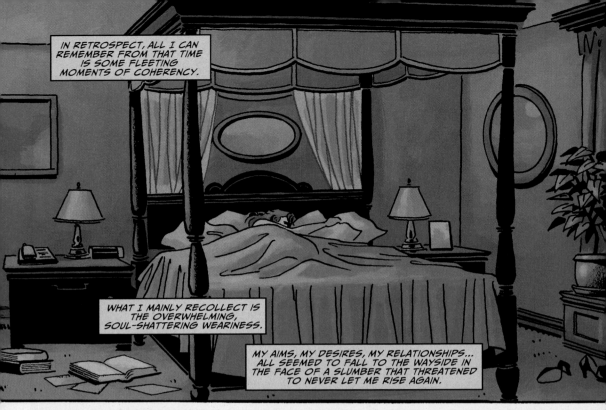

IN RETROSPECT, ALL I CAN REMEMBER FROM THAT TIME IS SOME FLEETING MOMENTS OF COHERENCY.

WHAT I MAINLY RECOLLECT IS THE OVERWHELMING, SOUL-SHATTERING WEARINESS.

MY AIMS, MY DESIRES, MY RELATIONSHIPS... ALL SEEMED TO FALL TO THE WAYSIDE IN THE FACE OF A SLUMBER THAT THREATENED TO NEVER LET ME RISE AGAIN.

RING RING

AND THE SIBILANT, SOLITARY VOICE THAT COMMANDED MY EVERY ACTION.

Unhh--?

H-HELLO...?

GOOD EVENING, MY DEAR MISS MADISON. I TRUST YOU ARE FEELING WELL?

YES... YES, I--

I'M CALLING TO SUMMON YOU TO ANOTHER OF OUR... SESSIONS. YOU UNDERSTAND?

YES, I...

YOU WILL RETURN TO THE CASTLE.

YOU WILL LEAVE AS SOON AS YOU ARE ABLE.

Y-YES, I...I WILL-- I'M...

...ON MY WAY--

KLNK--

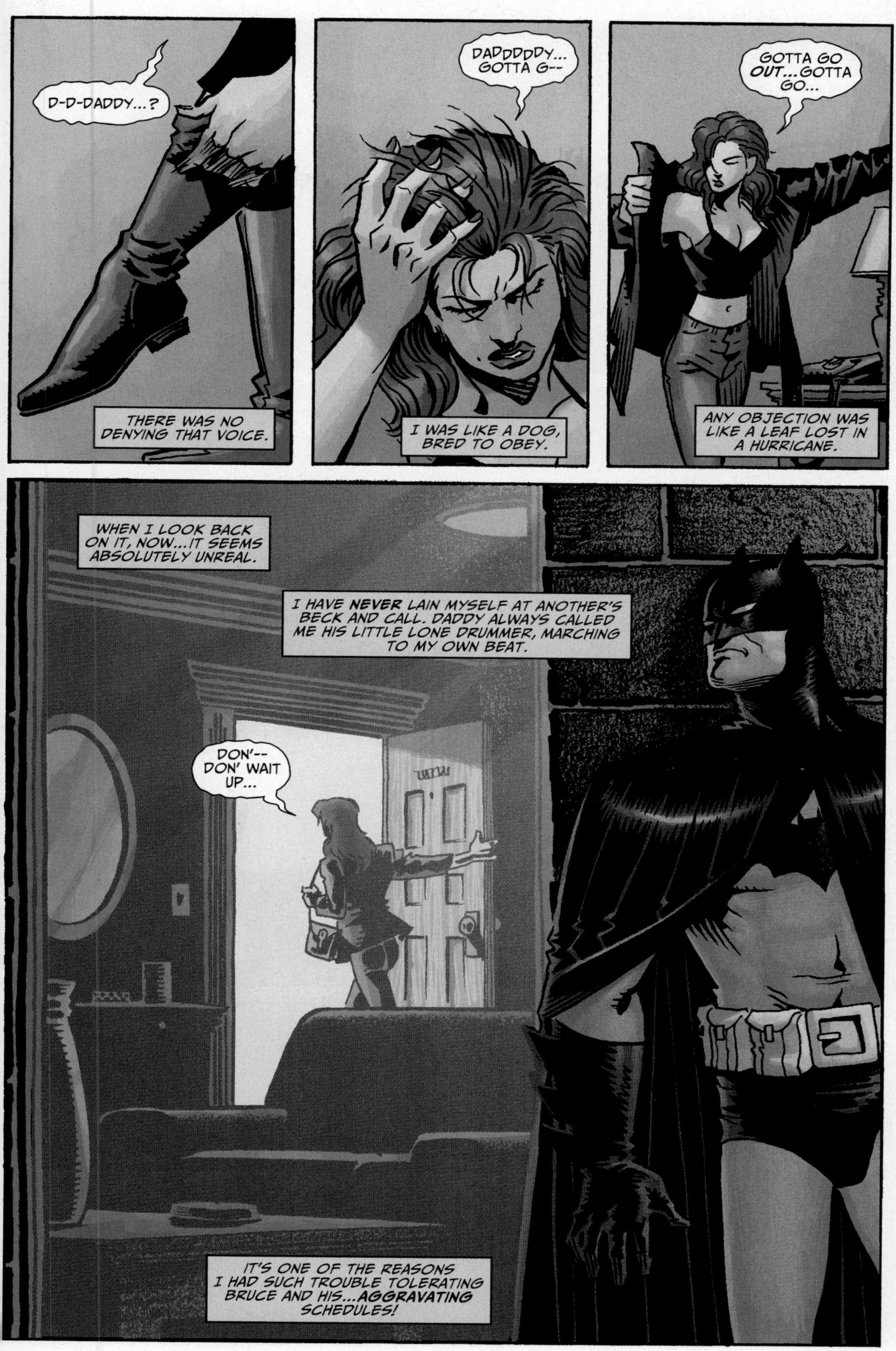
D-D-DADDY...?
THERE WAS NO DENYING THAT VOICE.
DADDDDDY... GOTTA G--
I WAS LIKE A DOG, BRED TO OBEY.
GOTTA GO OUT... GOTTA GO...
ANY OBJECTION WAS LIKE A LEAF LOST IN A HURRICANE.
WHEN I LOOK BACK ON IT, NOW... IT SEEMS ABSOLUTELY UNREAL.
I HAVE NEVER LAIN MYSELF AT ANOTHER'S BECK AND CALL. DADDY ALWAYS CALLED ME HIS LITTLE LONE DRUMMER, MARCHING TO MY OWN BEAT.
DON'-- DON' WAIT UP...
IT'S ONE OF THE REASONS I HAD SUCH TROUBLE TOLERATING BRUCE AND HIS... AGGRAVATING SCHEDULES!

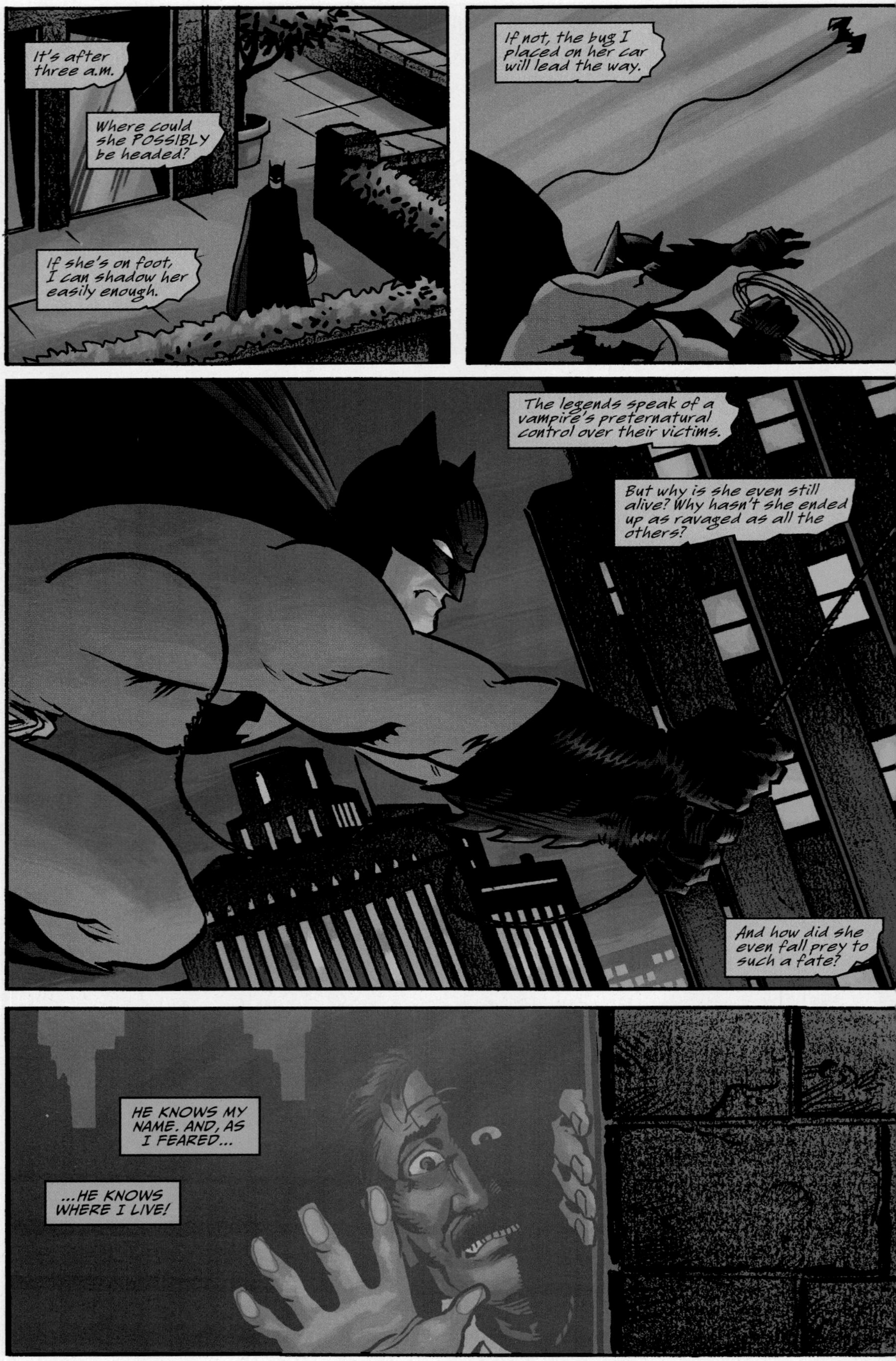
It's after three a.m.
Where could she POSSIBLY be headed?
If she's on foot, I can shadow her easily enough.
If not, the bug I placed on her car will lead the way.
The legends speak of a vampire's preternatural control over their victims.
But why is she even still alive? Why hasn't she ended up as ravaged as all the others?
And how did she even fall prey to such a fate?
HE KNOWS MY NAME. AND, AS I FEARED...
...HE KNOWS WHERE I LIVE!

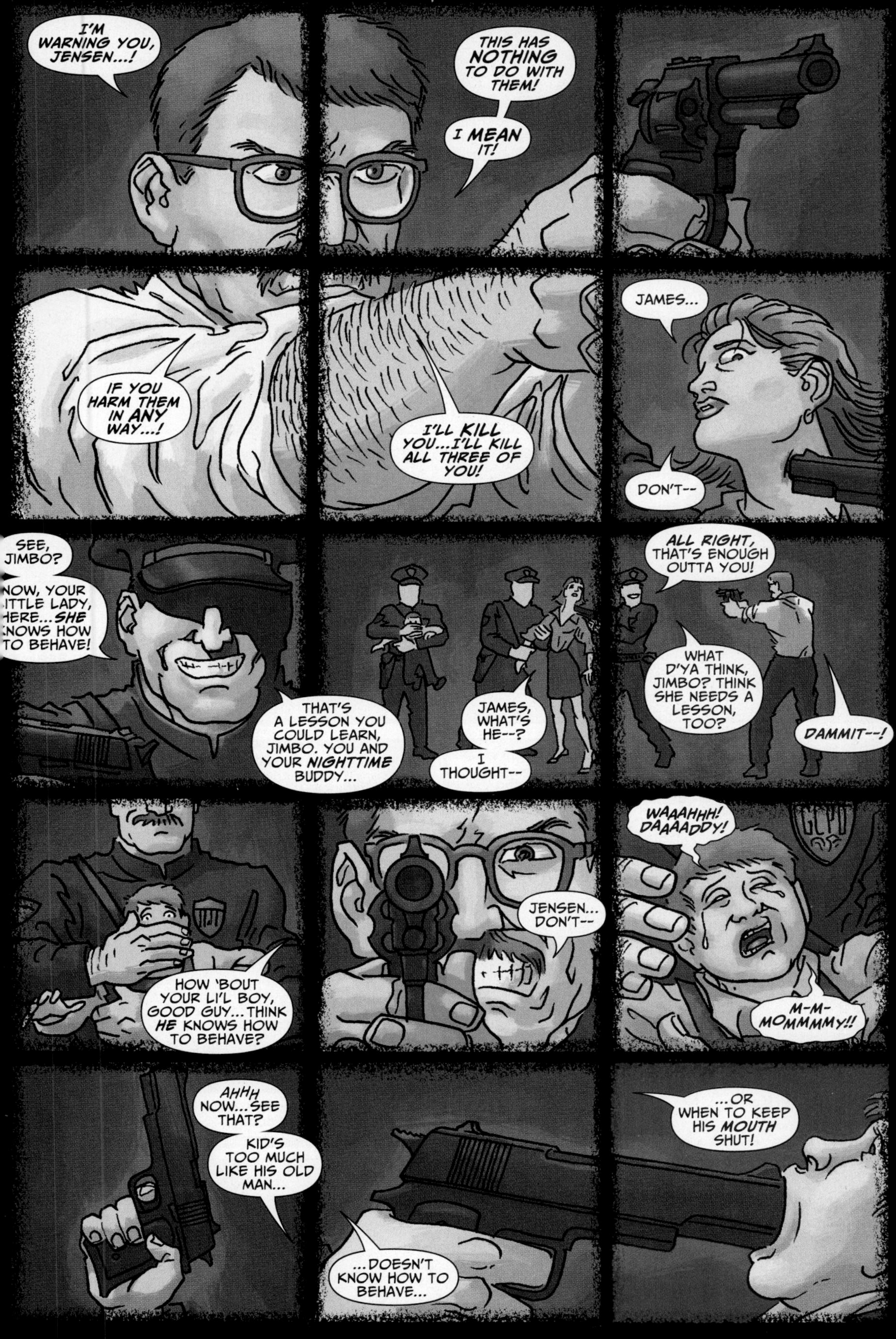
I'M WARNING YOU, JENSEN...!
THIS HAS NOTHING TO DO WITH THEM!
I MEAN IT!
IF YOU HARM THEM IN ANY WAY...!
I'LL KILL YOU...I'LL KILL ALL THREE OF YOU!
JAMES...
DON'T--
SEE, JIMBO?
NOW, YOUR LITTLE LADY, HERE...SHE KNOWS HOW TO BEHAVE!
THAT'S A LESSON YOU COULD LEARN, JIMBO. YOU AND YOUR NIGHTTIME BUDDY...
JAMES, WHAT'S HE--?
I THOUGHT--
ALL RIGHT, THAT'S ENOUGH OUTTA YOU!
WHAT D'YA THINK, JIMBO? THINK SHE NEEDS A LESSON, TOO?
DAMMIT--!
HOW 'BOUT YOUR LI'L BOY, GOOD GUY...THINK HE KNOWS HOW TO BEHAVE?
JENSEN... DON'T--
WAAAHHH! DAAAADDY!
M-M-MOMMMMY!!
AHHH NOW...SEE THAT?
KID'S TOO MUCH LIKE HIS OLD MAN...
...DOESN'T KNOW HOW TO BEHAVE...
...OR WHEN TO KEEP HIS MOUTH SHUT!

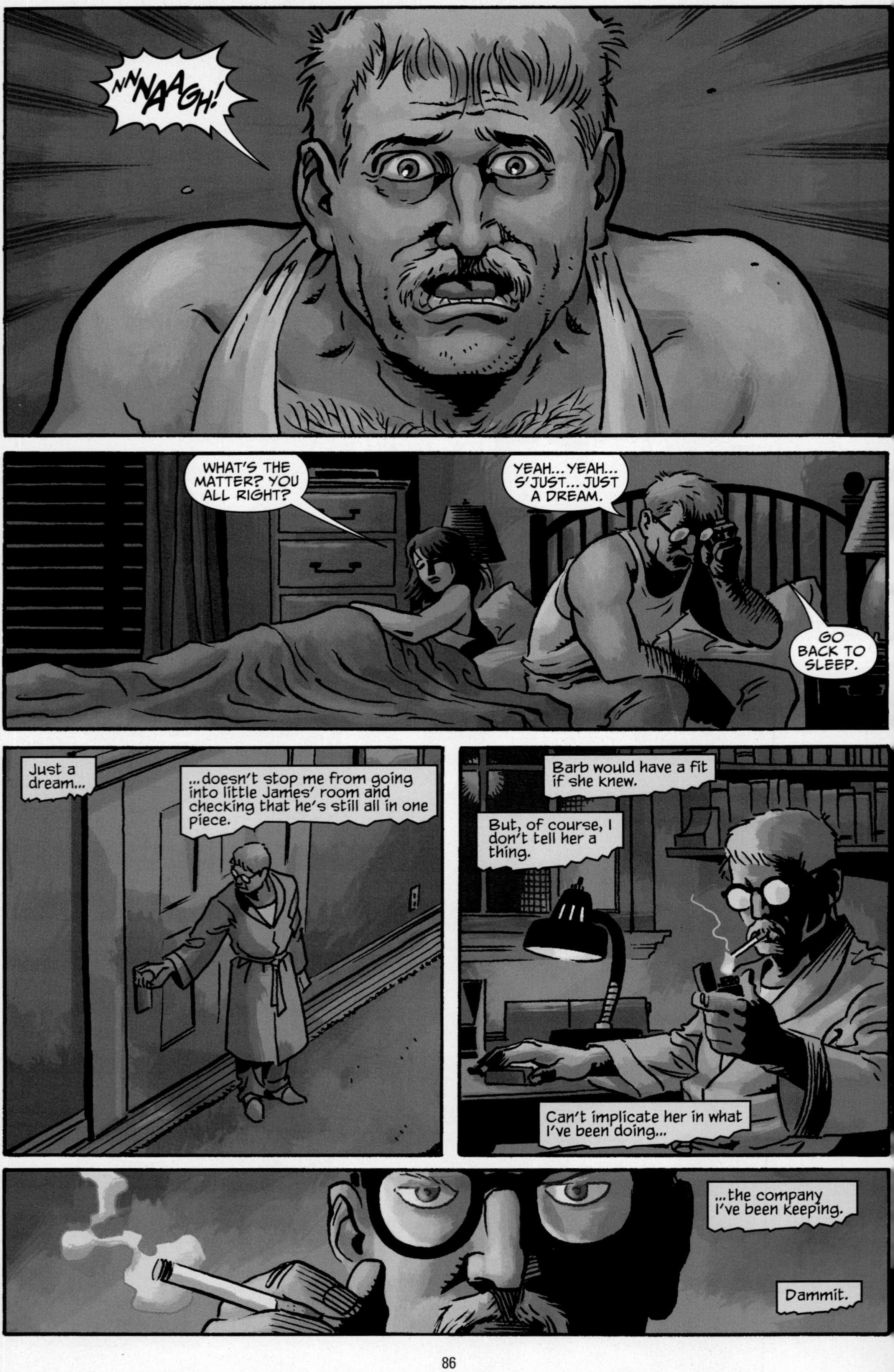
NNNAAGH!
WHAT'S THE MATTER? YOU ALL RIGHT?
YEAH... YEAH... S'JUST... JUST A DREAM.
GO BACK TO SLEEP.
Just a dream...
...doesn't stop me from going into little James' room and checking that he's still all in one piece.
Barb would have a fit if she knew.
But, of course, I don't tell her a thing.
Can't implicate her in what I've been doing...
...the company I've been keeping.
Dammit.

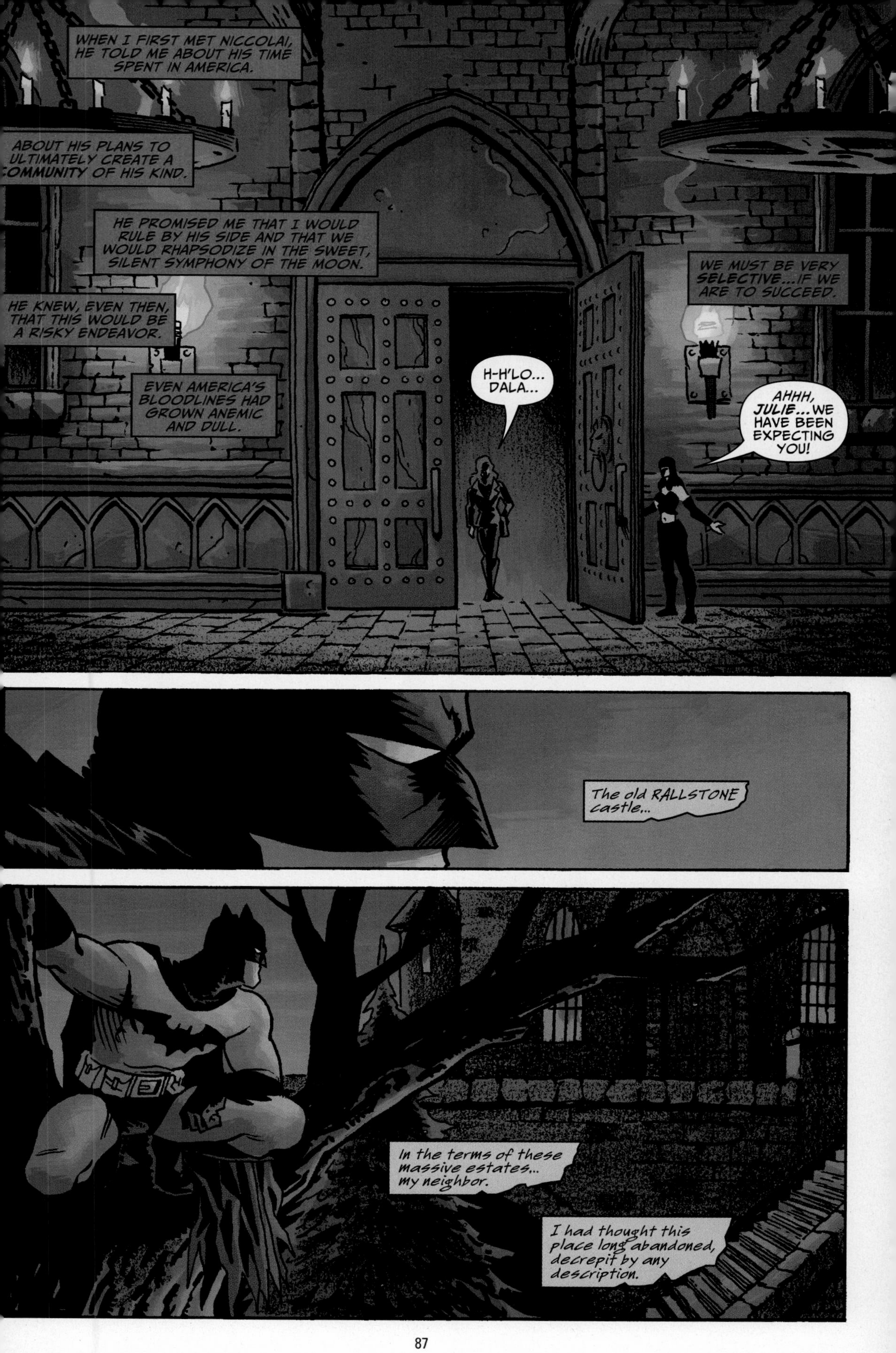
WHEN I FIRST MET NICCOLAI, HE TOLD ME ABOUT HIS TIME SPENT IN AMERICA.
ABOUT HIS PLANS TO ULTIMATELY CREATE A COMMUNITY OF HIS KIND.
HE PROMISED ME THAT I WOULD RULE BY HIS SIDE AND THAT WE WOULD RHAPSODIZE IN THE SWEET, SILENT SYMPHONY OF THE MOON.
HE KNEW, EVEN THEN, THAT THIS WOULD BE A RISKY ENDEAVOR.
EVEN AMERICA'S BLOODLINES HAD GROWN ANEMIC AND DULL.
WE MUST BE VERY SELECTIVE...IF WE ARE TO SUCCEED.
H-H'LO... DALA...
AHHH, JULIE...WE HAVE BEEN EXPECTING YOU!
The old RALLSTONE castle...
In the terms of these massive estates... my neighbor.
I had thought this place long abandoned, decrepit by any description.

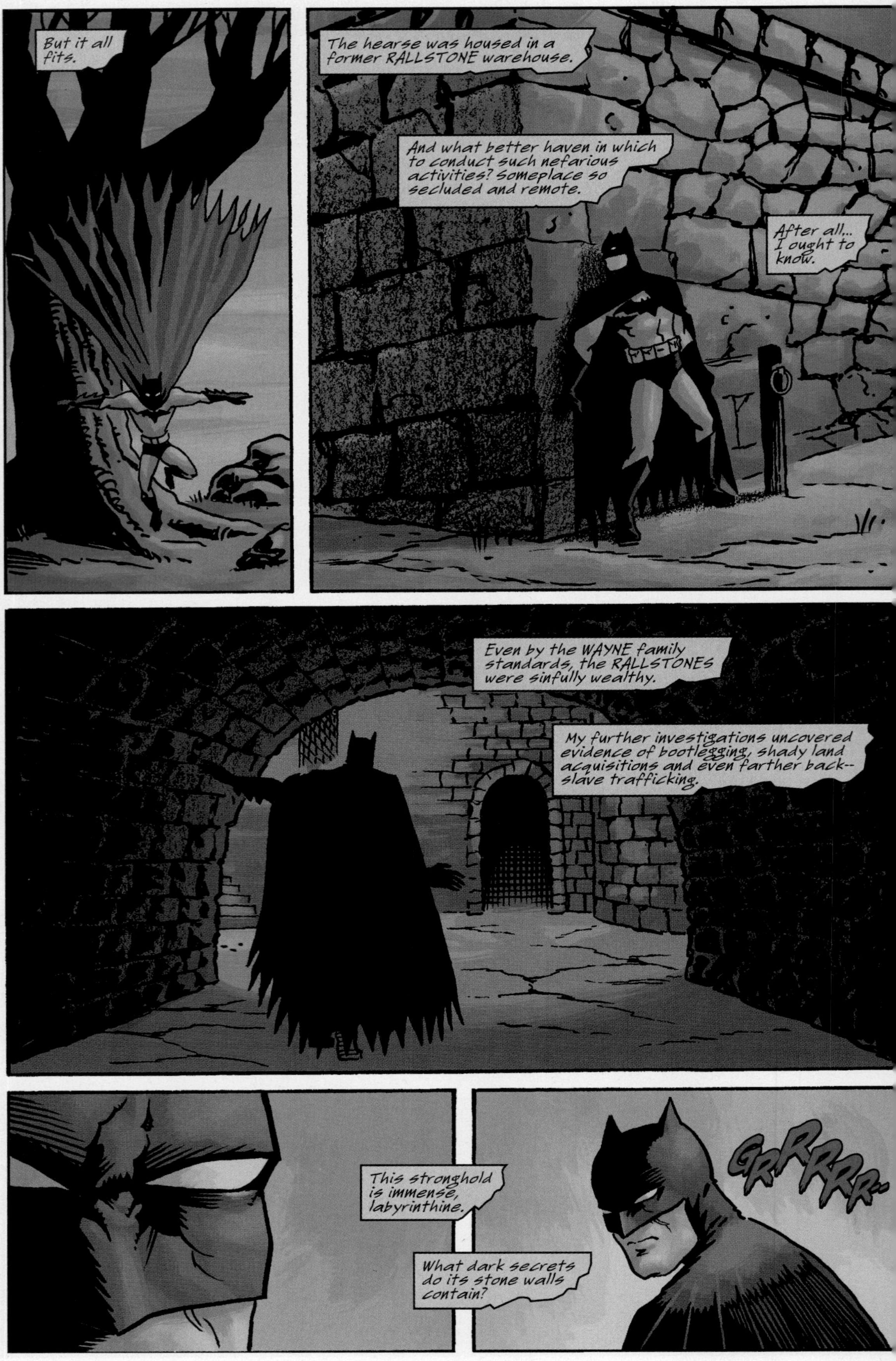
But it all fits.
The hearse was housed in a former RALLSTONE warehouse.
And what better haven in which to conduct such nefarious activities? Someplace so secluded and remote.
After all... I ought to know.
Even by the WAYNE family standards, the RALLSTONES were sinfully wealthy.
My further investigations uncovered evidence of bootlegging, shady land acquisitions and even farther back--slave trafficking.
This stronghold is immense, labyrinthine.
What dark secrets do its stone walls contain?
GRRRRR-

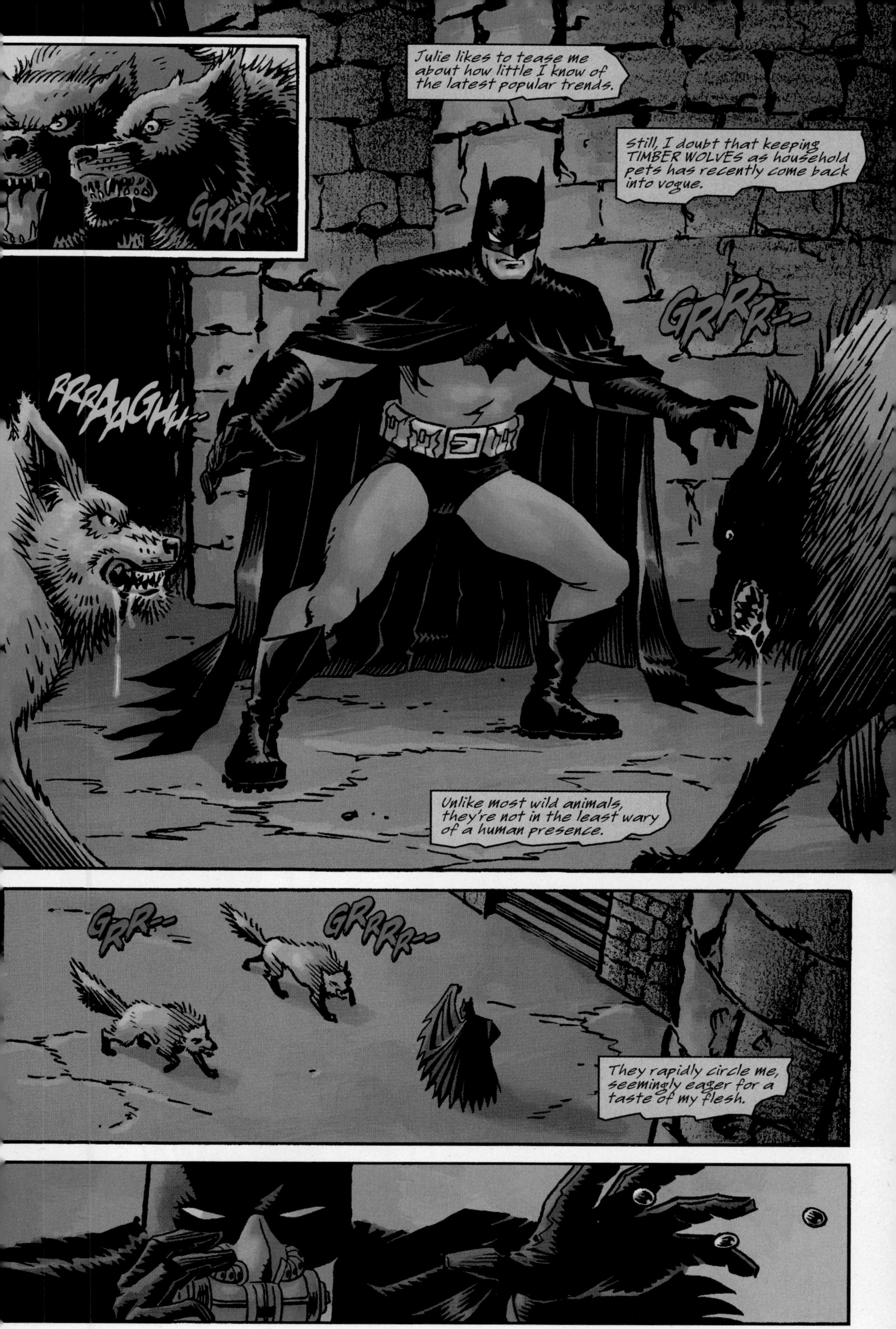
GRRR--
Julie likes to tease me about how little I know of the latest popular trends.
Still, I doubt that keeping TIMBER WOLVES as household pets has recently come back into vogue.
GRRR--
RRRAAAGHH--
Unlike most wild animals, they're not in the least wary of a human presence.
GRR--
GRRRR--
They rapidly circle me, seemingly eager for a taste of my flesh.

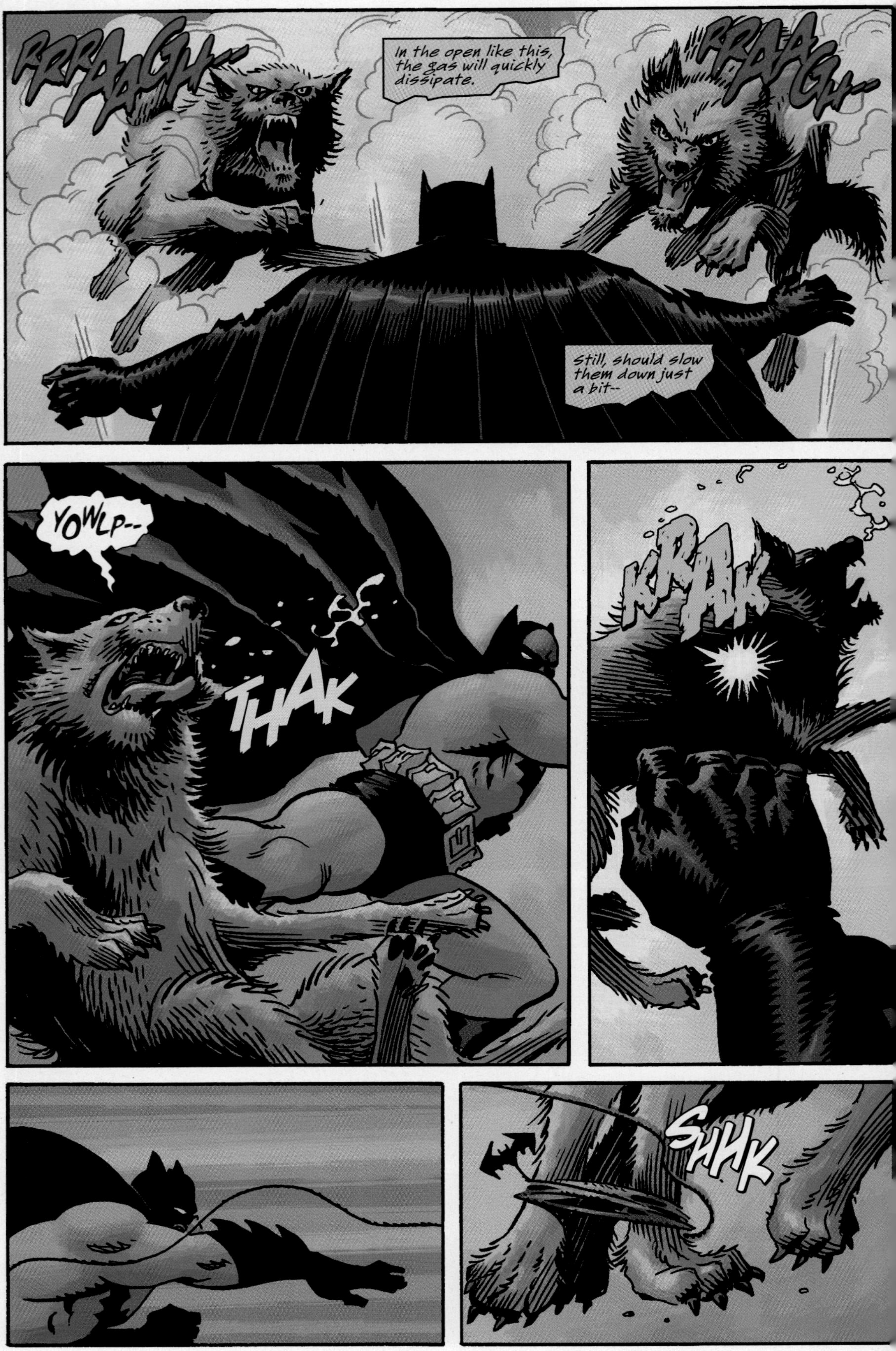
RRRAAAGH--
In the open like this, the gas will quickly dissipate.
RRRAAAGH--
Still, should slow them down just a bit--
YOWLP--
THAK
KRAK
SHUK

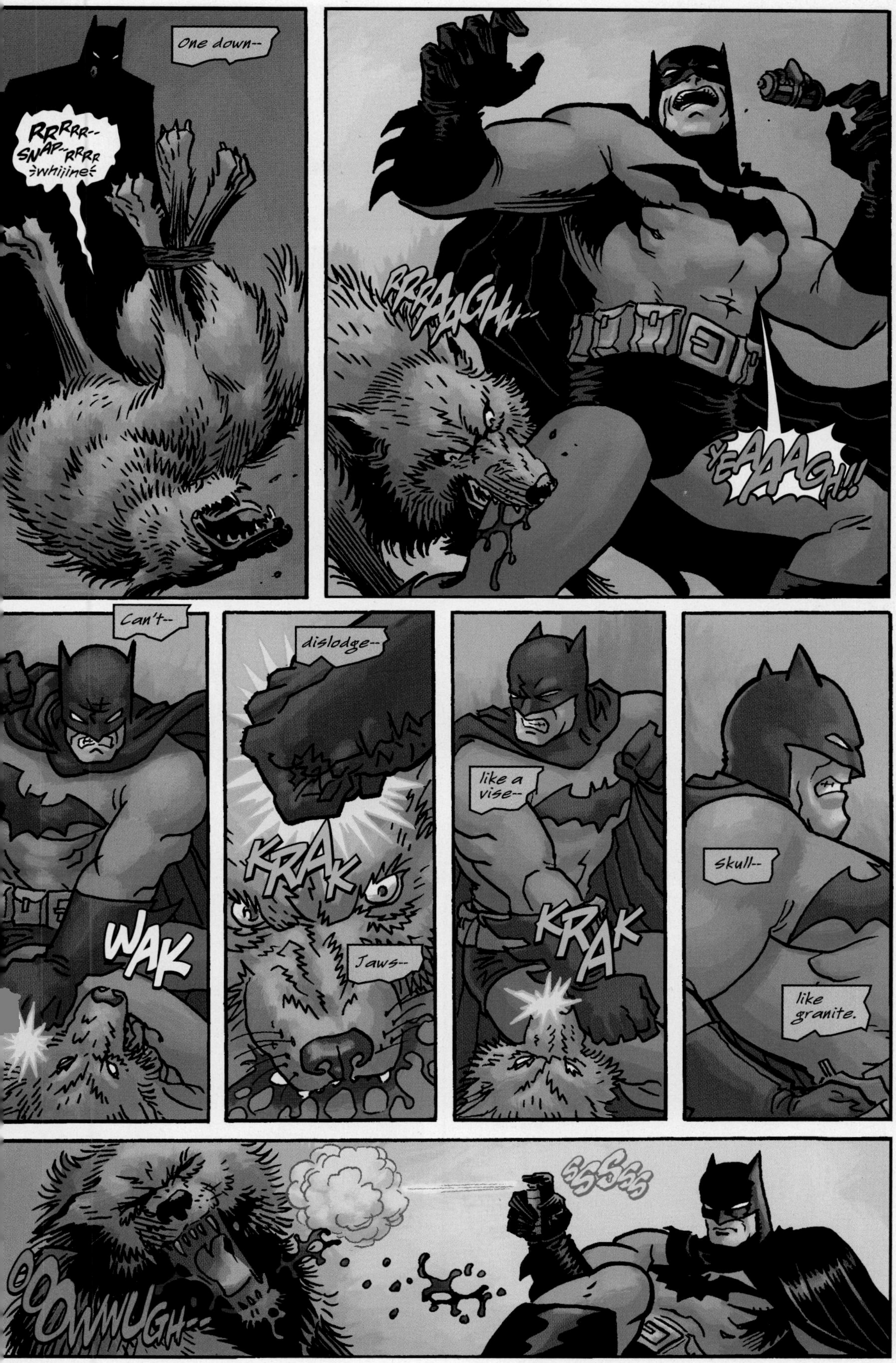
One down--
RRRRR-- SNAP--RRRR
whiiine
RRRAAGH...
YEAAAAGH!!
Can't--
WAK
dislodge--
KRAK
Jaws--
like a vise--
KRAK
Skull--
like granite.
SSSSS
OOOWWUGH

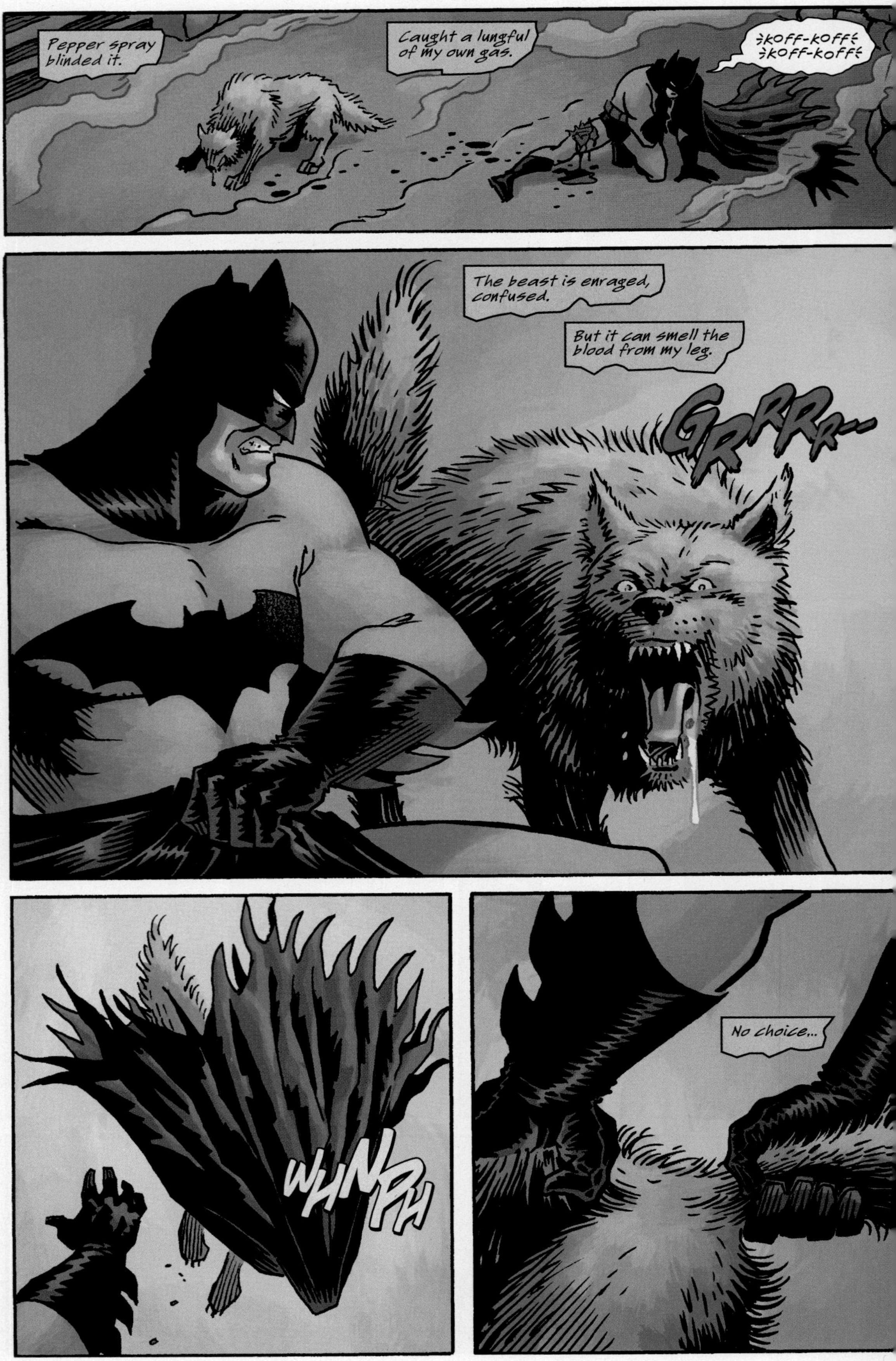
Pepper spray blinded it.
Caught a lungful of my own gas.
KOFF-KOFF KOFF-KOFF
The beast is enraged, confused.
But it can smell the blood from my leg.
GRRRR--
WHNPH
No choice...

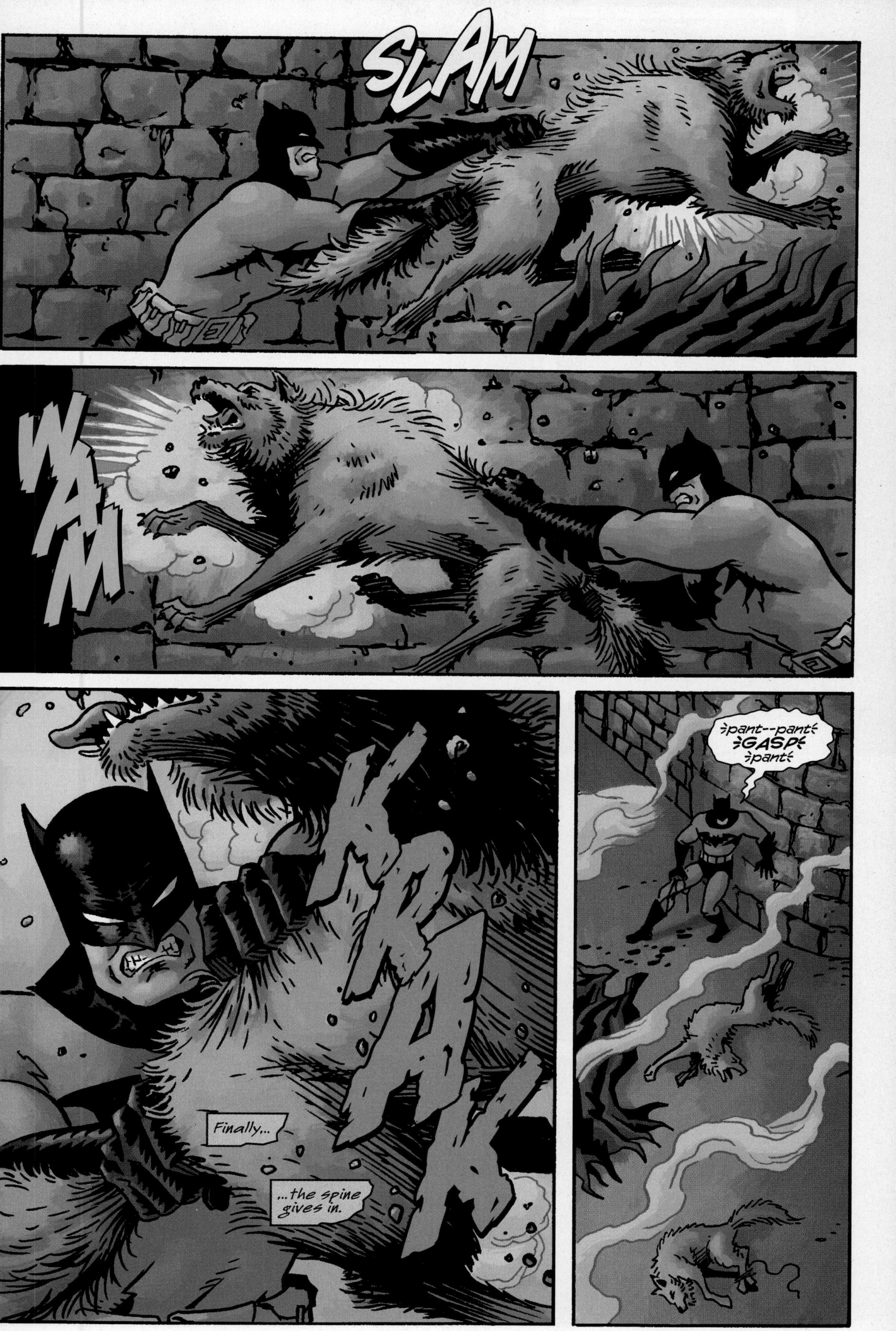
SLAM
WAM
Finally...
...the spine gives in.
pant--pant
GASP
pant

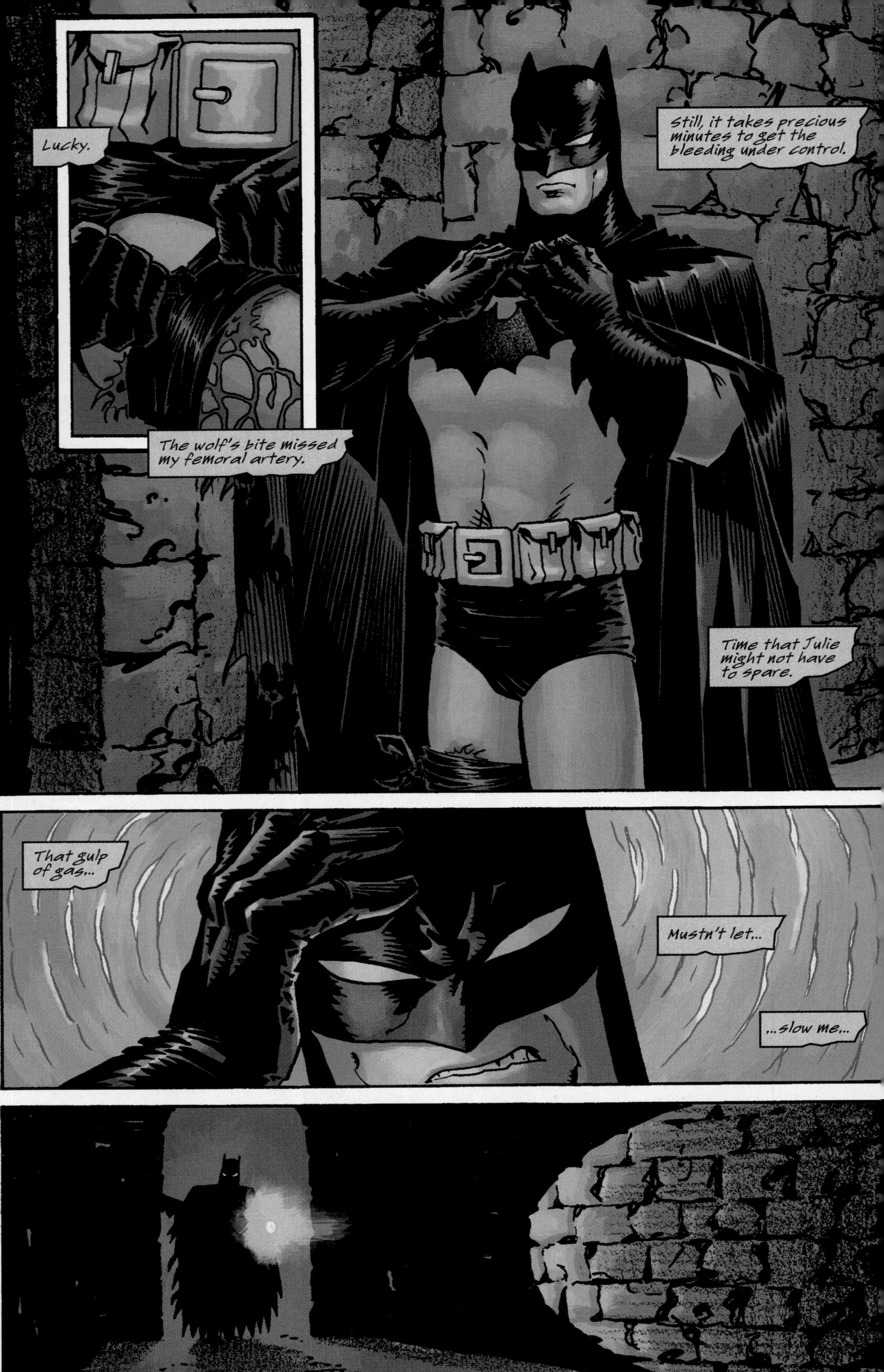

Lucky.
The wolf's bite missed my femoral artery.
Still, it takes precious minutes to get the bleeding under control.
Time that Julie might not have to spare.
That gulp of gas...
Mustn't let...
...slow me...

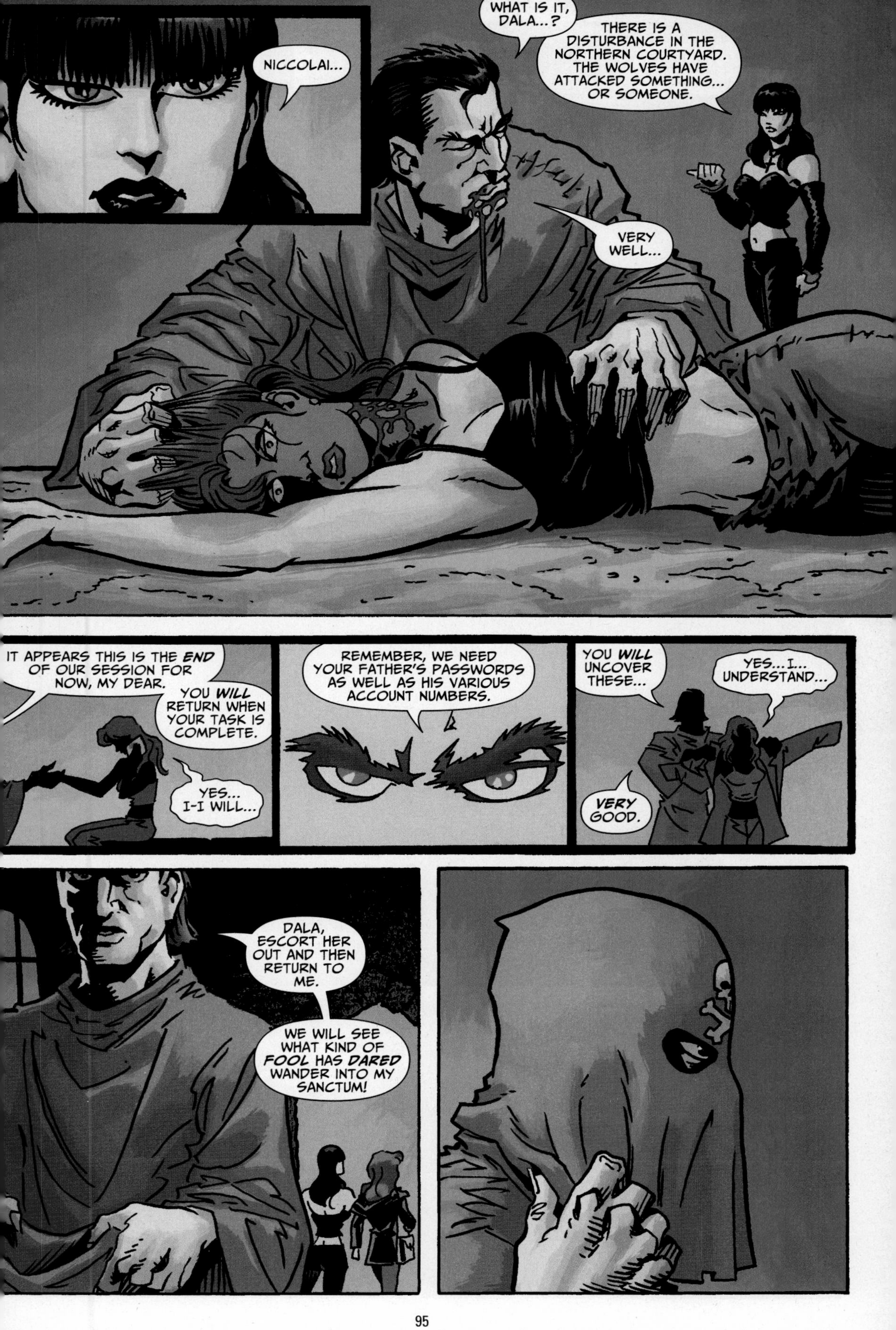
NICCOLAI...
WHAT IS IT, DALA...?
THERE IS A DISTURBANCE IN THE NORTHERN COURTYARD. THE WOLVES HAVE ATTACKED SOMETHING... OR SOMEONE.
VERY WELL...
IT APPEARS THIS IS THE *END* OF OUR SESSION FOR NOW, MY DEAR.
YOU *WILL* RETURN WHEN YOUR TASK IS COMPLETE.
YES... I-I WILL...
REMEMBER, WE NEED YOUR FATHER'S PASSWORDS AS WELL AS HIS VARIOUS ACCOUNT NUMBERS.
YOU *WILL* UNCOVER THESE...
YES... I... UNDERSTAND...
VERY GOOD.
DALA, ESCORT HER OUT AND THEN RETURN TO ME.
WE WILL SEE WHAT KIND OF *FOOL* HAS *DARED* WANDER INTO MY SANCTUM!

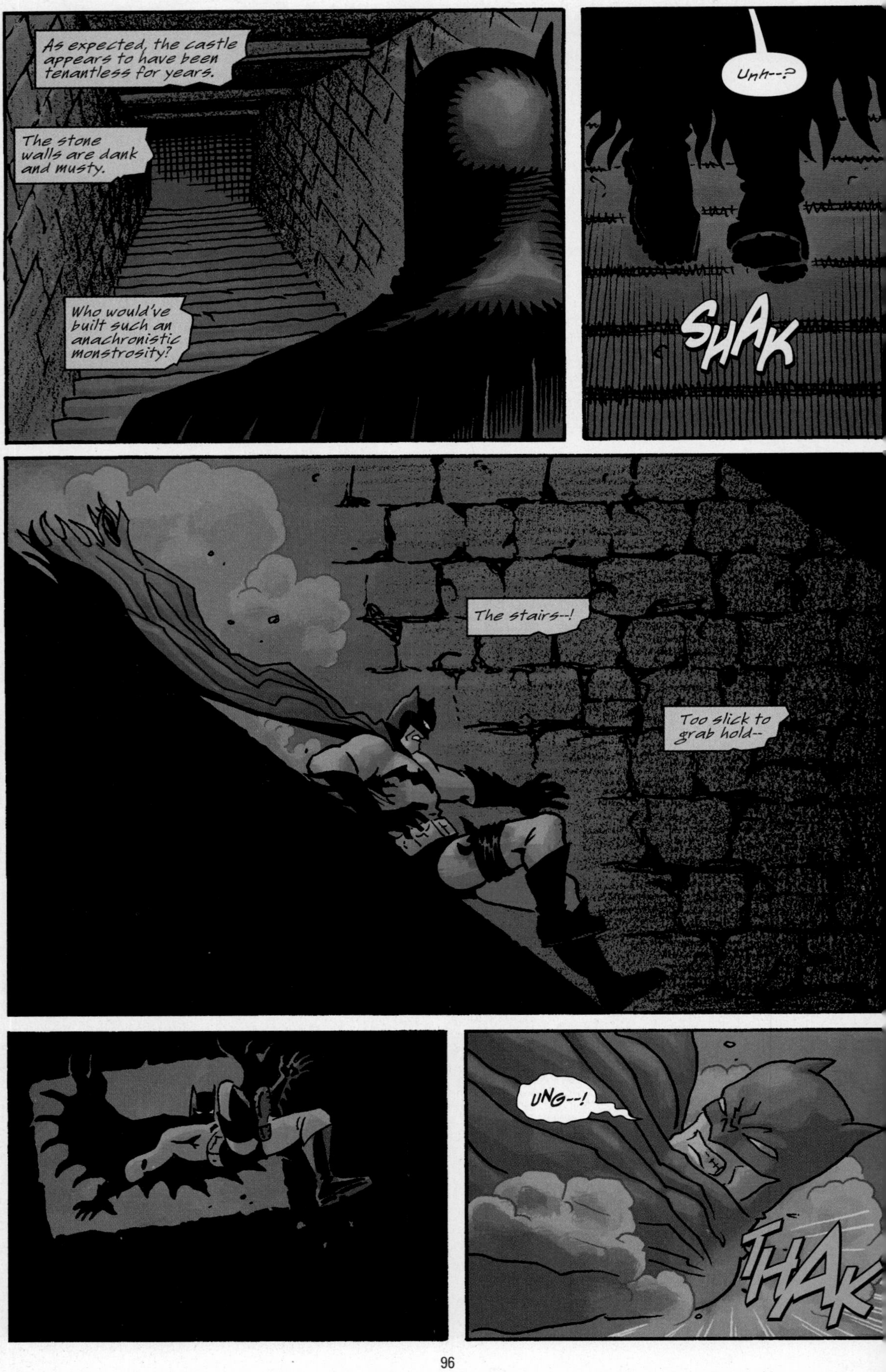

As expected, the castle appears to have been tenantless for years.
The stone walls are dank and musty.
Who would've built such an anachronistic monstrosity?
Unh--?
SHAK
The stairs--!
Too slick to grab hold--
UNG--!
THAK

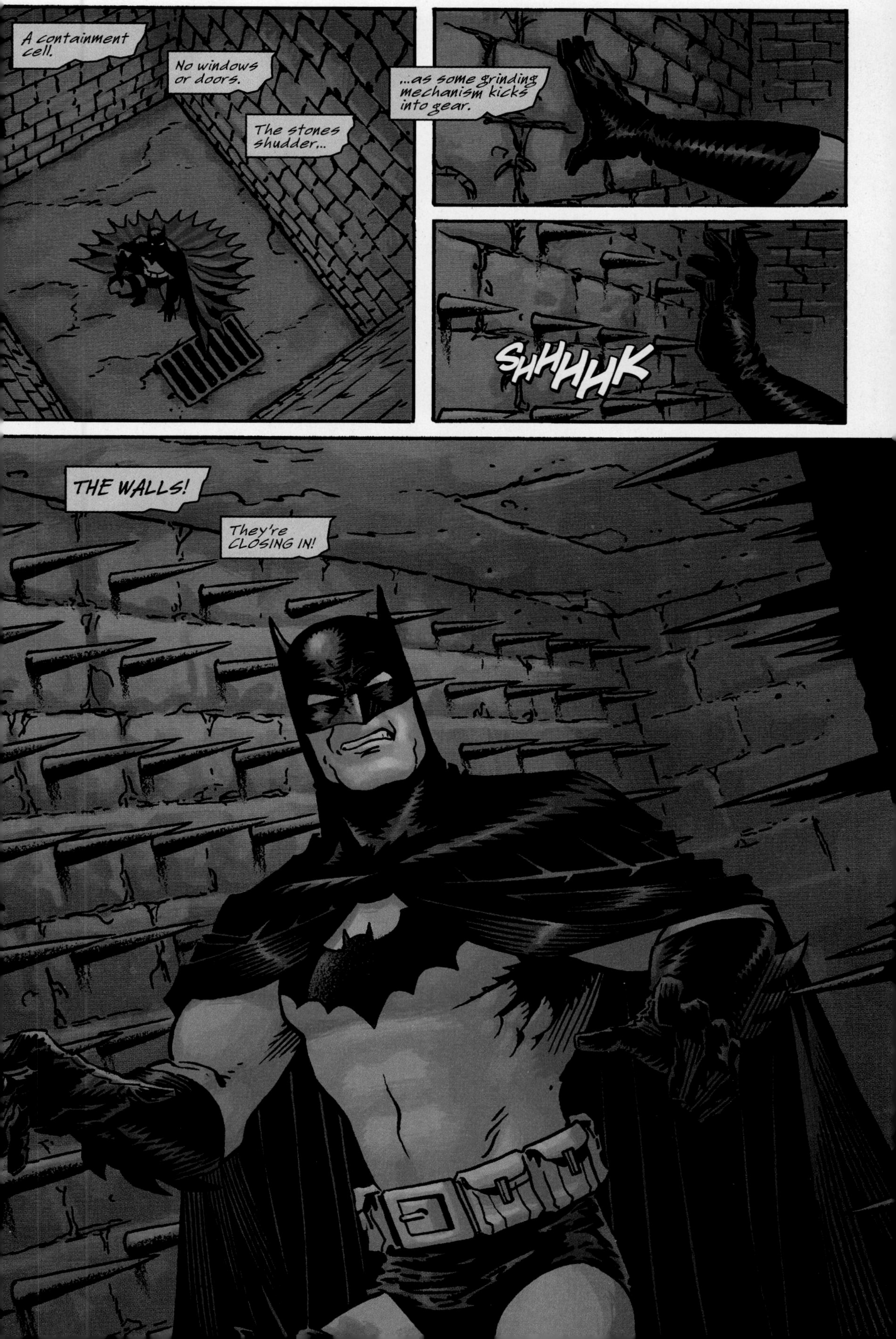
A containment cell.
No windows or doors.
The stones shudder...
...as some grinding mechanism kicks into gear.
SHHHHK
THE WALLS!
They're CLOSING IN!

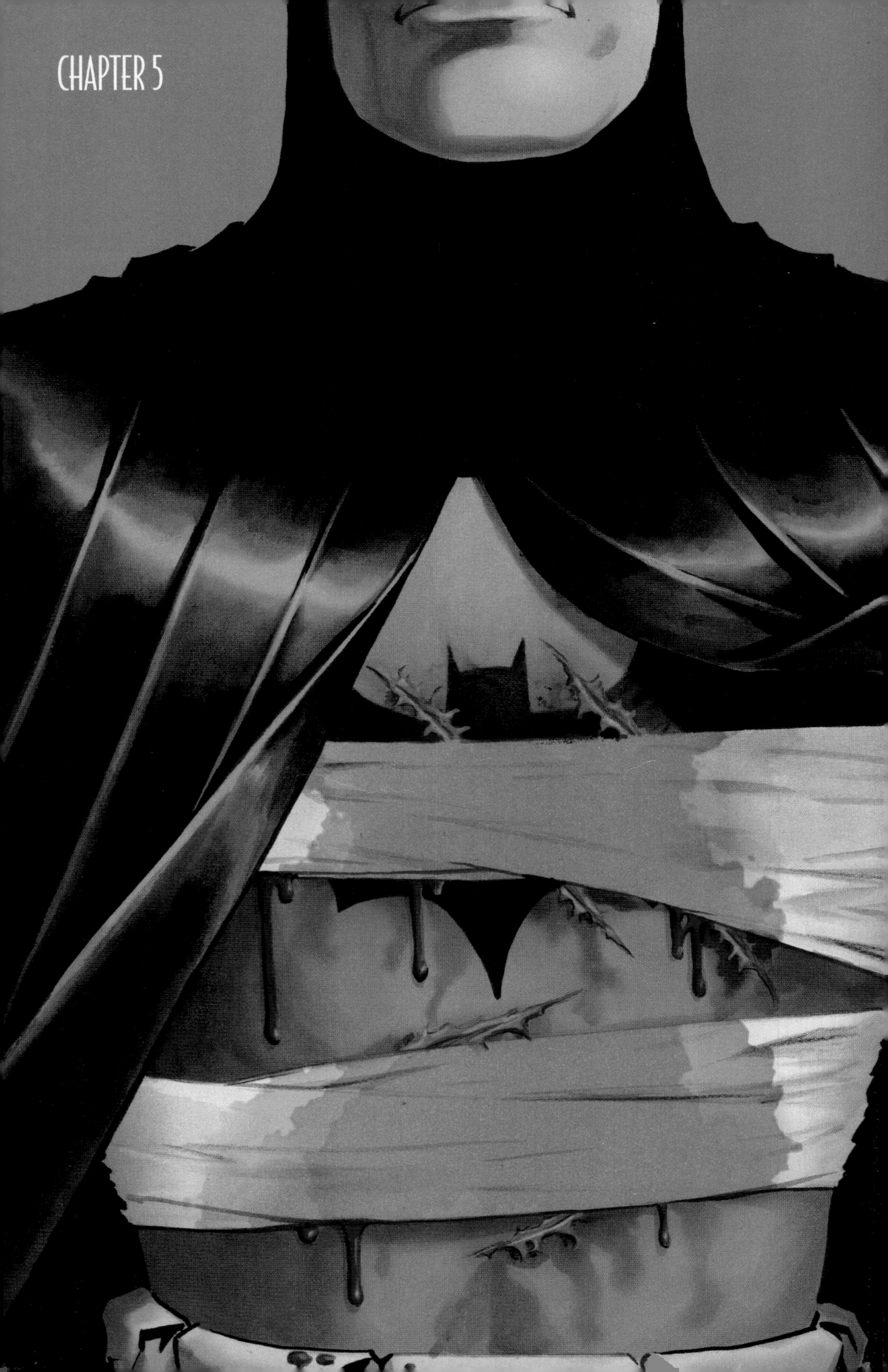
CHAPTER 5

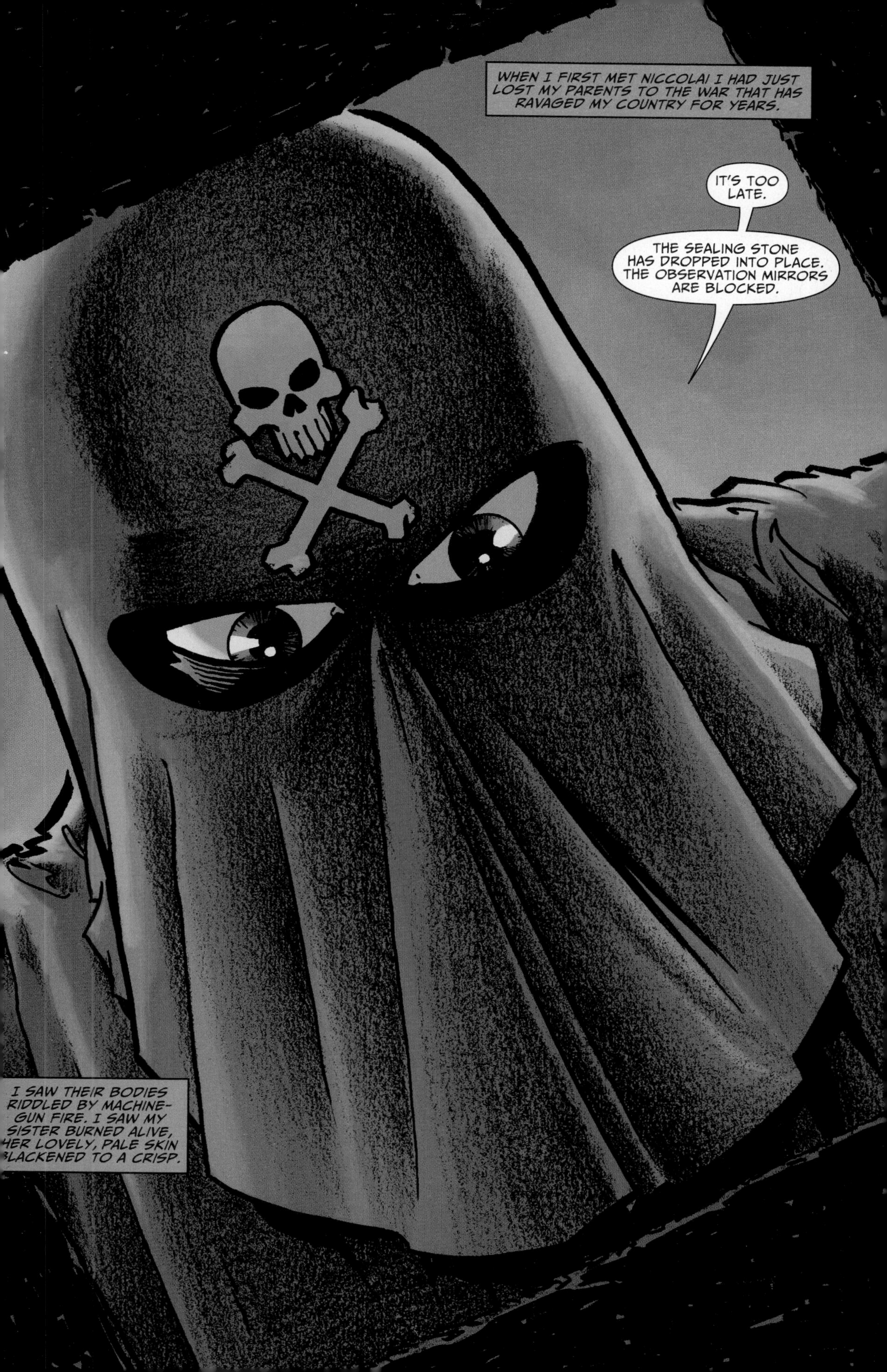
WHEN I FIRST MET NICCOLAI I HAD JUST LOST MY PARENTS TO THE WAR THAT HAS RAVAGED MY COUNTRY FOR YEARS.
IT'S TOO LATE.
THE SEALING STONE HAS DROPPED INTO PLACE. THE OBSERVATION MIRRORS ARE BLOCKED.
I SAW THEIR BODIES RIDDLED BY MACHINE-GUN FIRE. I SAW MY SISTER BURNED ALIVE, HER LOVELY, PALE SKIN BLACKENED TO A CRISP.

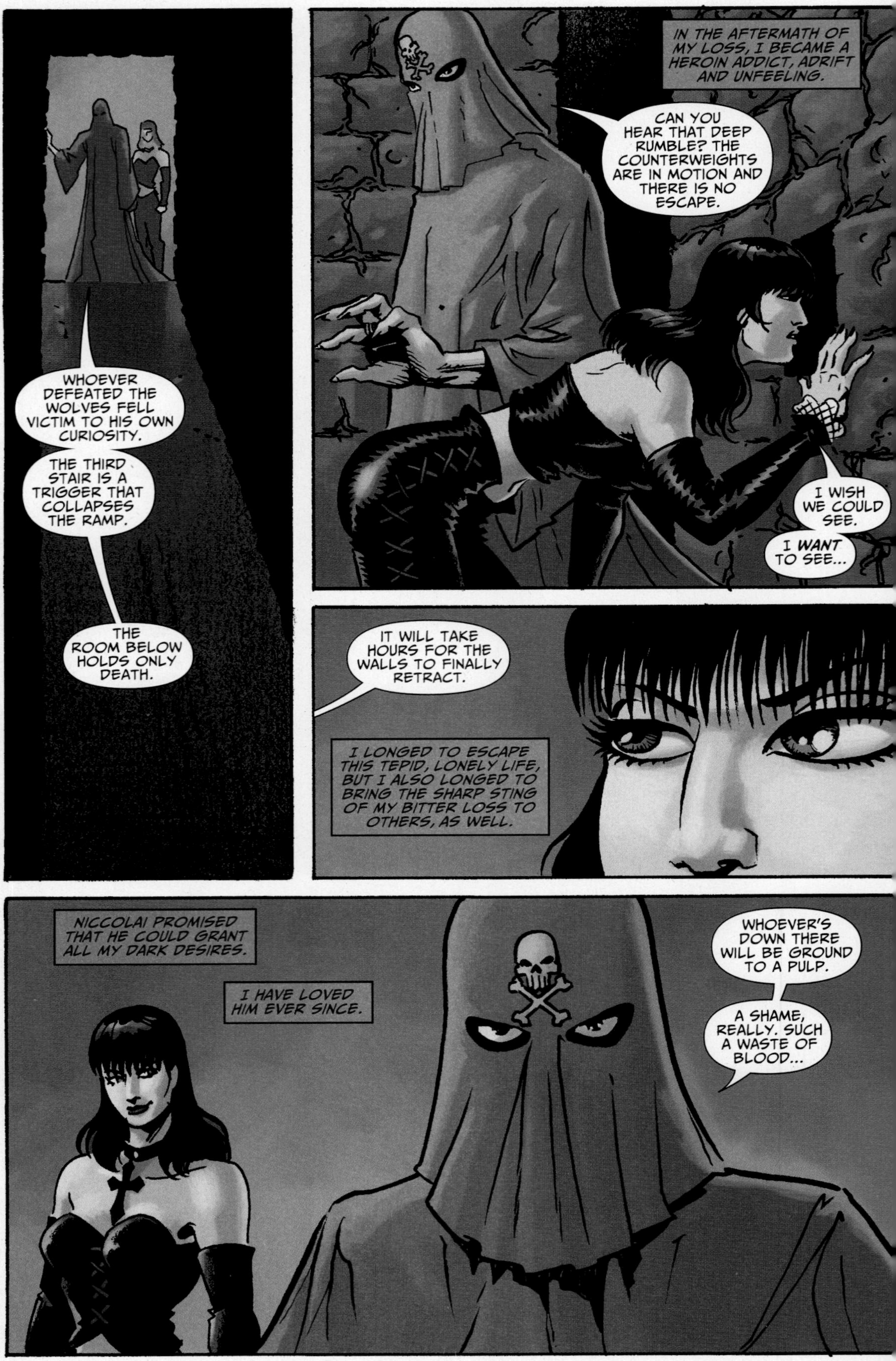
WHOEVER DEFEATED THE WOLVES FELL VICTIM TO HIS OWN CURIOSITY.
THE THIRD STAIR IS A TRIGGER THAT COLLAPSES THE RAMP.
THE ROOM BELOW HOLDS ONLY DEATH.
IN THE AFTERMATH OF MY LOSS, I BECAME A HEROIN ADDICT, ADRIFT AND UNFEELING.
CAN YOU HEAR THAT DEEP RUMBLE? THE COUNTERWEIGHTS ARE IN MOTION AND THERE IS NO ESCAPE.
I WISH WE COULD SEE.
I WANT TO SEE...
IT WILL TAKE HOURS FOR THE WALLS TO FINALLY RETRACT.
I LONGED TO ESCAPE THIS TEPID, LONELY LIFE, BUT I ALSO LONGED TO BRING THE SHARP STING OF MY BITTER LOSS TO OTHERS, AS WELL.
NICCOLAI PROMISED THAT HE COULD GRANT ALL MY DARK DESIRES.
I HAVE LOVED HIM EVER SINCE.
WHOEVER'S DOWN THERE WILL BE GROUND TO A PULP.
A SHAME, REALLY. SUCH A WASTE OF BLOOD...

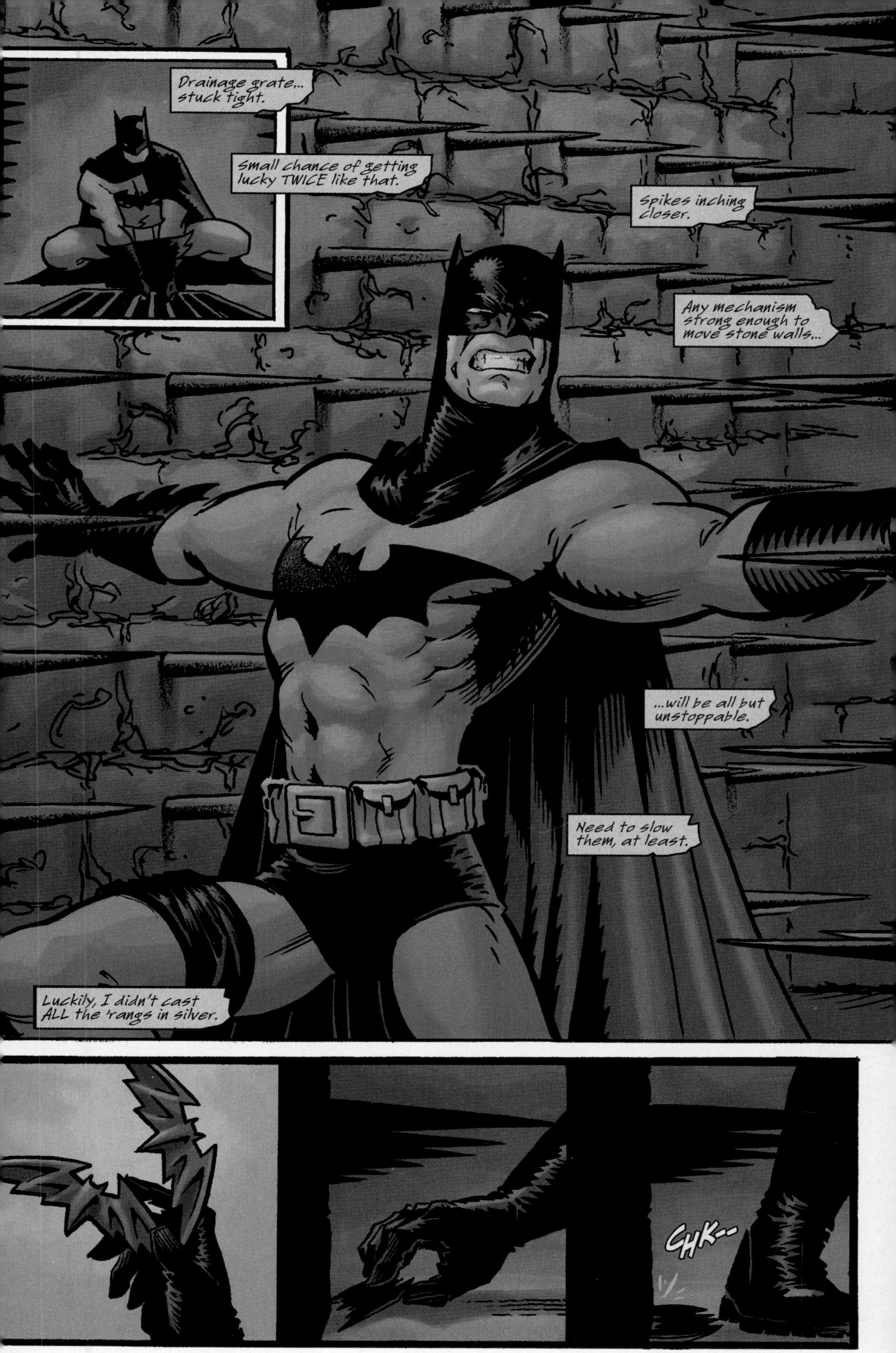

Drainage grate... stuck tight.
Small chance of getting lucky TWICE like that.
Spikes inching closer.
Any mechanism strong enough to move stone walls...
...will be all but unstoppable.
Need to slow them, at least.
Luckily, I didn't cast ALL the 'rangs in silver.
CHK--

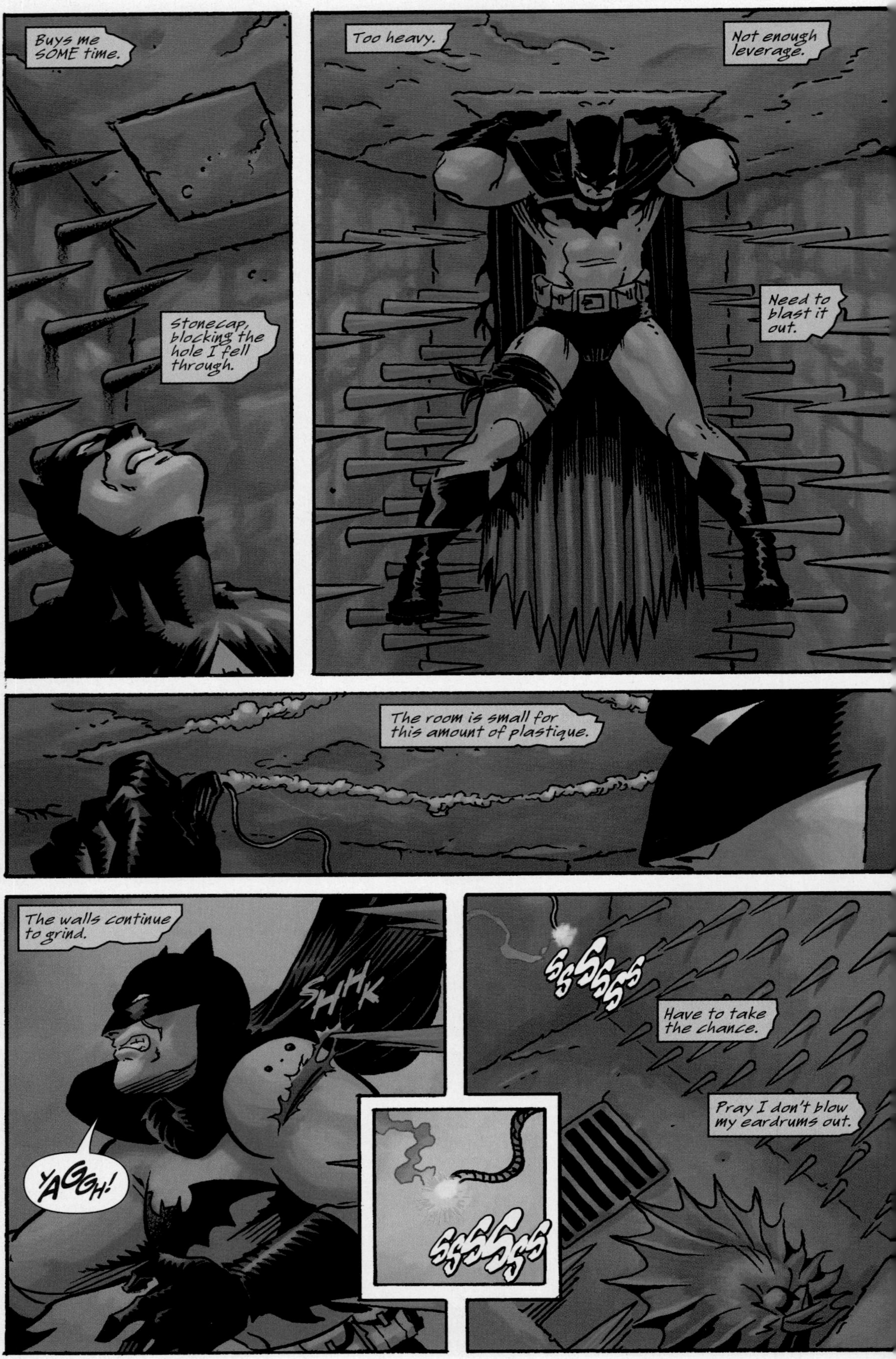
Buys me SOME time.
Stonecap, blocking the hole I fell through.
Too heavy.
Not enough leverage.
Need to blast it out.
The room is small for this amount of plastique.
The walls continue to grind.
SHHK
YAGGH!
SSSSSSS
SSSSSS
Have to take the chance.
Pray I don't blow my eardrums out.

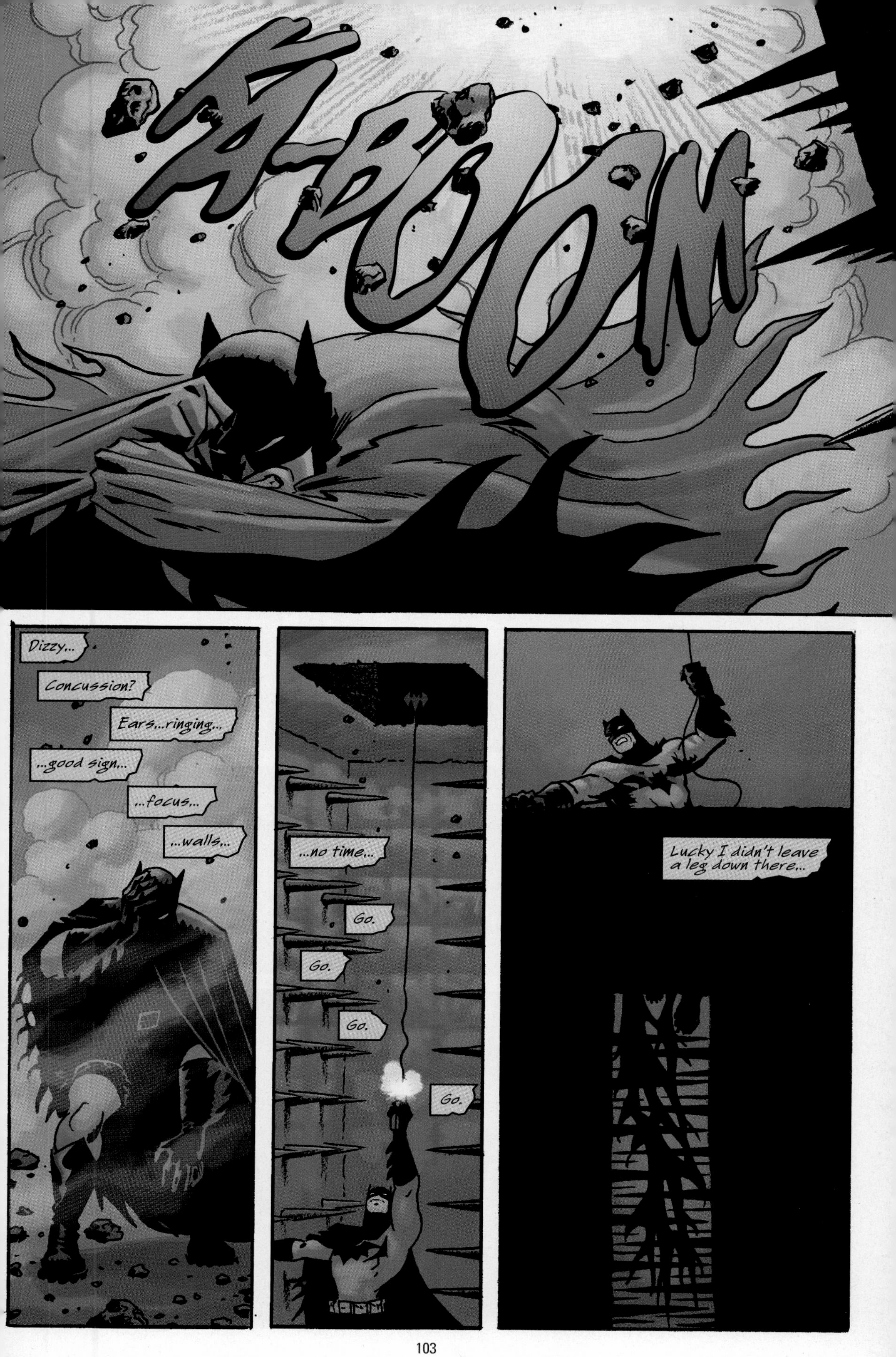
KA-BOOM
Dizzy...
Concussion?
Ears...ringing...
...good sign...
...focus...
...walls...
...no time...
Go.
Go.
Go.
Go.
Lucky I didn't leave a leg down there...

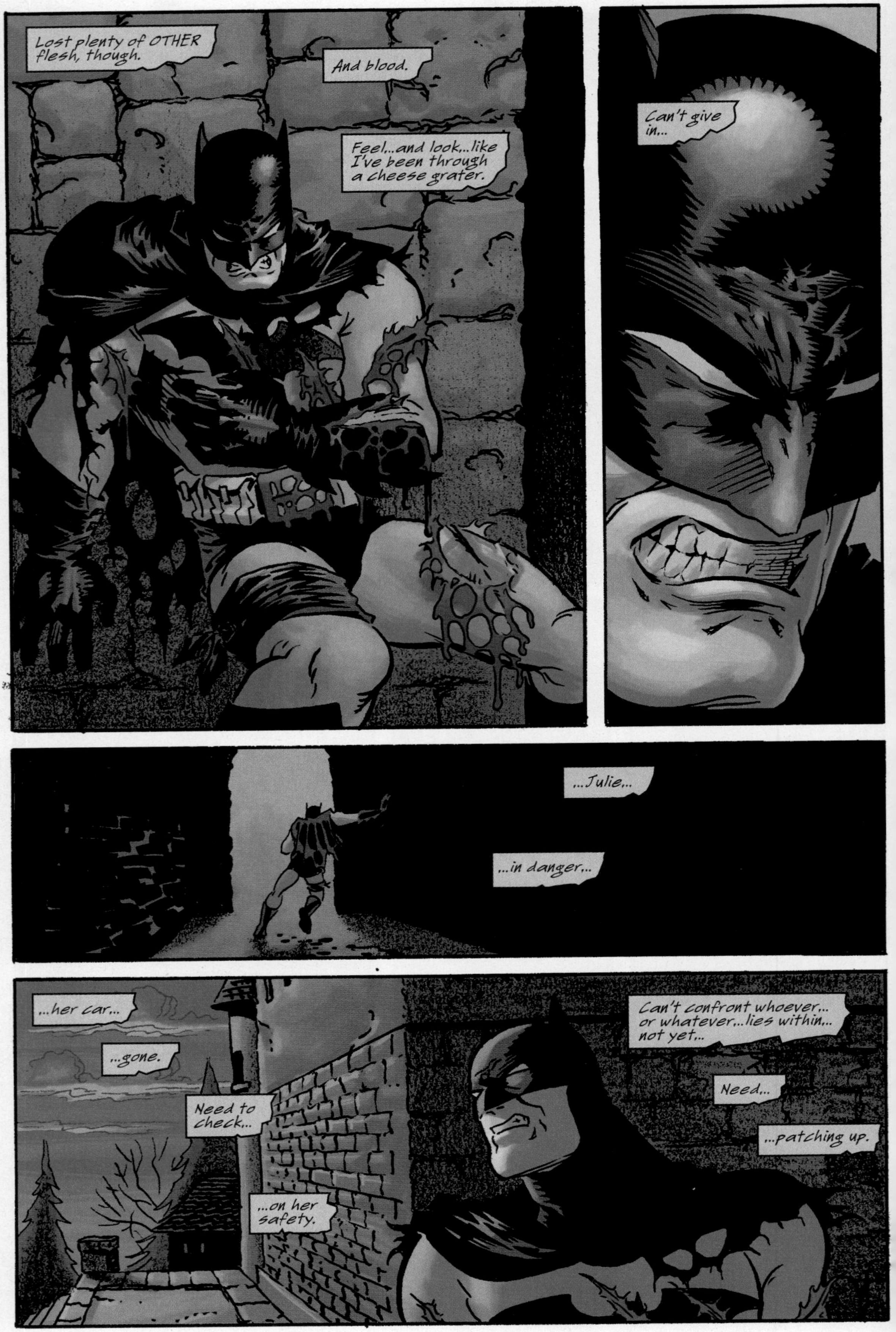
Lost plenty of OTHER flesh, though.
And blood.
Feel...and look...like I've been through a cheese grater.
Can't give in...
...Julie...
...in danger...
...her car...
...gone.
Need to check...
...on her safety.
Can't confront whoever... or whatever...lies within... not yet...
Need...
...patching up.

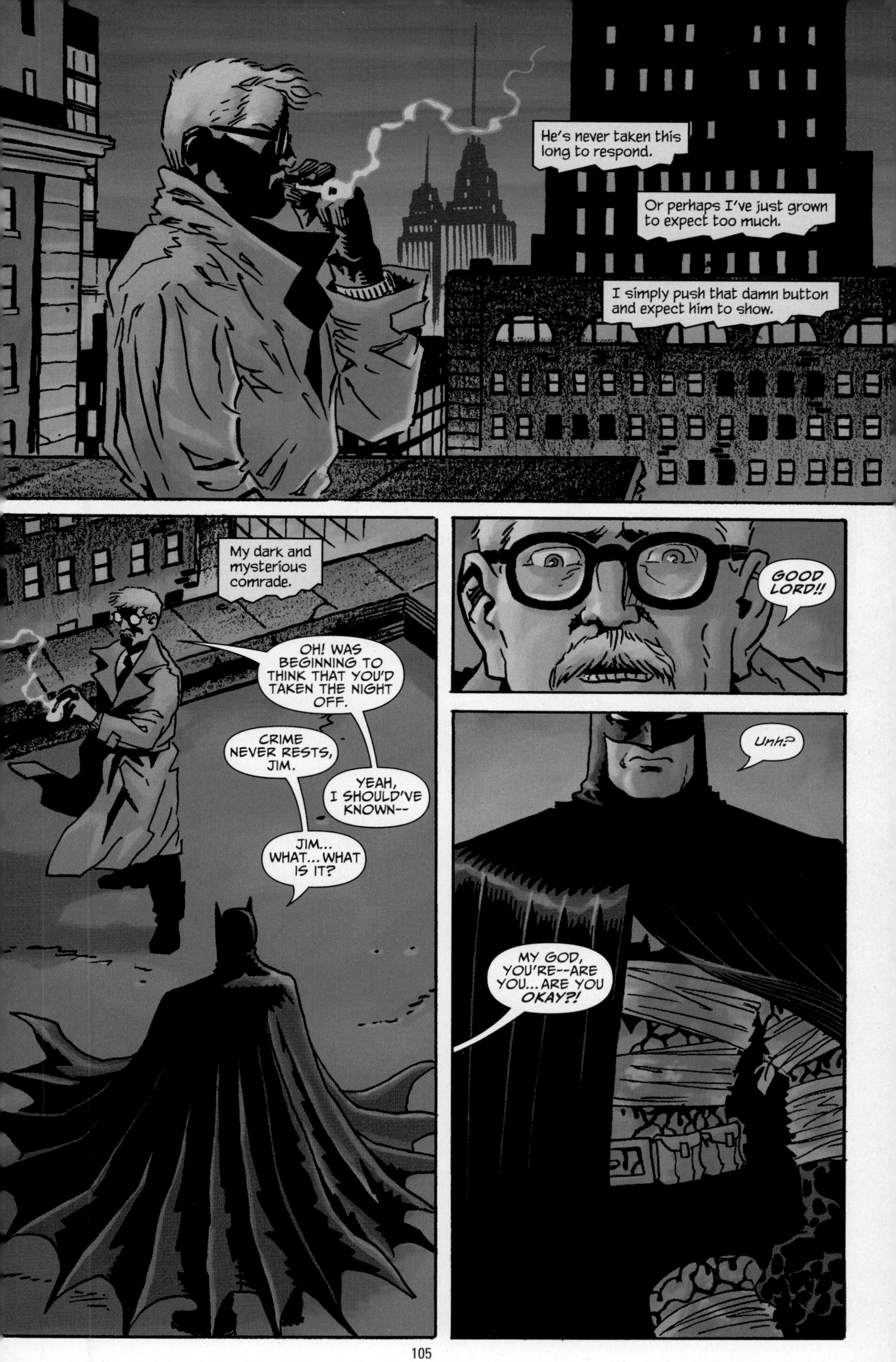
He's never taken this long to respond.
Or perhaps I've just grown to expect too much.
I simply push that damn button and expect him to show.
My dark and mysterious comrade.
OH! WAS BEGINNING TO THINK THAT YOU'D TAKEN THE NIGHT OFF.
CRIME NEVER RESTS, JIM.
YEAH, I SHOULD'VE KNOWN--
JIM... WHAT... WHAT IS IT?
GOOD LORD!!
Unh?
MY GOD, YOU'RE--ARE YOU... ARE YOU OKAY?!

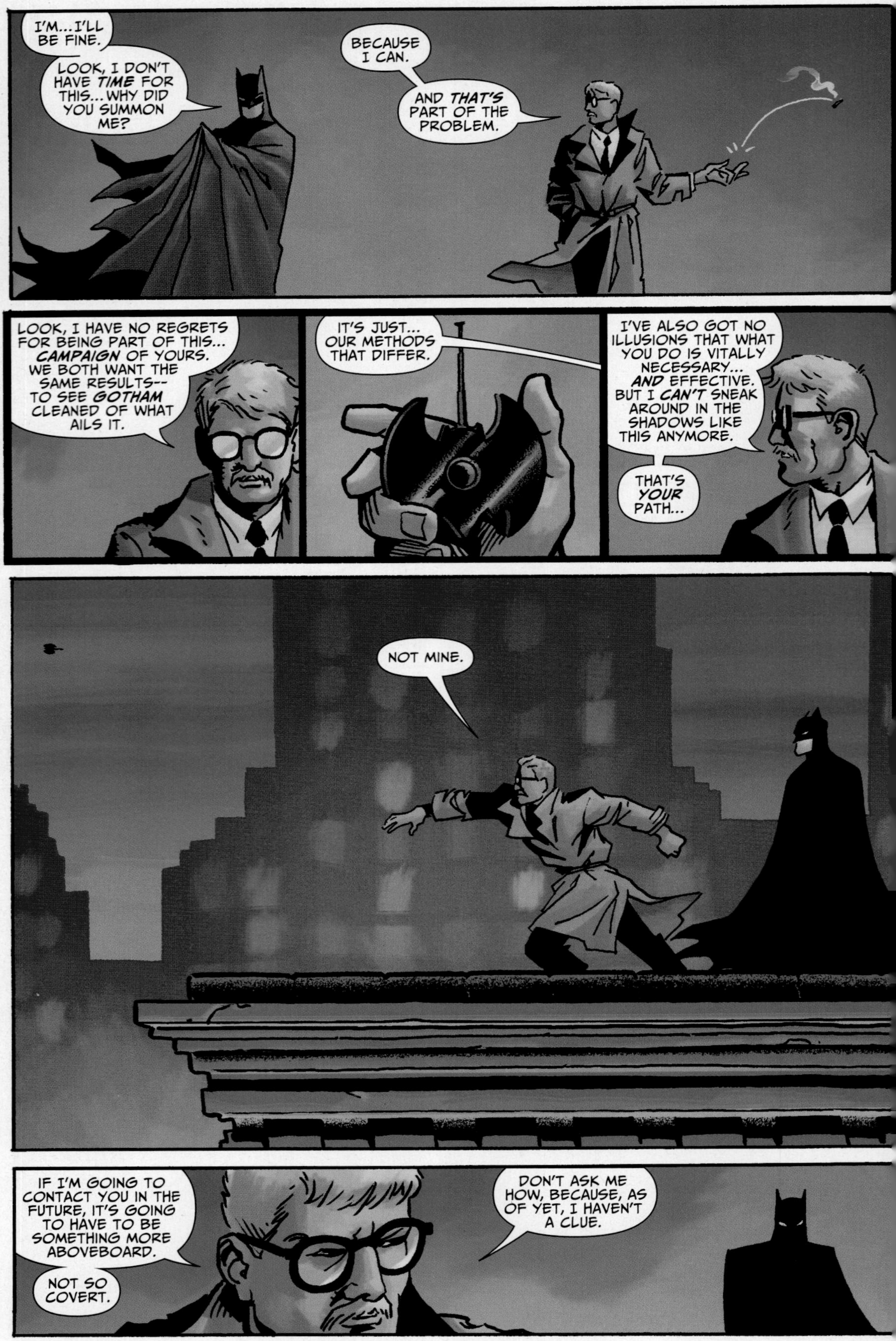
I'M...I'LL BE FINE.
LOOK, I DON'T HAVE TIME FOR THIS...WHY DID YOU SUMMON ME?
BECAUSE I CAN.
AND THAT'S PART OF THE PROBLEM.
LOOK, I HAVE NO REGRETS FOR BEING PART OF THIS... CAMPAIGN OF YOURS. WE BOTH WANT THE SAME RESULTS-- TO SEE GOTHAM CLEANED OF WHAT AILS IT.
IT'S JUST... OUR METHODS THAT DIFFER.
I'VE ALSO GOT NO ILLUSIONS THAT WHAT YOU DO IS VITALLY NECESSARY... AND EFFECTIVE. BUT I CAN'T SNEAK AROUND IN THE SHADOWS LIKE THIS ANYMORE.
THAT'S YOUR PATH...
NOT MINE.
IF I'M GOING TO CONTACT YOU IN THE FUTURE, IT'S GOING TO HAVE TO BE SOMETHING MORE ABOVEBOARD.
NOT SO COVERT.
DON'T ASK ME HOW, BECAUSE, AS OF YET, I HAVEN'T A CLUE.

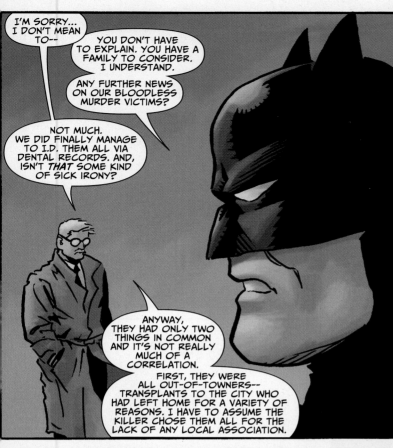

I'M SORRY... I DON'T MEAN TO--

YOU DON'T HAVE TO EXPLAIN. YOU HAVE A FAMILY TO CONSIDER. I UNDERSTAND.

ANY FURTHER NEWS ON OUR BLOODLESS MURDER VICTIMS?

NOT MUCH. WE DID FINALLY MANAGE TO I.D. THEM ALL VIA DENTAL RECORDS. AND, ISN'T *THAT* SOME KIND OF SICK IRONY?

ANYWAY, THEY HAD ONLY TWO THINGS IN COMMON AND IT'S NOT REALLY MUCH OF A CORRELATION.

FIRST, THEY WERE ALL OUT-OF-TOWNERS-- TRANSPLANTS TO THE CITY WHO HAD LEFT HOME FOR A VARIETY OF REASONS. I HAVE TO ASSUME THE KILLER CHOSE THEM ALL FOR THE LACK OF ANY LOCAL ASSOCIATION.

SECONDLY, AND I TEND TO THINK *THIS* IS MERE COINCIDENCE... THEY WERE *ALL* ONLY CHILDREN. NO SIBLINGS.

ONLY...?

YES. *WHY?* DO YOU THINK THAT'S SIGNIFIC--

Well...you all but ASKED for him to keep his distance.

Never really noticed the view from up here. Even after all this time.

Can really see quite far.

107

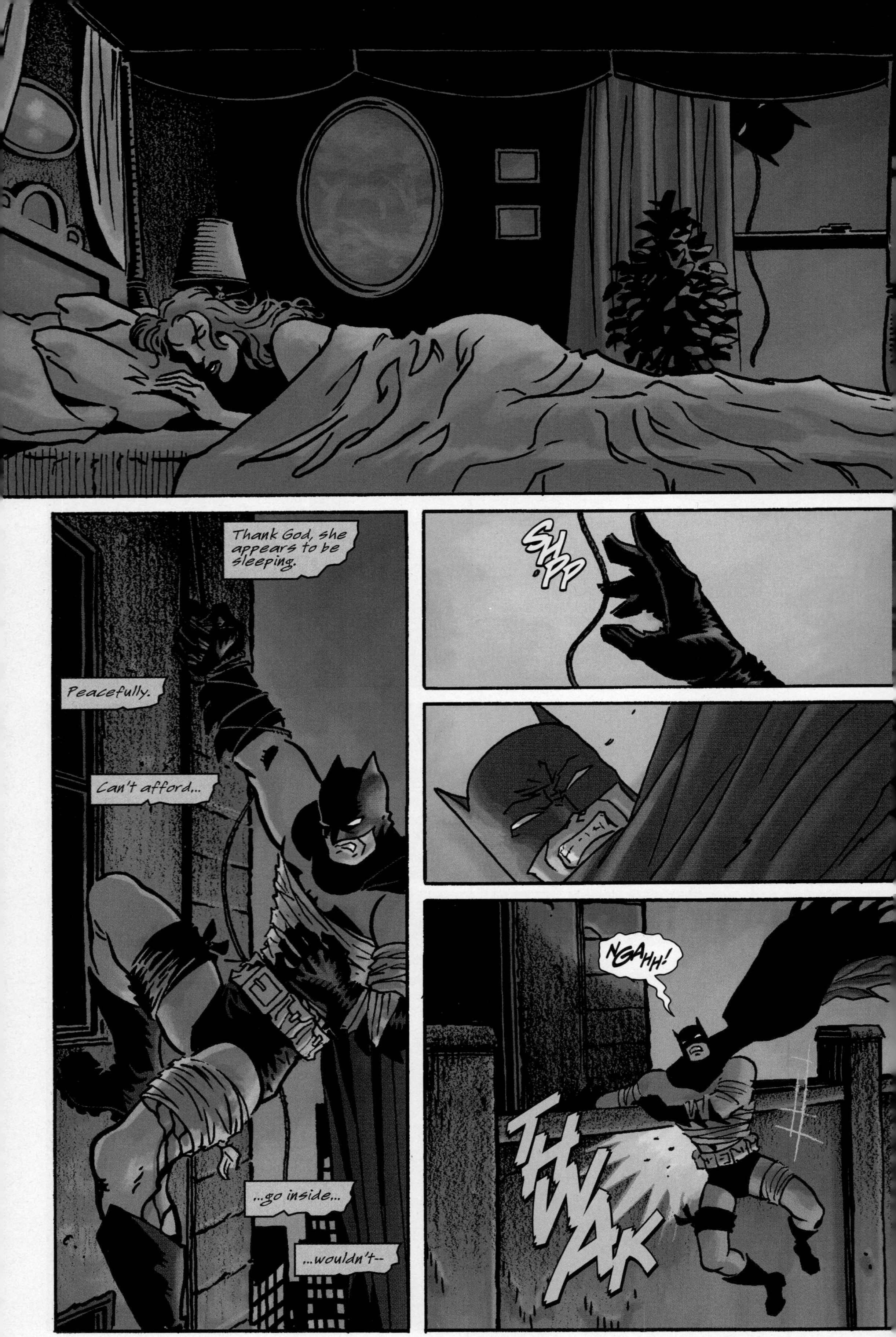
Thank God, she appears to be sleeping.
Peacefully.
Can't afford...
...go inside...
...wouldn't--
SHPP
NGAHH!
THWAK

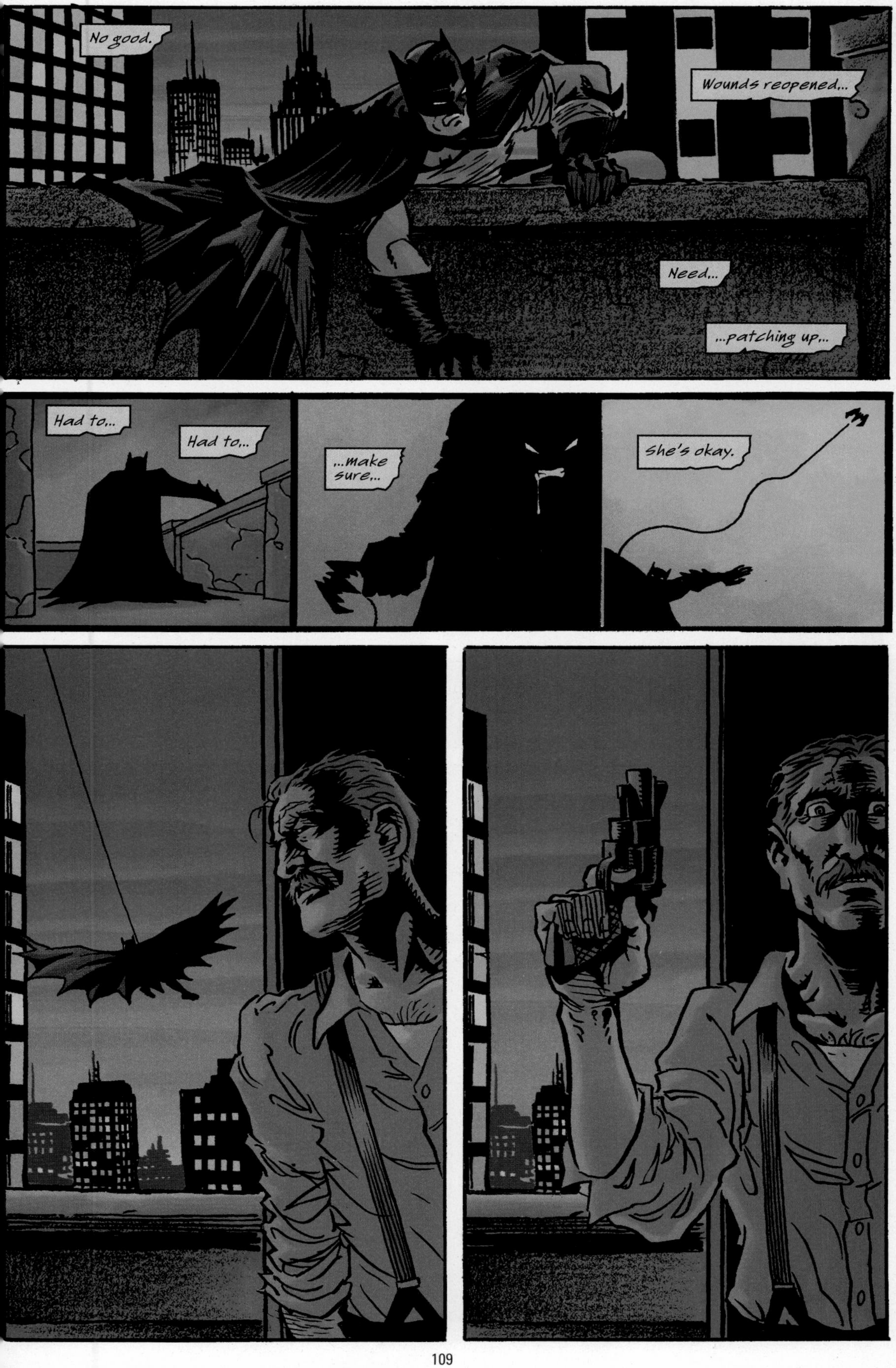
No good.
Wounds reopened...
Need...
...patching up...
Had to...
Had to...
...make sure...
She's okay.

I REMEMBER YOUR FATHER USED TO SPEAK OF THE RALLSTONE FAMILY.

HE SAID THEY WERE A STAIN ON GOTHAM'S REPUTATION AND ITS LIVELIHOOD.

A SIGN OF THINGS TO COME. EVEN THOUGH THEY'RE NO LONGER IN POWER, THEIR CORRUPTING INFLUENCE SEEMS TO HAVE SUNK INTO GOTHAM'S CURRENT LEGACY.

HE TRAVELED THROUGH EUROPE LIKE IT WAS HIS OWN PERSONAL PLAYGROUND, *REGARDLES* OF ANY POLITICAL STRIF THE RUMORS MAKE IT SOUND LIKE A ROVING BACCHANAL.

THE ONLY SURVIVING HEIR, *RICHARD RALLSTONE*, HAS BEEN, BY ALL ACCOUNTS, THE EPITOME OF INDOLENT YOUNG WEALTH.

RALLSTONE SCION HOME FROM ABROAD

FUTURE UNCERTAIN

RALLSTONE CASTLE FALLS INTO DISREPAIR

EVEN PUTS THE PUBLIC PERSONA OF BRUCE WAYNE TO SHAME.

HIS FATHER WAS THE LAST KNOWN RESIDENT OF THE "RALLSTONE CASTLE."

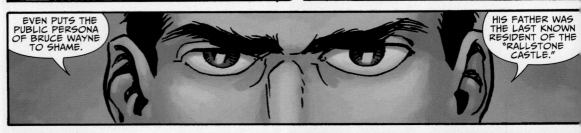

HE COMMITTED SUICIDE WHEN HE ULTIMATELY HAD TO DECLARE BANKRUPTCY.

THE CASTLE'S DEED IS *STILL* LISTED IN RICHARD RALLSTONE'S NAME--OWWCH!

EASY THERE, "DOC!"

IT'S NOT *MY* FAULT YOU CAN'T SEEM TO REMAIN UNINJURED FOR MORE THAN A FEW DAYS AT A TIME.

NOW THEN, IS THAT ALL? NO OTHER LACERATIONS, LESIONS, CONTUSIONS OR ABRASIONS THAT NEED TENDING TO?

NO, NO... THAT'S FINE. I THINK YOU GOT THEM ALL. BESIDES, I DON'T KNOW IF I COULD *STAND* ANY MORE OF THE *TREATMENTS!*

OHH... DON'T BE SUCH A BABY! HERE...

LET ME BANDAGE THOSE LAST STITCHES.

THANKS, ALFRED.

ALL IN THE LINE OF DUTY, SIR.

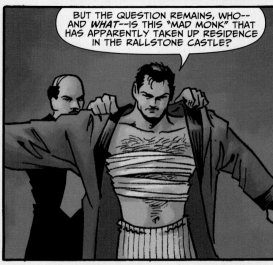

BUT THE QUESTION REMAINS, WHO-- AND *WHAT*--IS THIS "MAD MONK" THAT HAS APPARENTLY TAKEN UP RESIDENCE IN THE RALLSTONE CASTLE?

IF IT *IS*, IN FACT, RICHARD RALLSTONE, HAVE HIS HEDONISTIC WORLD TRAVELS LEFT HIM WITH A HORRIBLE AND BLOODTHIRSTY PSYCHOSIS?

IN ANY CASE, REAL OR IMAGINED, BOTH VAMPIRES AND GOTHAM'S *OTHER* CREATURE OF THE NIGHT MUST SLEEP DURING THE DAYTIME.

YOU REALLY NEED TO REST UP THOSE WOUNDS, SIR.

OR HAS HE ACTUALLY FALLEN PREY TO SOME CURSE AND CONDITION THAT EXISTS OUTSIDE THE RATIONAL WORLD?

ON THE OTHER HAND, THERE *IS* A MAN IN METROPOLIS WHO CAN ACTUALLY FLY AND BEND STEEL IN HIS BARE HANDS--

SIR...

ALL RIGHT, ALFRED. ALL RIGHT.

D-D-DADDY...?

ARE Y-- ARE YOU H-HERE? DADDY, I--

CAN'T *BELIEVE* I SLEPT SO... SO LONG--

I HAVE ALWAYS THOUGHT OF MYSELF AS A MAN WHO FACES UP TO HIS RESPONSIBILITIES.

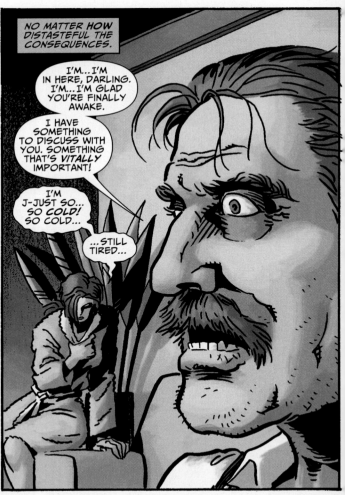

NO MATTER *HOW* DISTASTEFUL THE CONSEQUENCES.

I'M...I'M IN HERE, DARLING. I'M...I'M GLAD YOU'RE FINALLY AWAKE.

I HAVE SOMETHING TO DISCUSS WITH YOU. SOMETHING THAT'S *VITALLY* IMPORTANT!

I'M J-JUST SO... SO *COLD!* SO COLD...

...STILL TIRED...

...AND IT'S *SOOOO* BRIGHT! CAN'T WE...CAN'T WE DRAW THE SHADES?

DARLING...

...I KNOW I...I HAVEN'T BEEN AS *HONEST* WITH YOU AS I SHOULD HAVE BEEN, LATELY.

YOU HAVE TO UNDERSTAND, THIS ISN'T EASY FOR ME.

LORD KNOWS, I'VE BEEN ASHAMED OF WHAT I DID BUT, NOW... NOW I FIND MYSELF--

...OH, GOD...

--FORCED INTO ACTIONS THAT MIGHT...MIGHT ULTIMATELY PROVE DISASTROUS.

DADDY, I DON'T...

...WHA-- WHAT ARE YOU TALKING AB--

YOU KNOW I AM A MAN OF PRINCIPLE...*AND* OF COMPROMISE. BUT *THIS* SITUATION HAS PROVEN UNYIELDING. AND IT DEMANDS AN END!

HERE...

WHAT... WHAT'S TH--?

A COPY OF MY WILL.

ALONG WITH VITAL INFORMATION IN REGARD TO MY VARIOUS HOLDINGS, TRUSTS AND ACCOUNTS--ALONG WITH ALL THE NECESSARY PASSWORDS.

OH, MY DEAR... IF, FOR SOME REASON, I NEVER GET TO SEE-- NOR HOLD YOU AGAIN... REMEMBER ME AS A MAN OF MY WORD.

REMEMBER... YOUR FATHER DEARLY LOVED YOU.

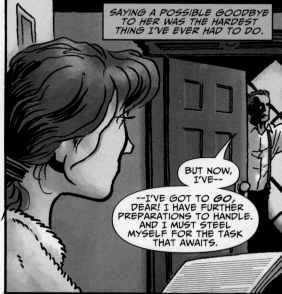

SAYING A POSSIBLE GOODBYE TO HER WAS THE HARDEST THING I'VE EVER HAD TO DO.

BUT NOW, I'VE--

--I'VE GOT TO GO, DEAR! I HAVE FURTHER PREPARATIONS TO HANDLE. AND I MUST STEEL MYSELF FOR THE TASK THAT AWAITS.

SOON, I WILL CONFRONT THE SECOND HARDEST.

'KAY, DADDY...

G'BYE, DADDY...

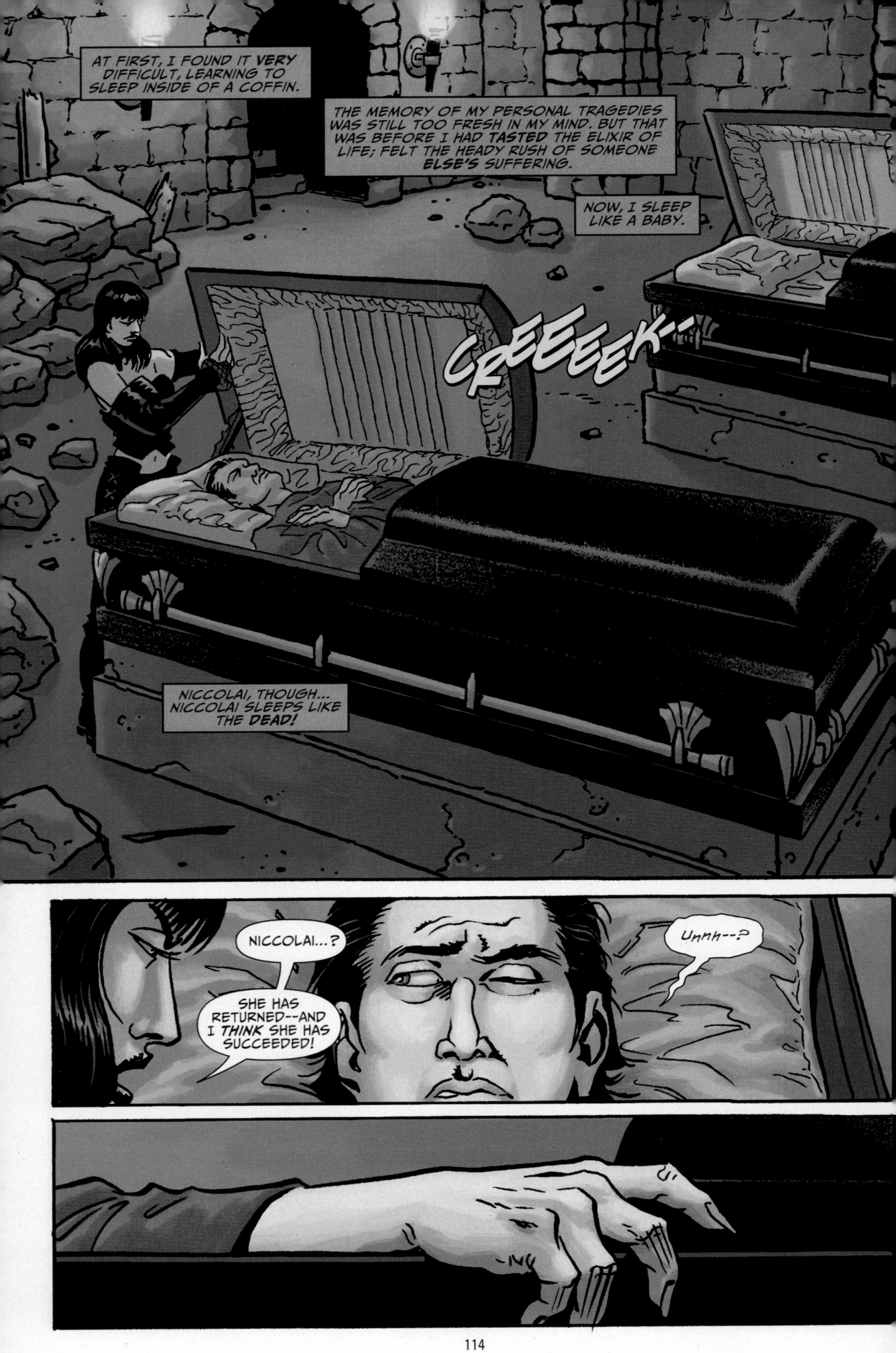
AT FIRST, I FOUND IT VERY DIFFICULT, LEARNING TO SLEEP INSIDE OF A COFFIN.
THE MEMORY OF MY PERSONAL TRAGEDIES WAS STILL TOO FRESH IN MY MIND. BUT THAT WAS BEFORE I HAD TASTED THE ELIXIR OF LIFE; FELT THE HEADY RUSH OF SOMEONE ELSE'S SUFFERING.
NOW, I SLEEP LIKE A BABY.
CREEEEEK--
NICCOLAI, THOUGH... NICCOLAI SLEEPS LIKE THE DEAD!
NICCOLAI...?
SHE HAS RETURNED--AND I THINK SHE HAS SUCCEEDED!
Unnh--?

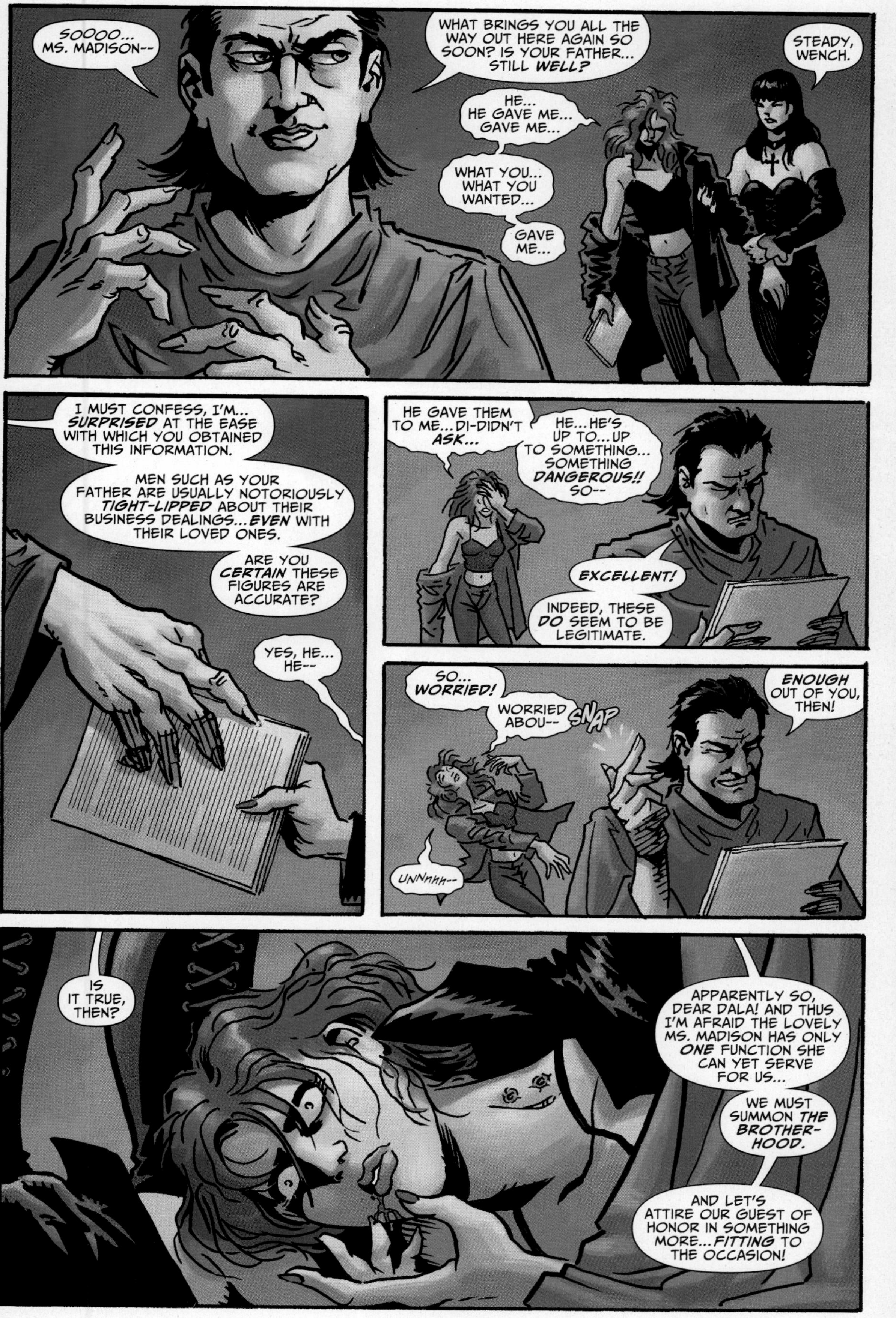
SOOOO... MS. MADISON--
WHAT BRINGS YOU ALL THE WAY OUT HERE AGAIN SO SOON? IS YOUR FATHER... STILL WELL?
STEADY, WENCH.
HE... HE GAVE ME... GAVE ME...
WHAT YOU... WHAT YOU WANTED...
GAVE ME...
I MUST CONFESS, I'M... SURPRISED AT THE EASE WITH WHICH YOU OBTAINED THIS INFORMATION.
MEN SUCH AS YOUR FATHER ARE USUALLY NOTORIOUSLY TIGHT-LIPPED ABOUT THEIR BUSINESS DEALINGS...EVEN WITH THEIR LOVED ONES.
ARE YOU CERTAIN THESE FIGURES ARE ACCURATE?
YES, HE... HE--
HE GAVE THEM TO ME...DI-DIDN'T ASK...
HE...HE'S UP TO...UP TO SOMETHING... SOMETHING DANGEROUS!! SO--
EXCELLENT!
INDEED, THESE DO SEEM TO BE LEGITIMATE.
SO... WORRIED!
WORRIED ABOU--
SNAP
ENOUGH OUT OF YOU, THEN!
UNNnhh--
IS IT TRUE, THEN?
APPARENTLY SO, DEAR DALA! AND THUS I'M AFRAID THE LOVELY MS. MADISON HAS ONLY ONE FUNCTION SHE CAN YET SERVE FOR US...
WE MUST SUMMON THE BROTHER-HOOD.
AND LET'S ATTIRE OUR GUEST OF HONOR IN SOMETHING MORE...FITTING TO THE OCCASION!

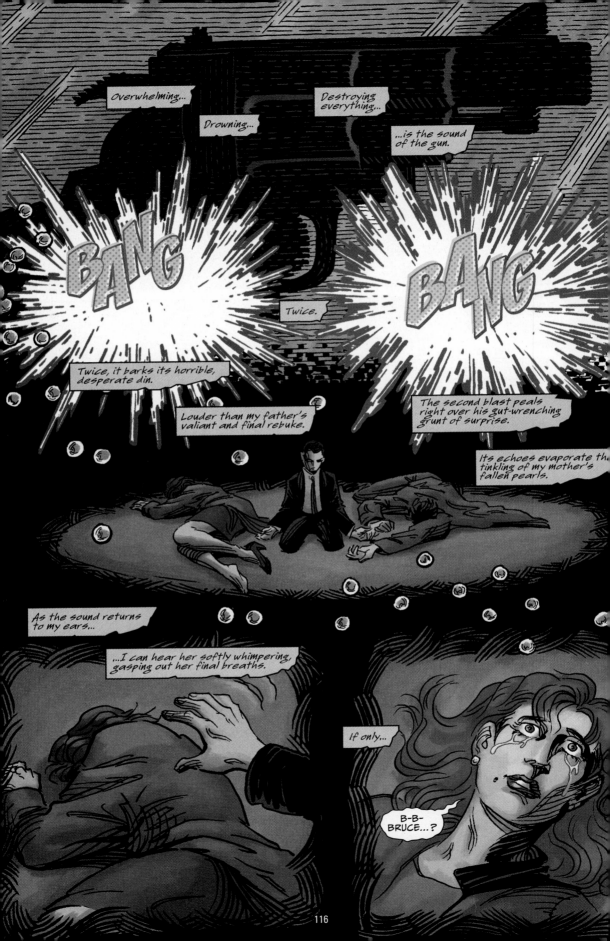

Overwhelming...

Drowning...

Destroying everything...

...is the sound of the gun.

BANG

BANG

Twice.

Twice, it barks its horrible, desperate din.

Louder than my father's valiant and final rebuke.

The second blast peals right over his gut-wrenching grunt of surprise.

Its echoes evaporate the tinkling of my mother's fallen pearls.

As the sound returns to my ears...

...I can hear her softly whimpering, gasping out her final breaths.

If only...

B-B-BRUCE...?

116

If only I knew how to save her...

JULIIIEEE!

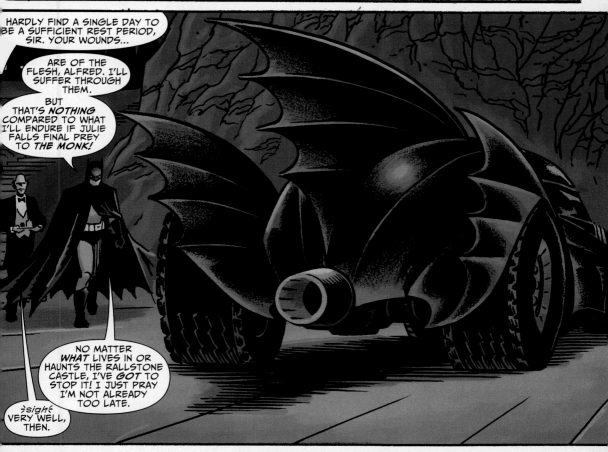

HARDLY FIND A SINGLE DAY TO BE A SUFFICIENT REST PERIOD, SIR. YOUR WOUNDS...

ARE OF THE FLESH, ALFRED. I'LL SUFFER THROUGH THEM.

BUT THAT'S *NOTHING* COMPARED TO WHAT I'LL ENDURE IF JULIE FALLS FINAL PREY TO *THE MONK!*

NO MATTER *WHAT* LIVES IN OR HAUNTS THE RALLSTONE CASTLE, I'VE *GOT* TO STOP IT! I JUST PRAY I'M NOT ALREADY TOO LATE.

ξsighξ VERY WELL, THEN.

HERE. THESE SHOULD HELP HOLD YOU TOGETHER, AT LEAST FOR TONIGHT.

WHAT *ARE* THEY?

ONE'S AN ADVANCED COAGULANT, IT *SHOULD* HELP KEEP YOU FROM BLEEDING--*TOO MUCH.* THE OTHERS ARE TO DULL THE PAIN AND MAKE SURE YOU STAY ALERT.

THANKS, ALFRED.

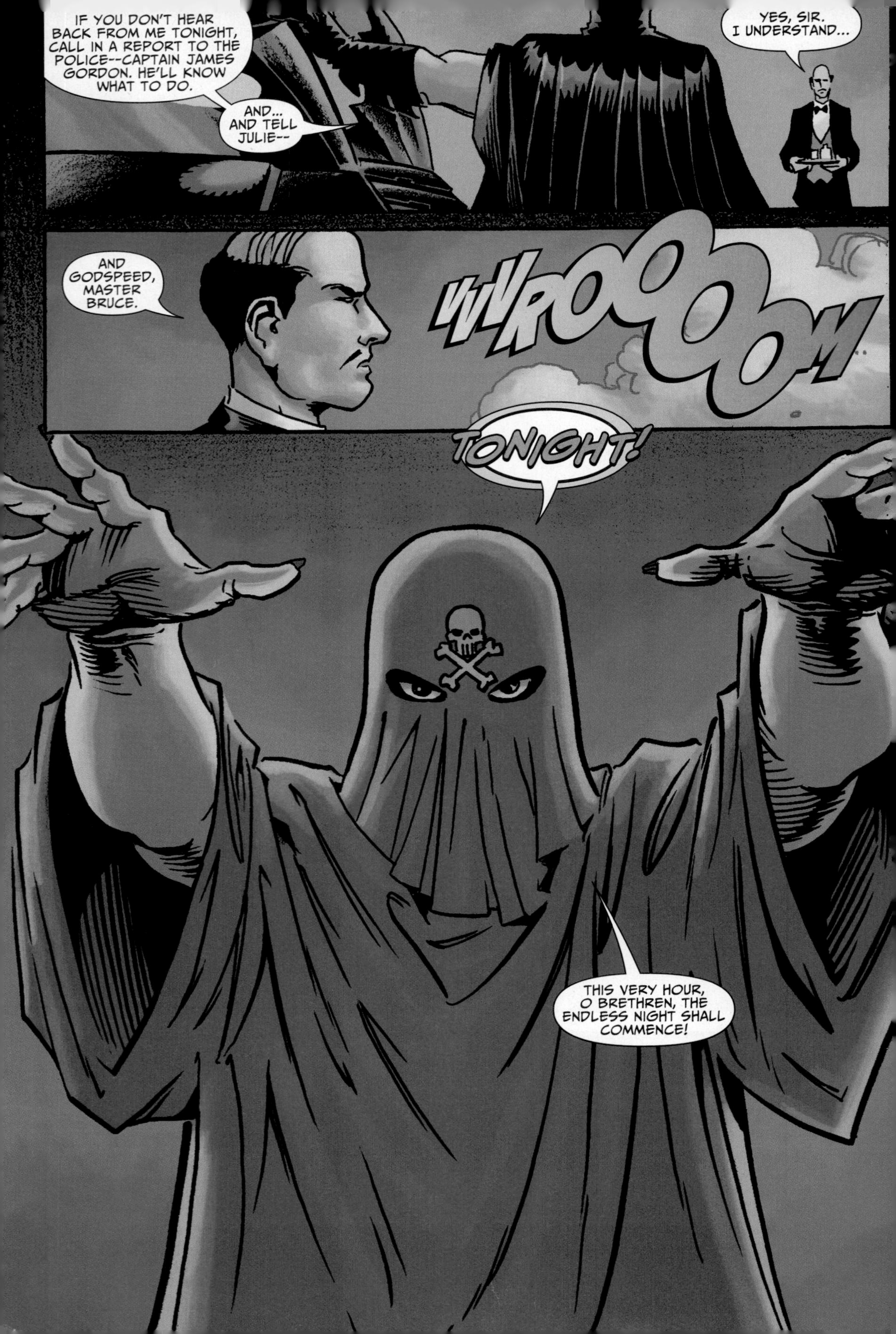
IF YOU DON'T HEAR BACK FROM ME TONIGHT, CALL IN A REPORT TO THE POLICE--CAPTAIN JAMES GORDON. HE'LL KNOW WHAT TO DO.
YES, SIR. I UNDERSTAND...
AND... AND TELL JULIE--
AND GODSPEED, MASTER BRUCE.
VVVROOOOOOM
TONIGHT!
THIS VERY HOUR, O BRETHREN, THE ENDLESS NIGHT SHALL COMMENCE!

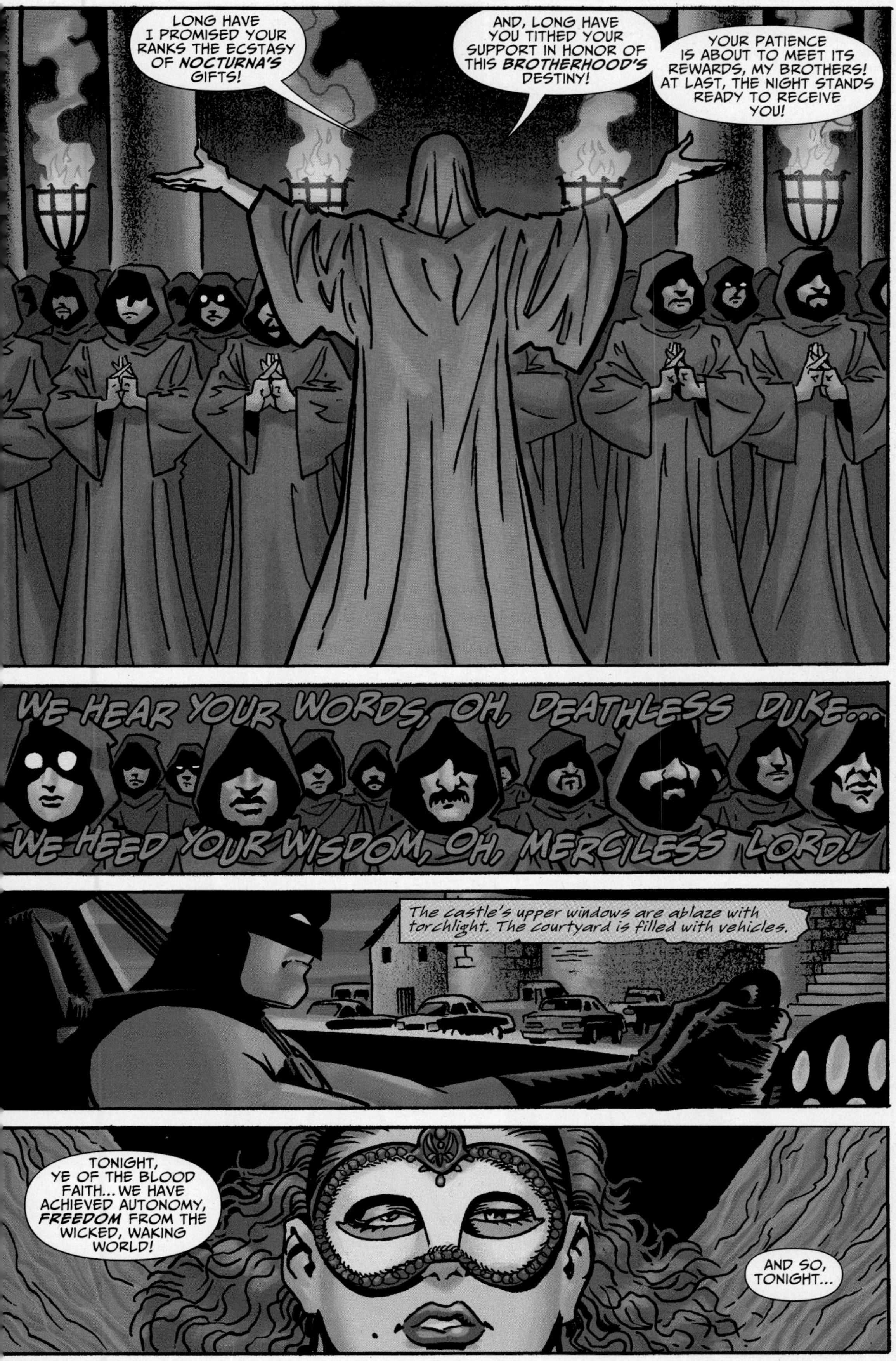
LONG HAVE I PROMISED YOUR RANKS THE ECSTASY OF NOCTURNA'S GIFTS!
AND, LONG HAVE YOU TITHED YOUR SUPPORT IN HONOR OF THIS BROTHERHOOD'S DESTINY!
YOUR PATIENCE IS ABOUT TO MEET ITS REWARDS, MY BROTHERS! AT LAST, THE NIGHT STANDS READY TO RECEIVE YOU!
WE HEAR YOUR WORDS, OH, DEATHLESS DUKE...
WE HEED YOUR WISDOM, OH, MERCILESS LORD!
The castle's upper windows are ablaze with torchlight. The courtyard is filled with vehicles.
TONIGHT, YE OF THE BLOOD FAITH... WE HAVE ACHIEVED AUTONOMY, FREEDOM FROM THE WICKED, WAKING WORLD!
AND SO, TONIGHT...

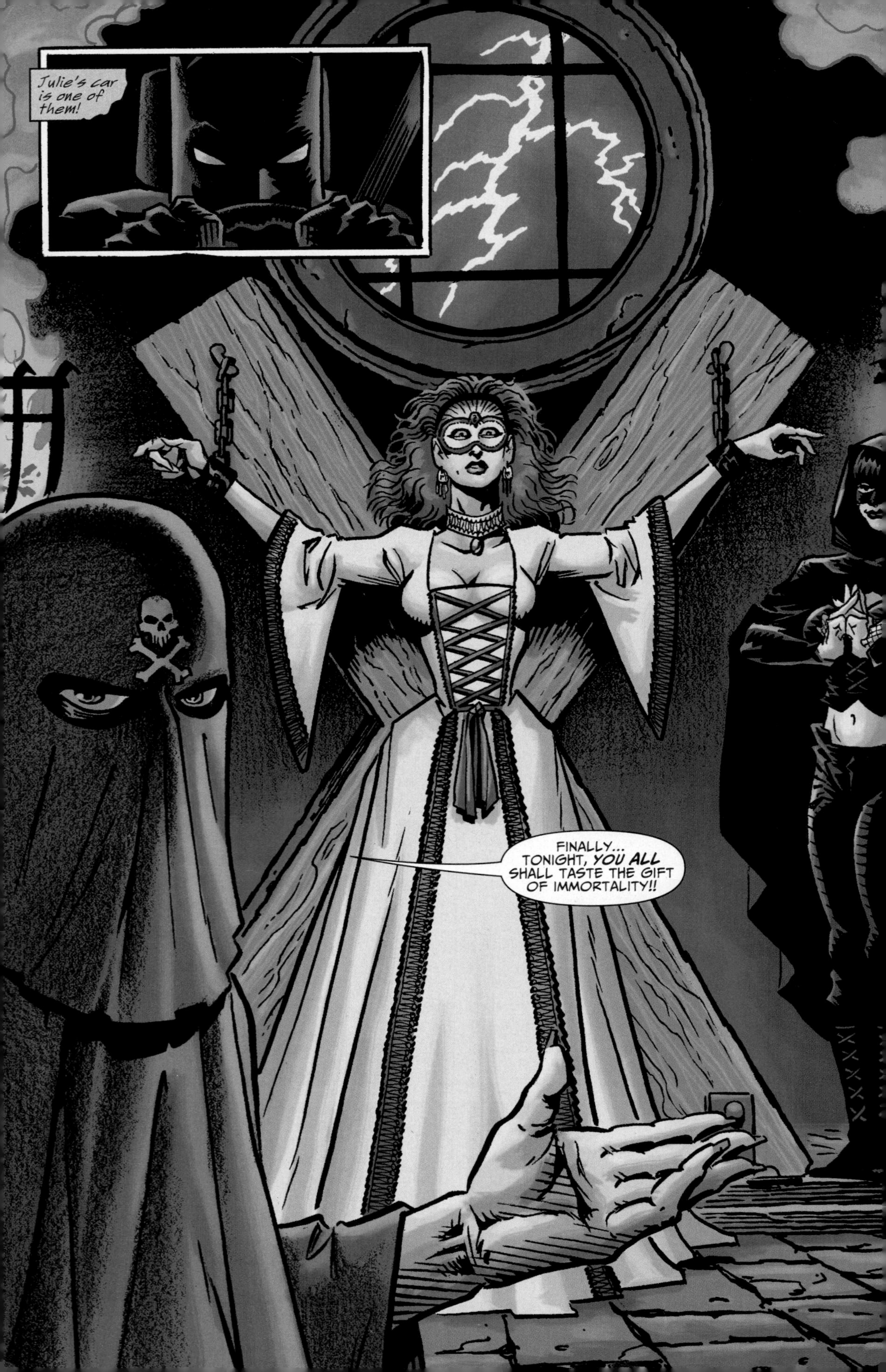
Julie's car is one of them!
FINALLY... TONIGHT, YOU ALL SHALL TASTE THE GIFT OF IMMORTALITY!!

CHAPTER 6

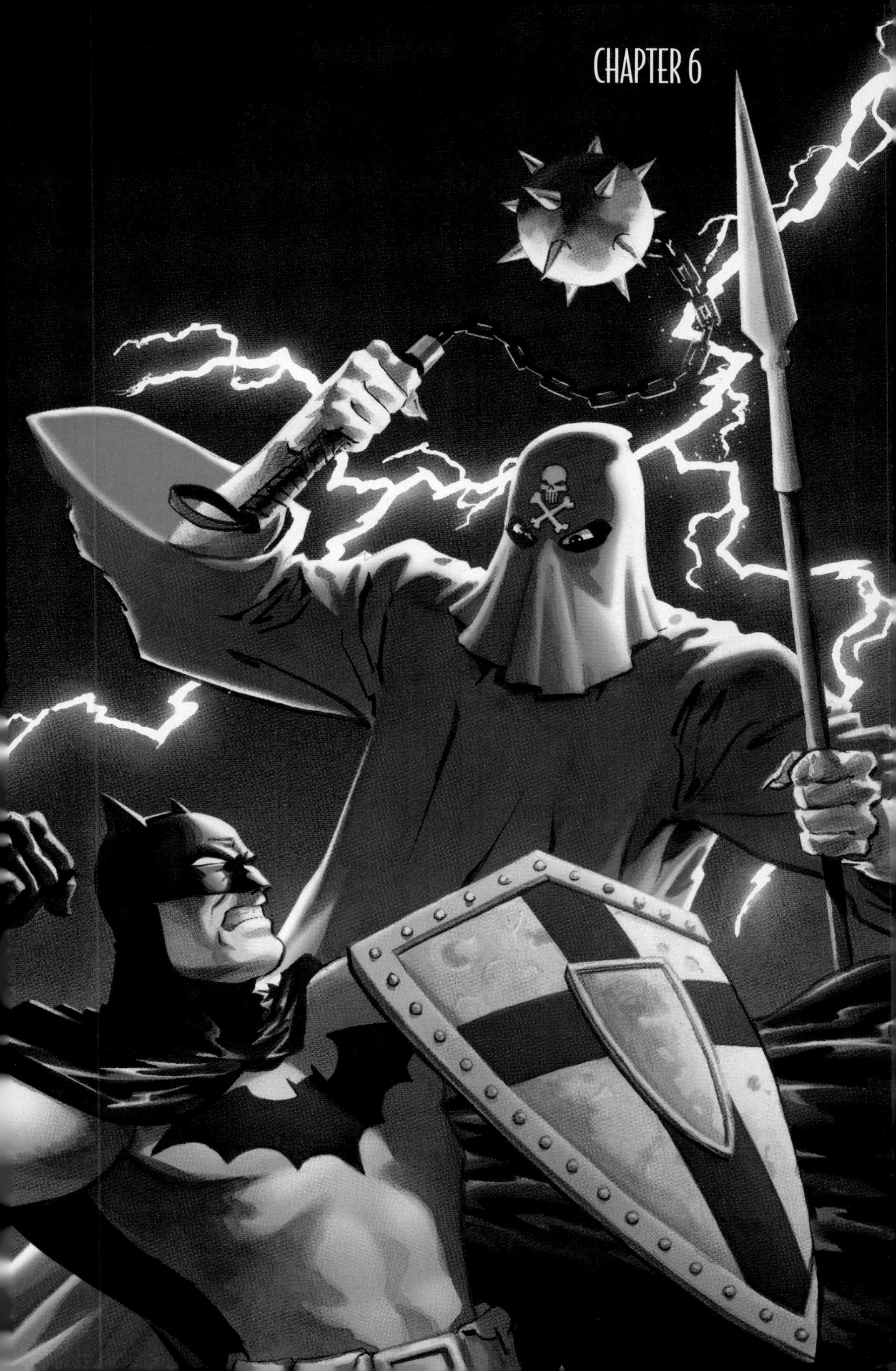

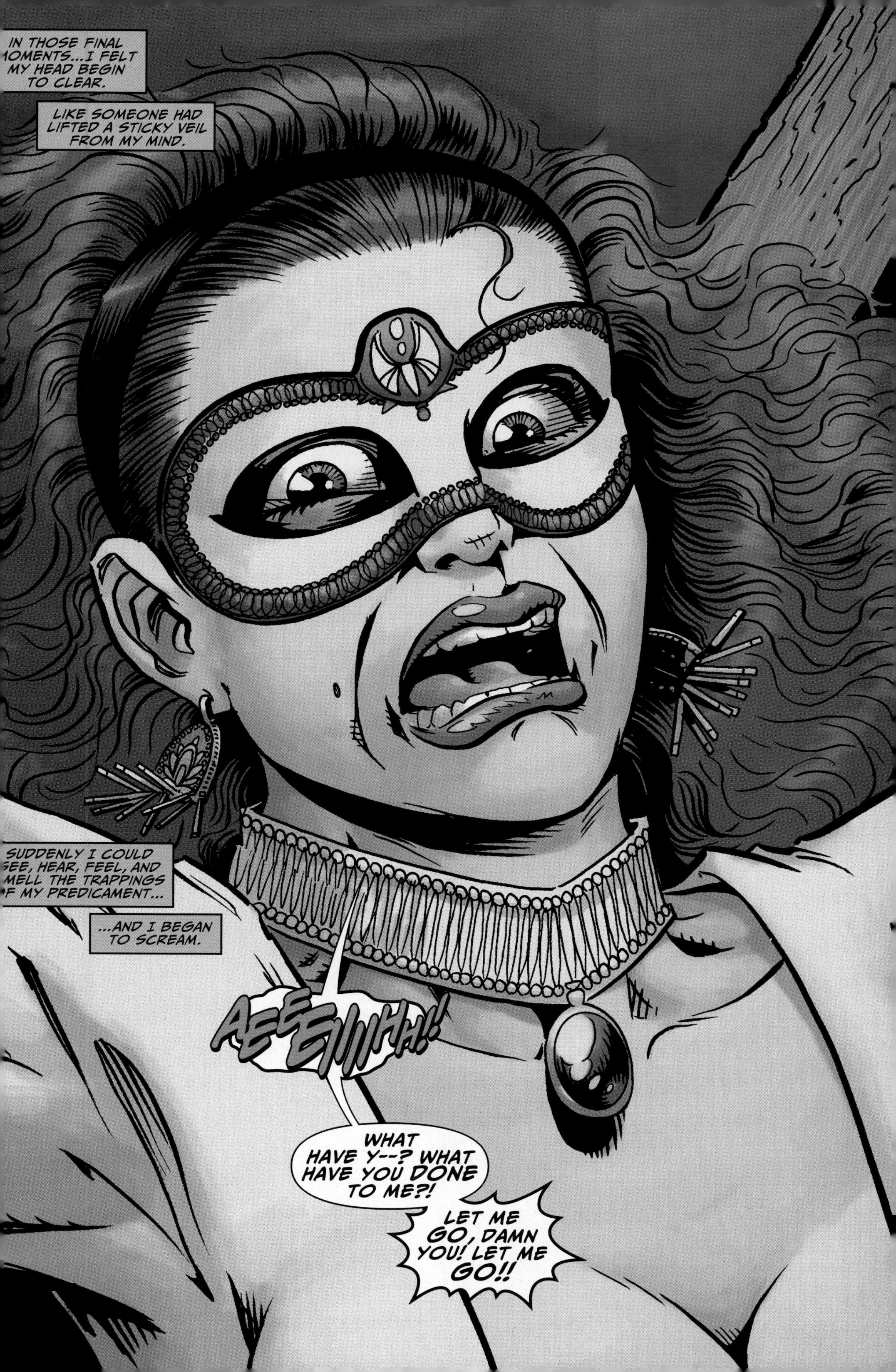
IN THOSE FINAL MOMENTS...I FELT MY HEAD BEGIN TO CLEAR.
LIKE SOMEONE HAD LIFTED A STICKY VEIL FROM MY MIND.
SUDDENLY I COULD SEE, HEAR, FEEL, AND SMELL THE TRAPPINGS OF MY PREDICAMENT...
...AND I BEGAN TO SCREAM.
AEEEIIIIHH!
WHAT HAVE Y--? WHAT HAVE YOU DONE TO ME?!
LET ME GO, DAMN YOU! LET ME GO!!

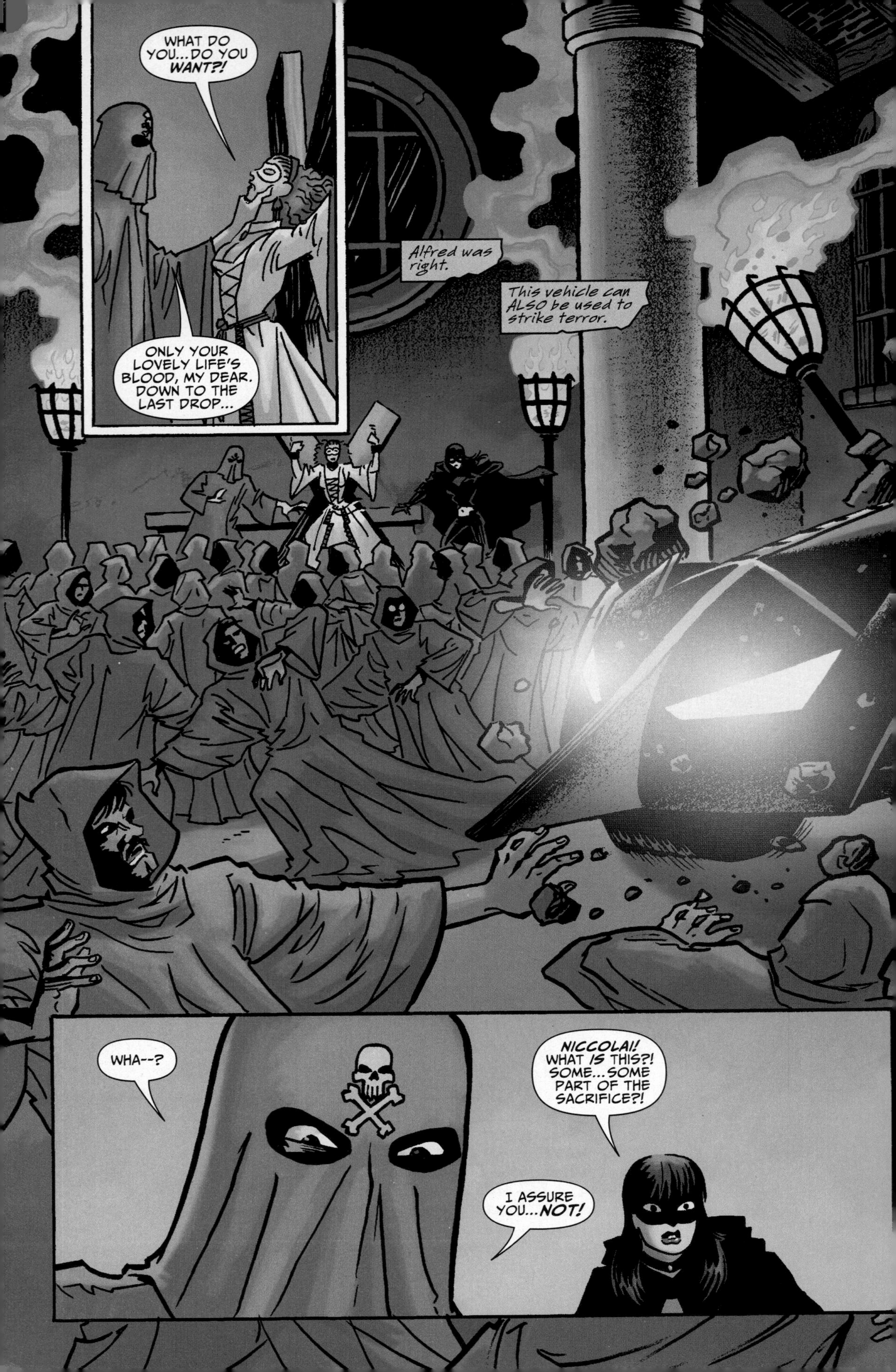
WHAT DO YOU...DO YOU WANT?!
ONLY YOUR LOVELY LIFE'S BLOOD, MY DEAR. DOWN TO THE LAST DROP...
Alfred was right.
This vehicle can ALSO be used to strike terror.
WHA--?
NICCOLAI! WHAT IS THIS?! SOME...SOME PART OF THE SACRIFICE?!
I ASSURE YOU...NOT!

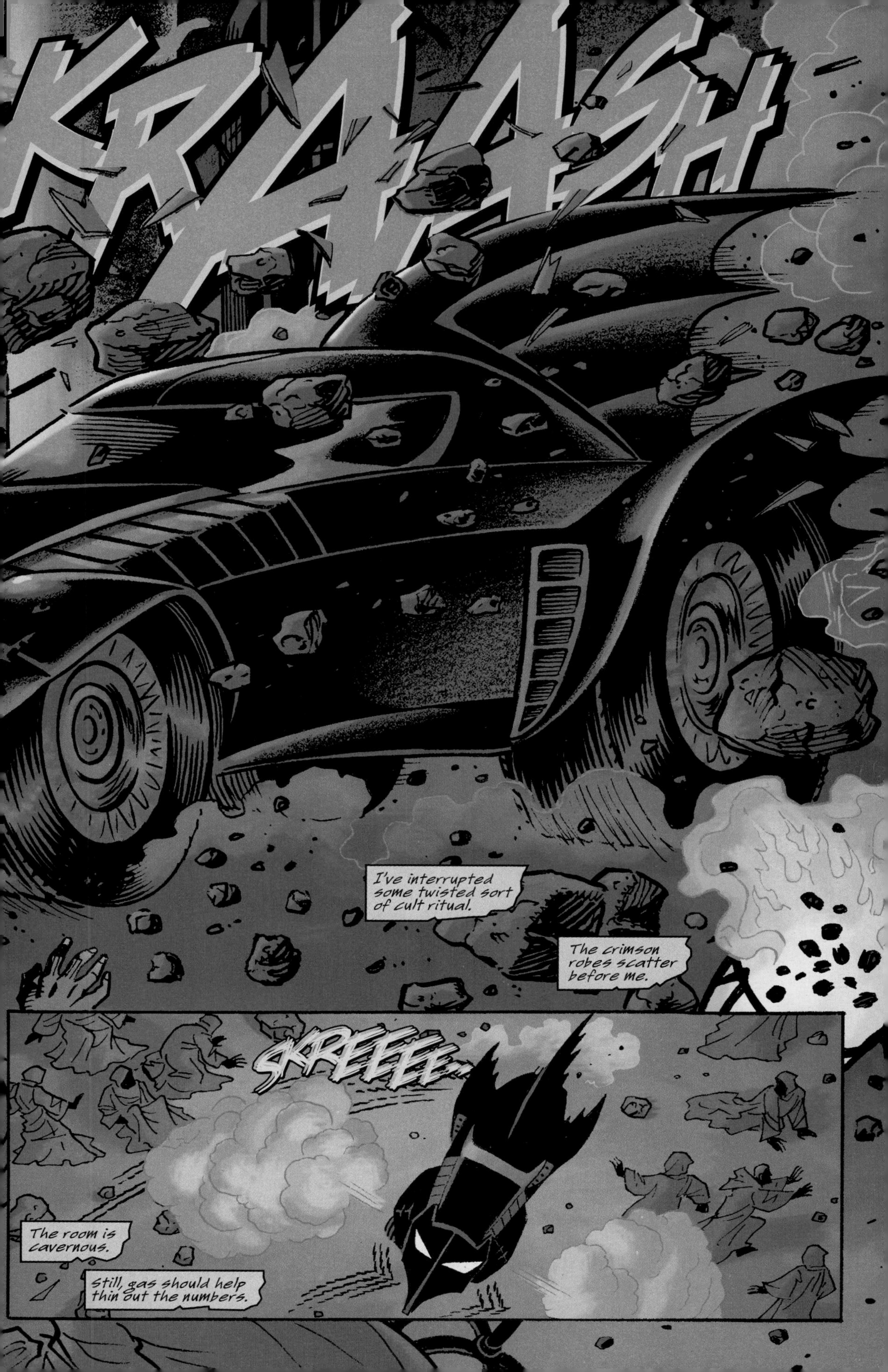
KRASH
I've interrupted some twisted sort of cult ritual.
The crimson robes scatter before me.
SKREEEEE...
The room is cavernous.
Still, gas should help thin out the numbers.

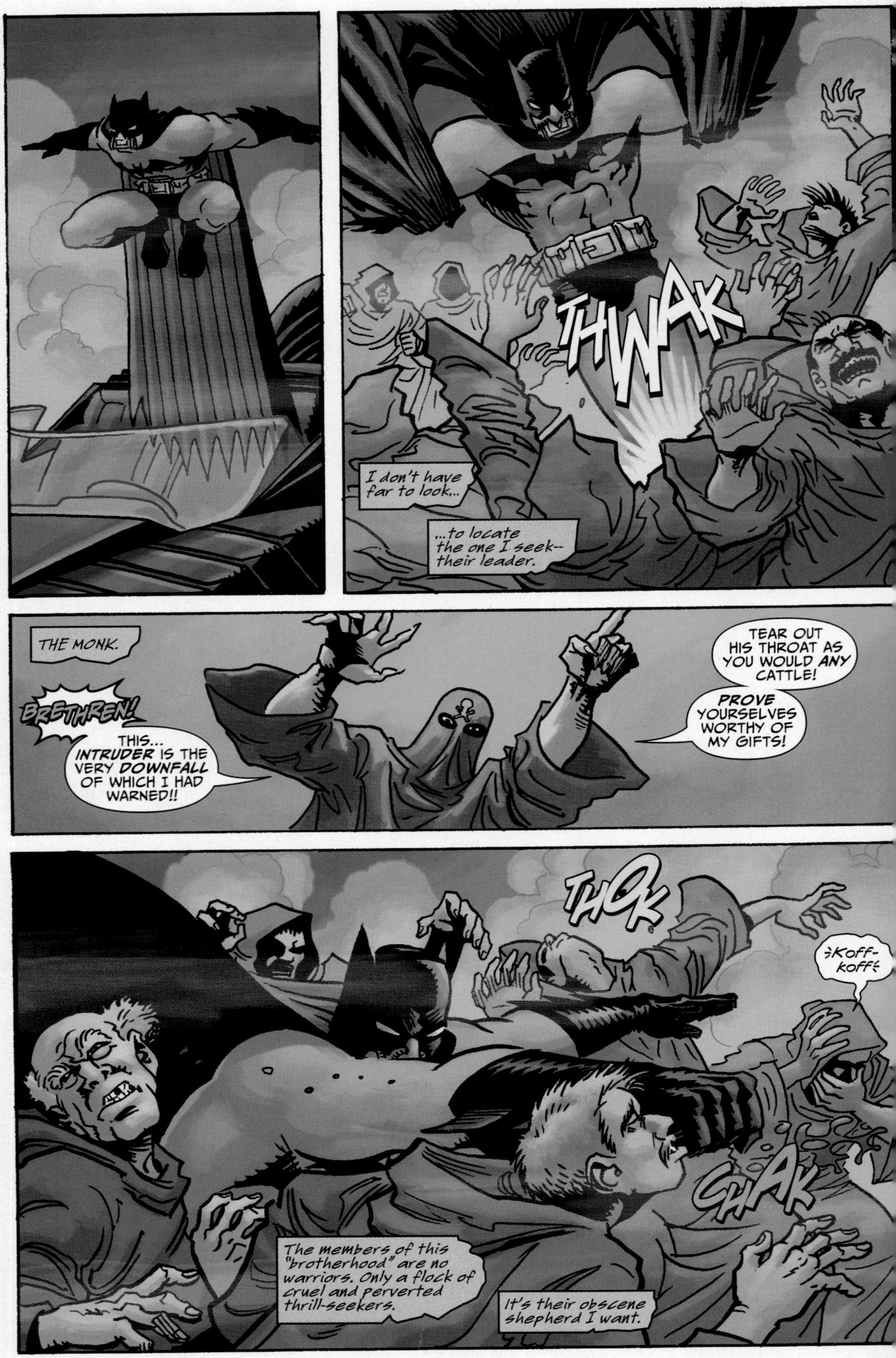
I don't have far to look...
...to locate the one I seek--their leader.
THWAK
THE MONK.
BRETHREN!
THIS... INTRUDER IS THE VERY DOWNFALL OF WHICH I HAD WARNED!!
TEAR OUT HIS THROAT AS YOU WOULD ANY CATTLE!
PROVE YOURSELVES WORTHY OF MY GIFTS!
THOK
KOFF-KOFF
CHAK
The members of this "brotherhood" are no warriors. Only a flock of cruel and perverted thrill-seekers.
It's their obscene shepherd I want.

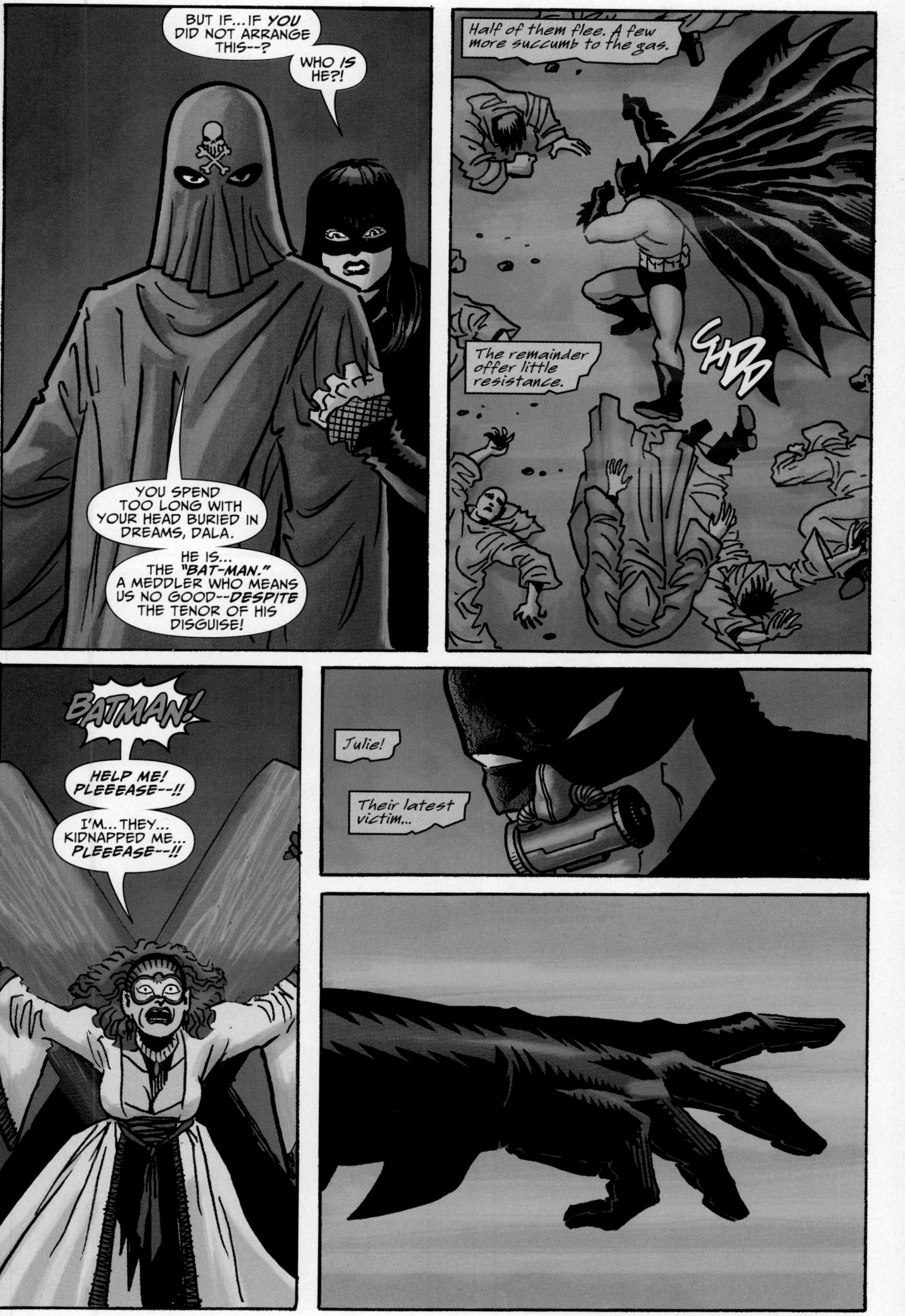
BUT IF... IF YOU DID NOT ARRANGE THIS--?
WHO IS HE?!
YOU SPEND TOO LONG WITH YOUR HEAD BURIED IN DREAMS, DALA.
HE IS... THE "BAT-MAN." A MEDDLER WHO MEANS US NO GOOD--DESPITE THE TENOR OF HIS DISGUISE!
Half of them flee. A few more succumb to the gas.
The remainder offer little resistance.
BATMAN!
HELP ME! PLEEEASE--!!
I'M... THEY... KIDNAPPED ME... PLEEEASE--!!
Julie!
Their latest victim...

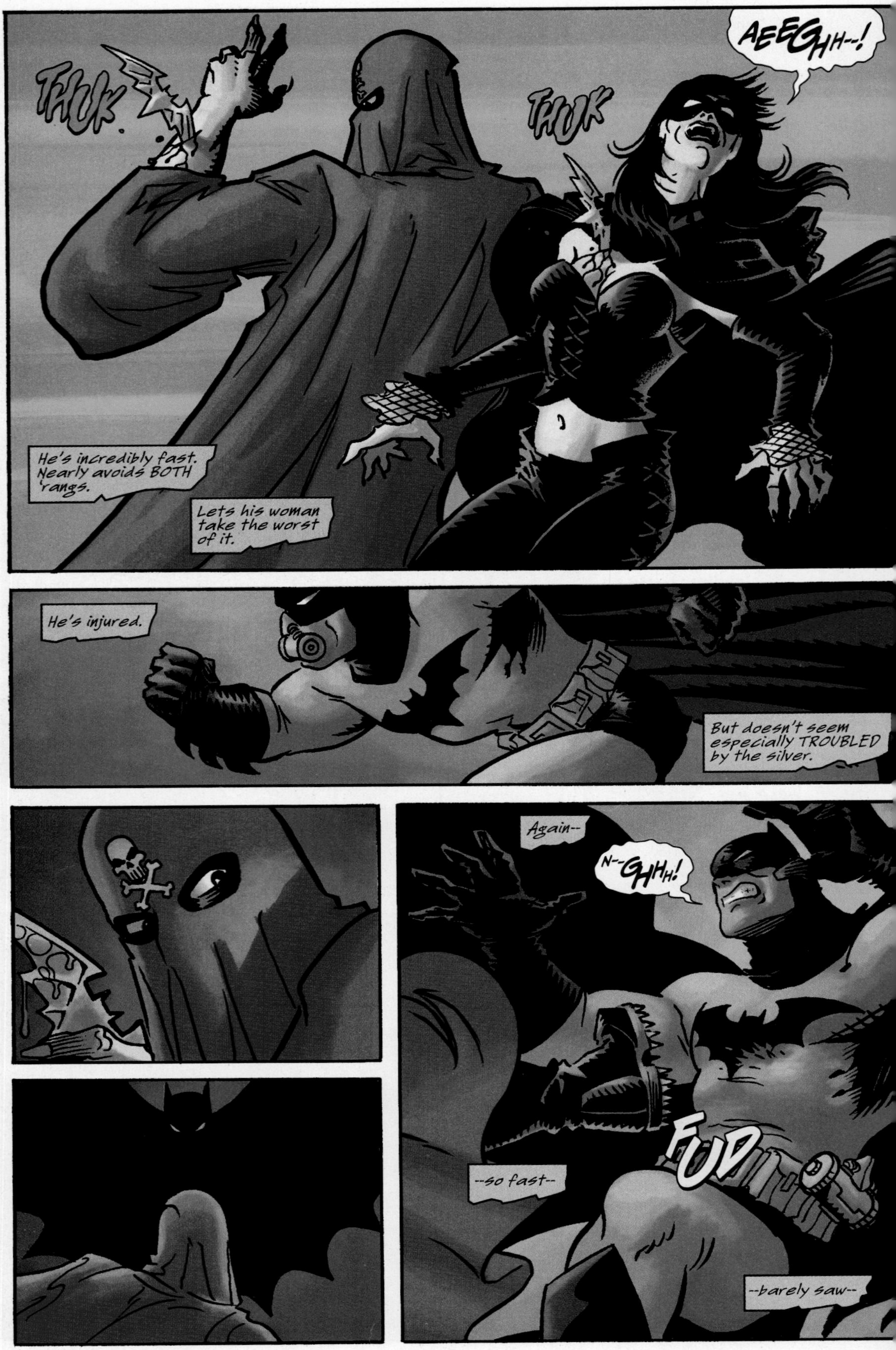
THUK
AEEGHH--!
THUK
He's incredibly fast. Nearly avoids BOTH 'rangs.
Lets his woman take the worst of it.
He's injured.
But doesn't seem especially TROUBLED by the silver.
Again--
N--GHHH!
FUD
--so fast--
--barely saw--

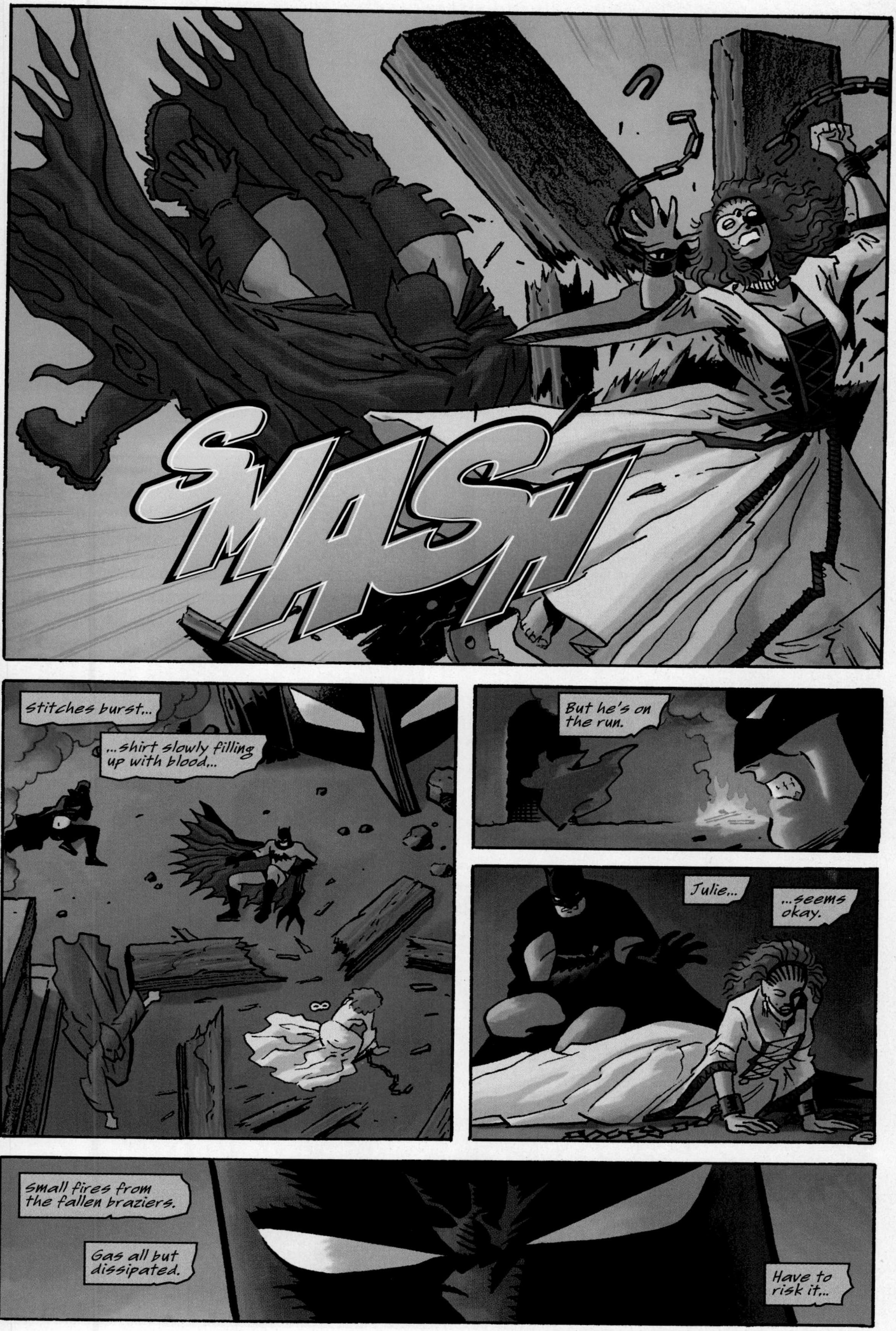
SMASH
Stitches burst...
...shirt slowly filling up with blood...
But he's on the run.
Julie...
...seems okay.
Small fires from the fallen braziers.
Gas all but dissipated.
Have to risk it...

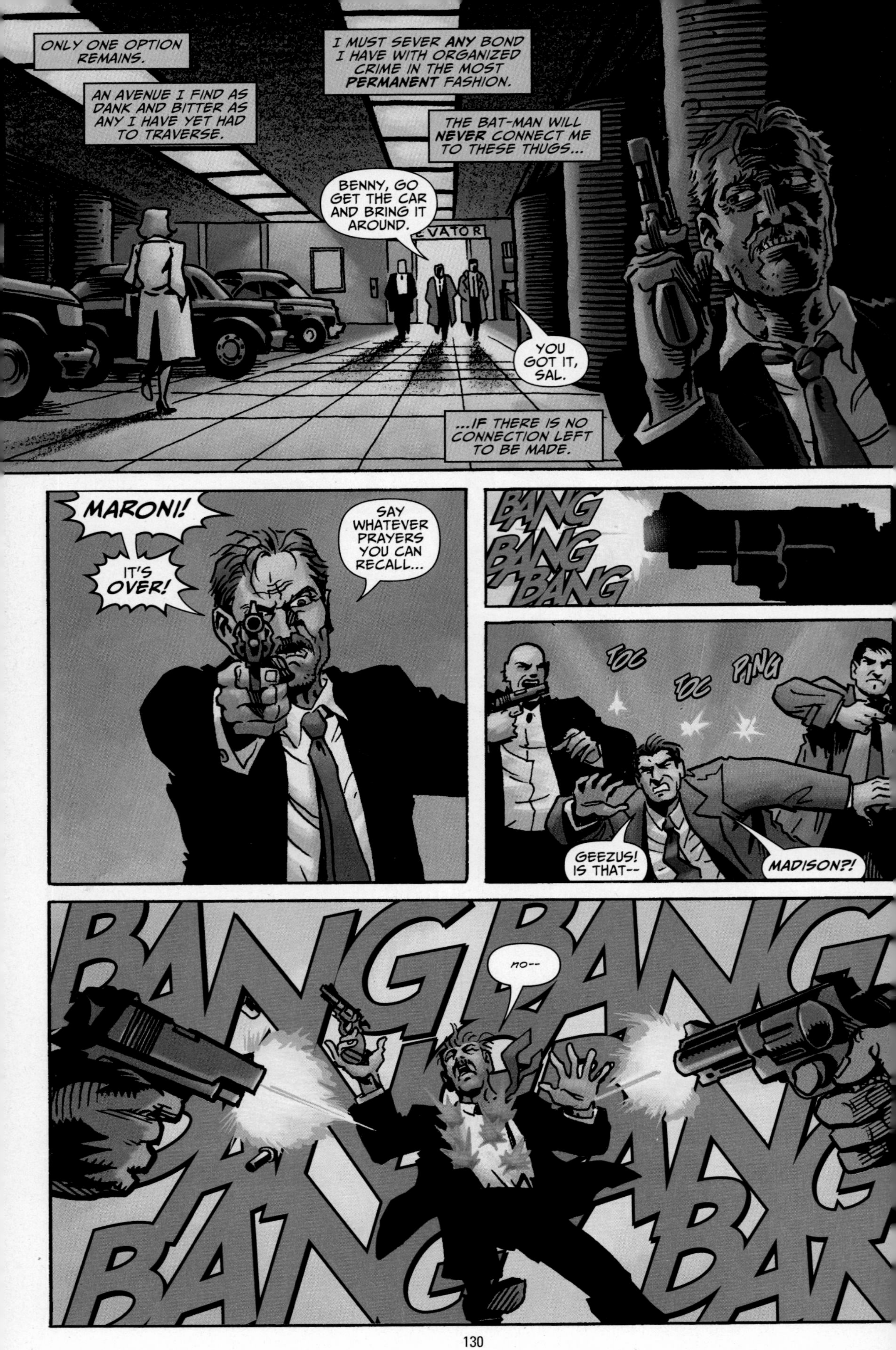
ONLY ONE OPTION REMAINS.
AN AVENUE I FIND AS DANK AND BITTER AS ANY I HAVE YET HAD TO TRAVERSE.
I MUST SEVER ANY BOND I HAVE WITH ORGANIZED CRIME IN THE MOST PERMANENT FASHION.
THE BAT-MAN WILL NEVER CONNECT ME TO THESE THUGS...
BENNY, GO GET THE CAR AND BRING IT AROUND.
YOU GOT IT, SAL.
...IF THERE IS NO CONNECTION LEFT TO BE MADE.
MARONI!
IT'S OVER!
SAY WHATEVER PRAYERS YOU CAN RECALL...
BANG
BANG
BANG
TOC
TOC
PING
GEEZUS! IS THAT--
MADISON?!
BANG BANG
NO--
BANG BANG BANG

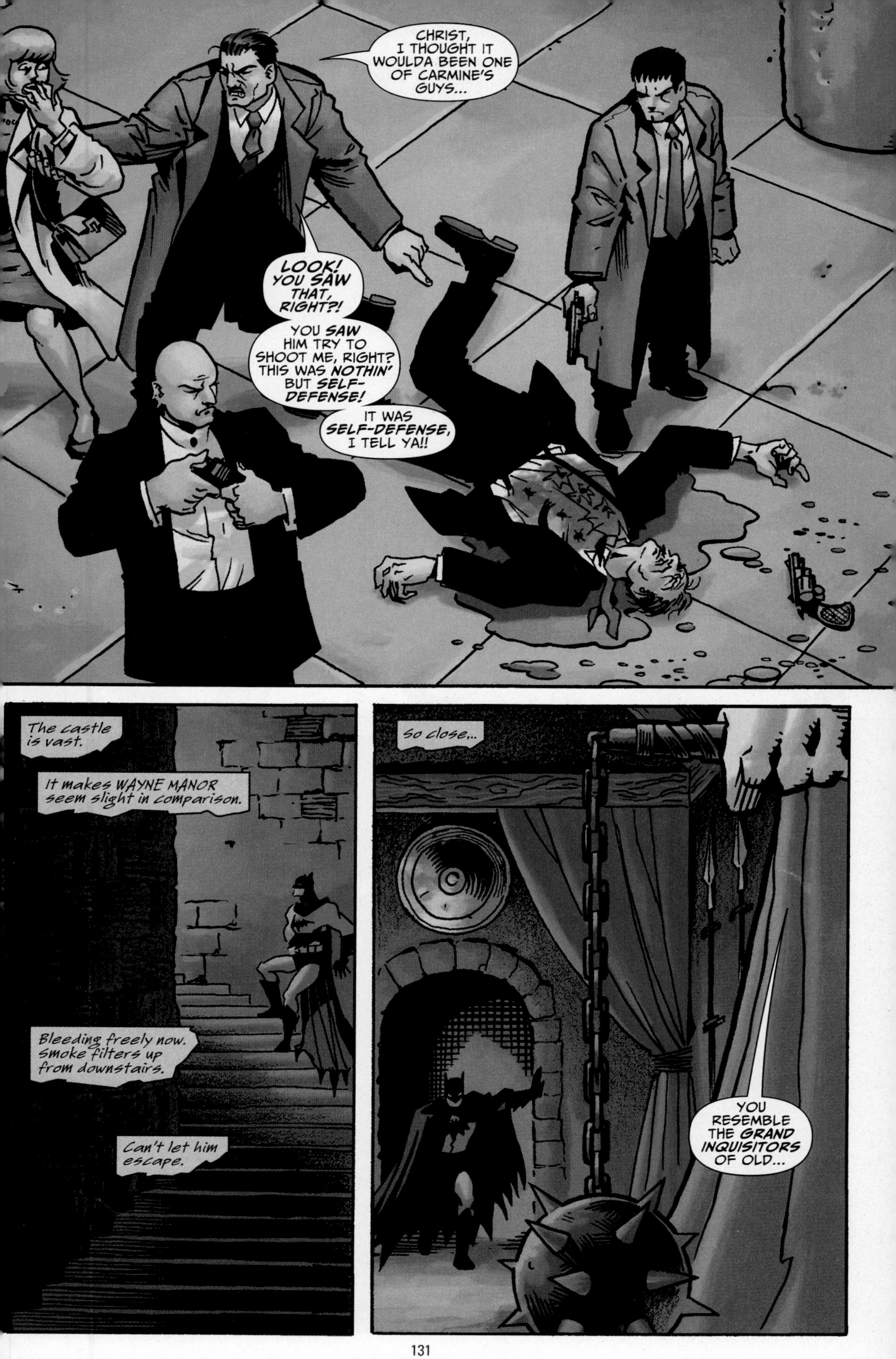
CHRIST, I THOUGHT IT WOULDA BEEN ONE OF CARMINE'S GUYS...
LOOK! YOU SAW THAT, RIGHT?!
YOU SAW HIM TRY TO SHOOT ME, RIGHT? THIS WAS NOTHIN' BUT SELF-DEFENSE!
IT WAS SELF-DEFENSE, I TELL YA!!
The castle is vast.
It makes WAYNE MANOR seem slight in comparison.
Bleeding freely now. Smoke filters up from downstairs.
Can't let him escape.
So close...
YOU RESEMBLE THE GRAND INQUISITORS OF OLD...

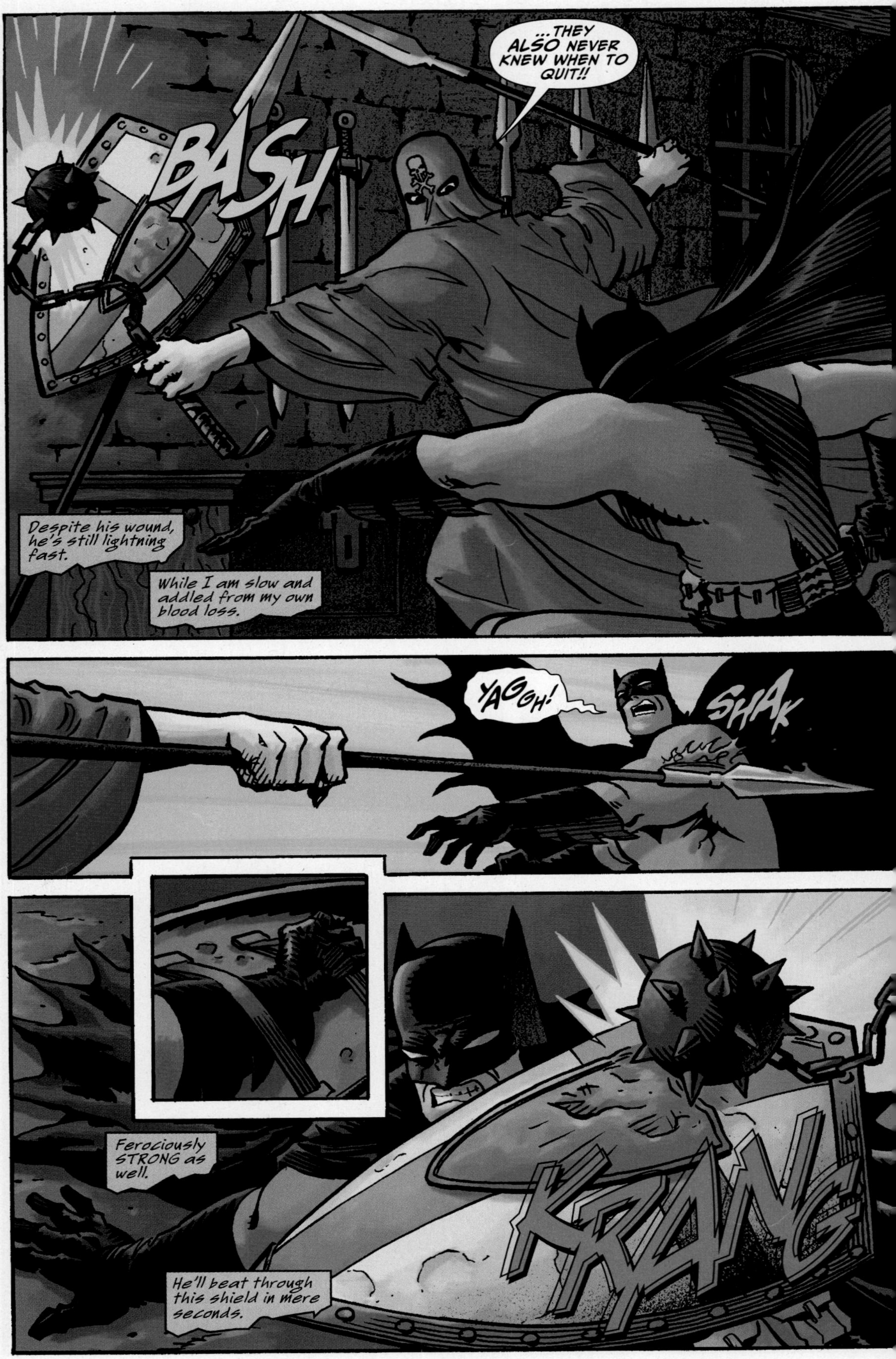
...THEY ALSO NEVER KNEW WHEN TO QUIT!!
BASH
Despite his wound, he's still lightning fast.
While I am slow and addled from my own blood loss.
YAGGH!
SHAK
Ferociously STRONG as well.
KRANG
He'll beat through this shield in mere seconds.

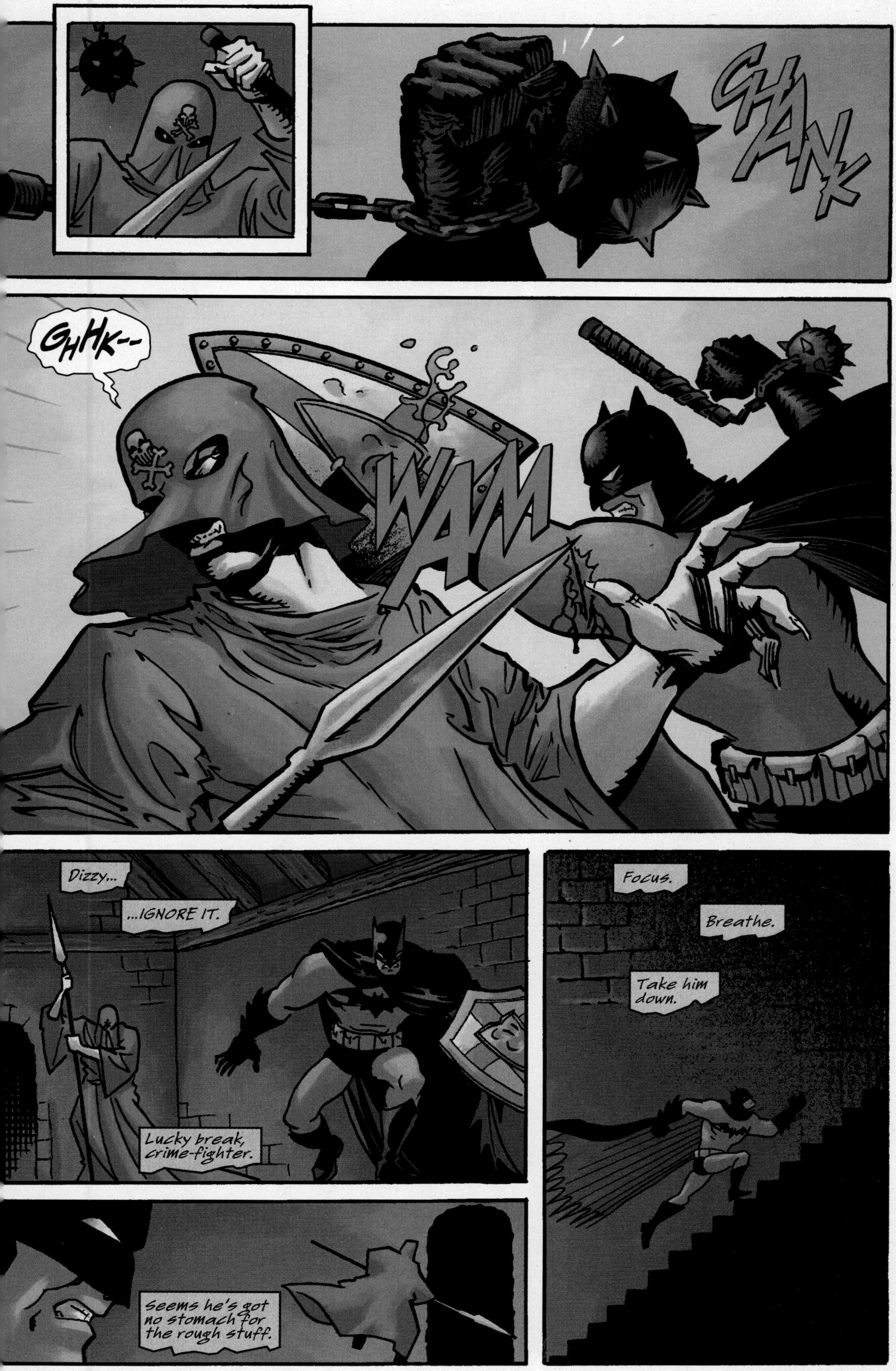

CHANK
GHHK--
WAM
Dizzy...
...IGNORE IT.
Lucky break, crime-fighter.
Focus.
Breathe.
Take him down.
Seems he's got no stomach for the rough stuff.

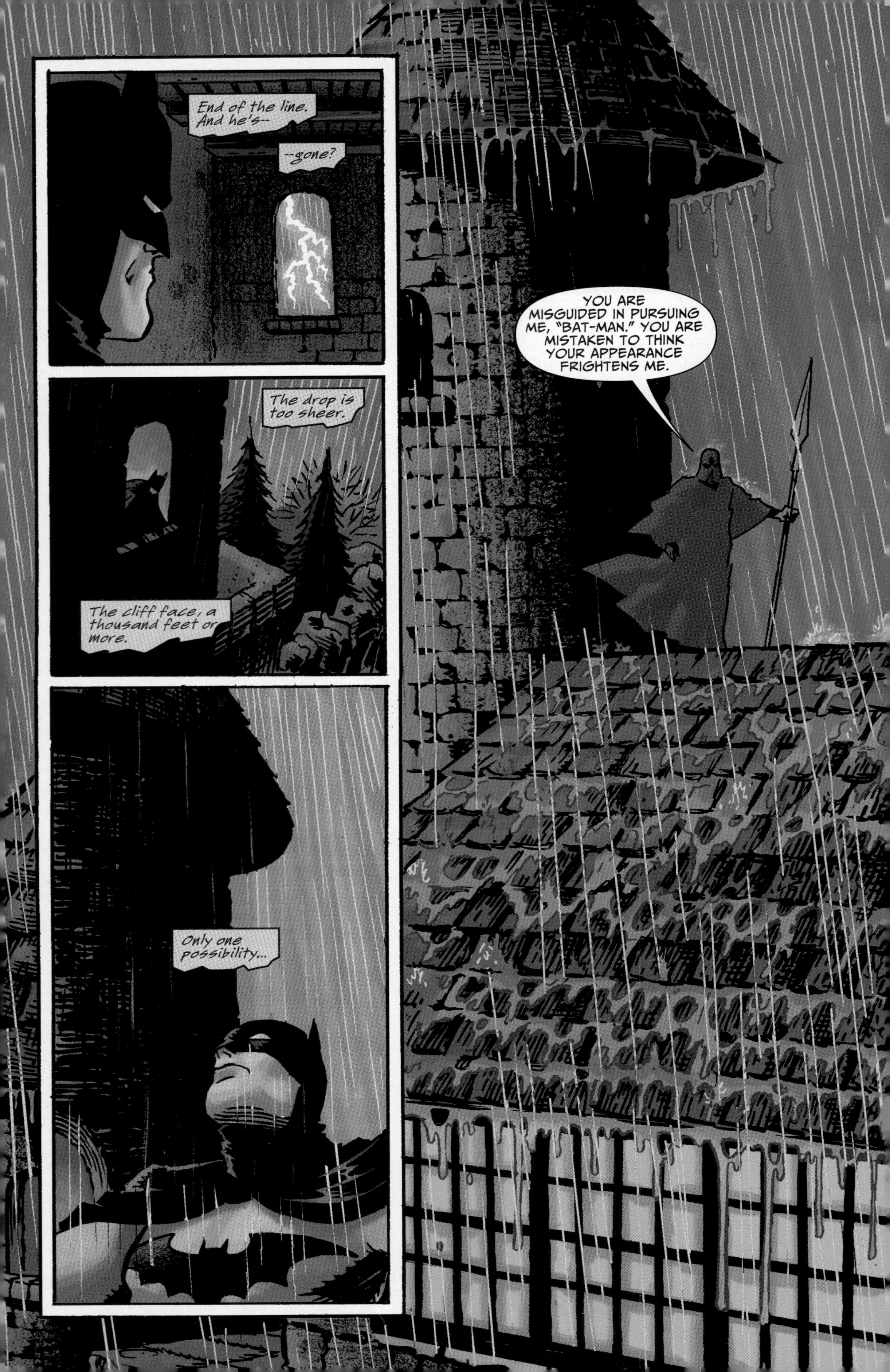
End of the line. And he's--
--gone?
The drop is too sheer.
The cliff face, a thousand feet or more.
Only one possibility...
YOU ARE MISGUIDED IN PURSUING ME, "BAT-MAN." YOU ARE MISTAKEN TO THINK YOUR APPEARANCE FRIGHTENS ME.

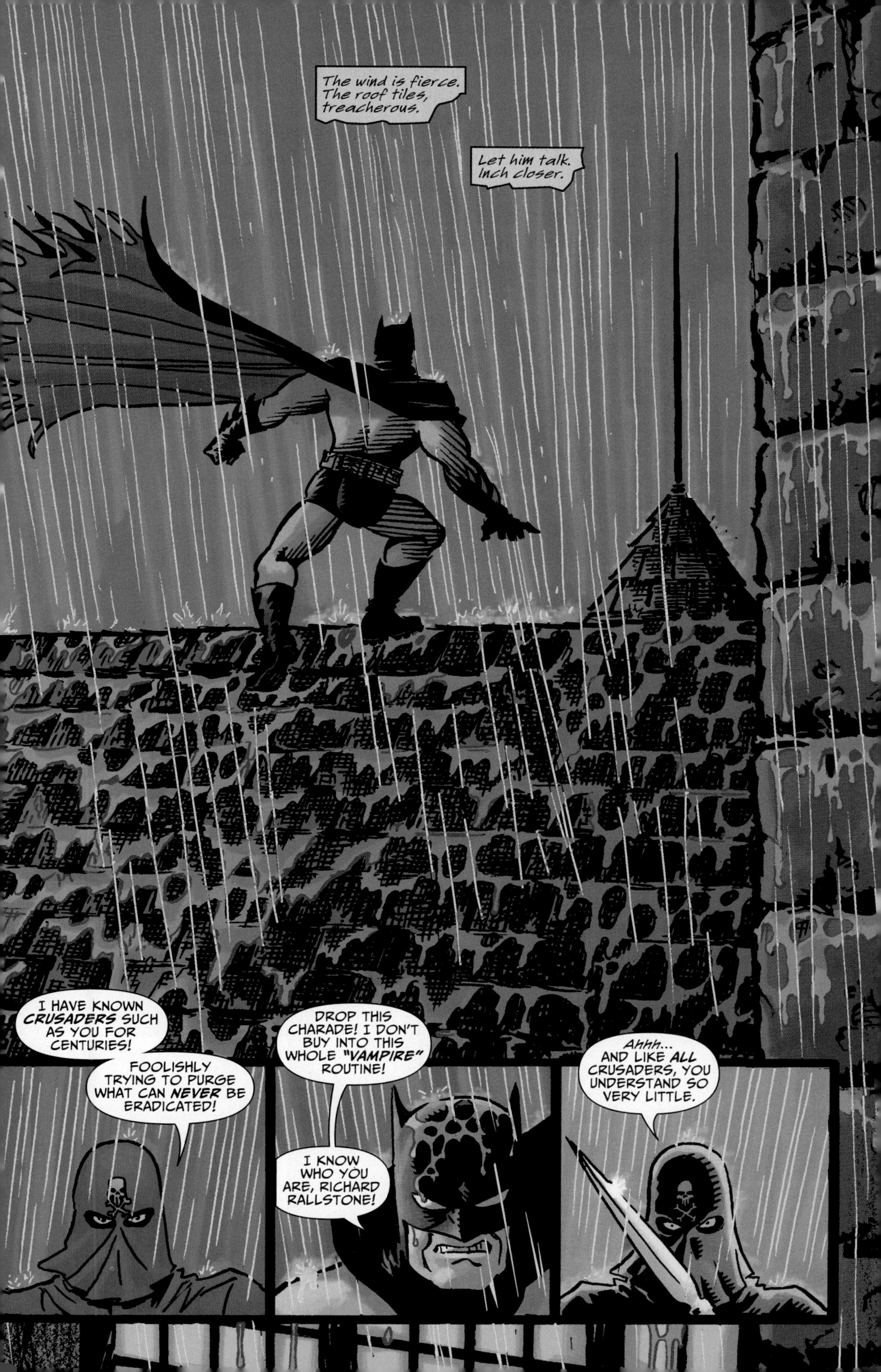
The wind is fierce. The roof tiles, treacherous.
Let him talk. Inch closer.
I HAVE KNOWN CRUSADERS SUCH AS YOU FOR CENTURIES!
FOOLISHLY TRYING TO PURGE WHAT CAN NEVER BE ERADICATED!
DROP THIS CHARADE! I DON'T BUY INTO THIS WHOLE "VAMPIRE" ROUTINE!
I KNOW WHO YOU ARE, RICHARD RALLSTONE!
Ahhh... AND LIKE ALL CRUSADERS, YOU UNDERSTAND SO VERY LITTLE.

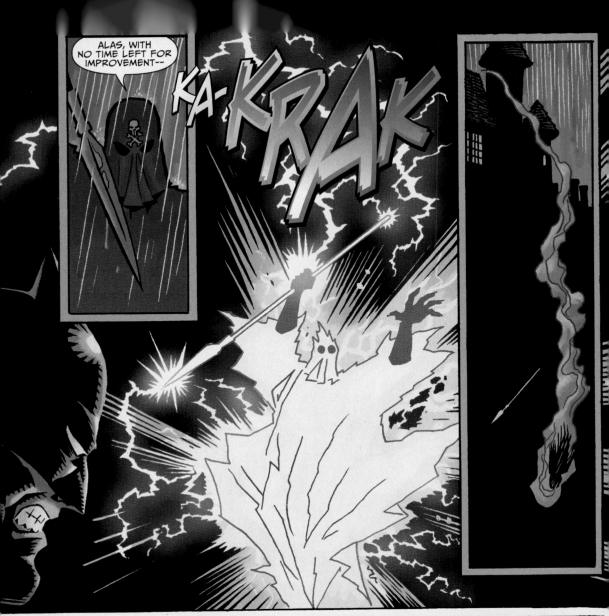

ALAS, WITH NO TIME LEFT FOR IMPROVEMENT--

KA-KRAK

His glowing arc winks out in the darkened depths below.

Time to take the hint and get off of this rooftop.

I can smell the smoke from beneath me.

Julie.

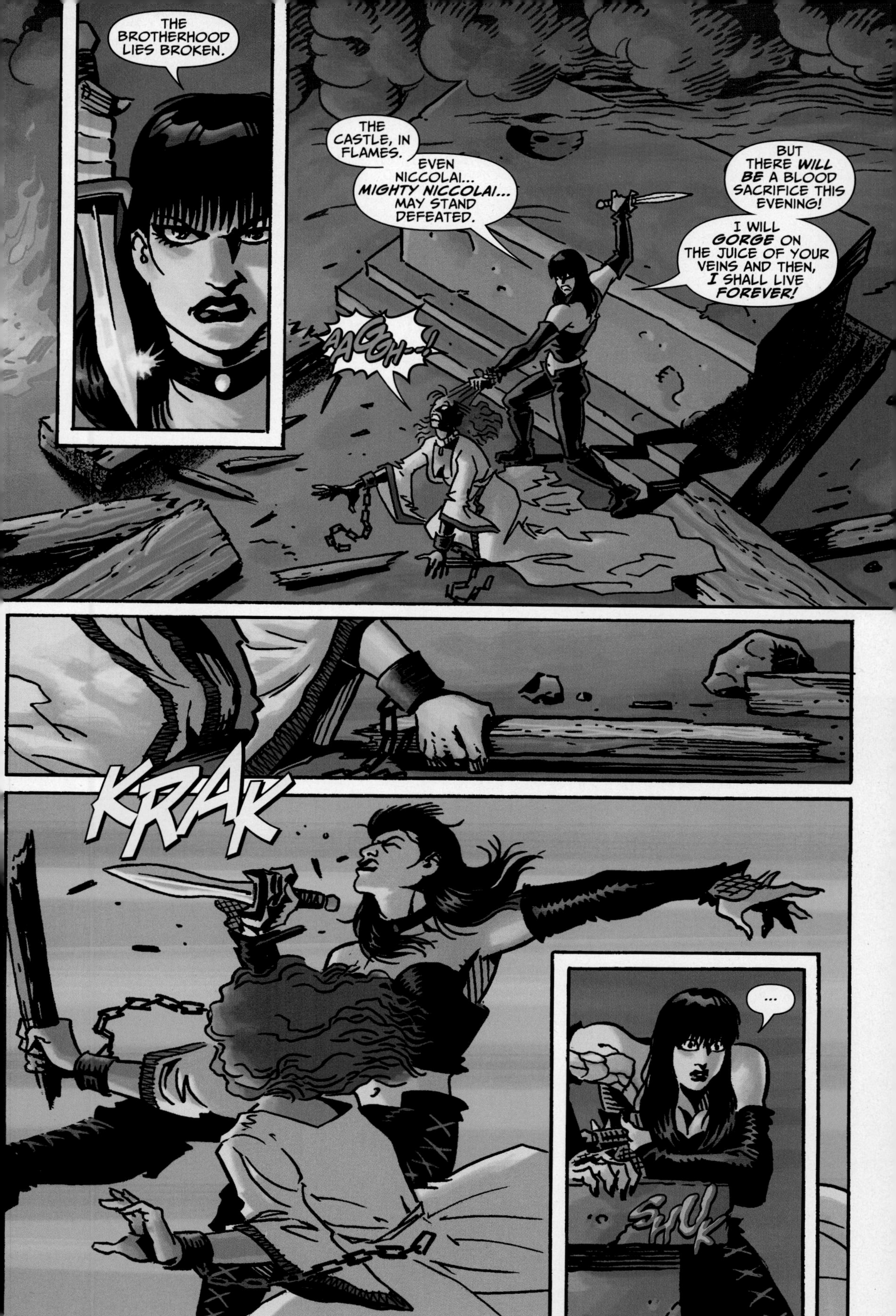
THE BROTHERHOOD LIES BROKEN.
THE CASTLE, IN FLAMES.
EVEN NICCOLAI... MIGHTY NICCOLAI... MAY STAND DEFEATED.
BUT THERE WILL BE A BLOOD SACRIFICE THIS EVENING!
I WILL GORGE ON THE JUICE OF YOUR VEINS AND THEN, I SHALL LIVE FOREVER!
AACCHH--!
KRAK
...
SHUK

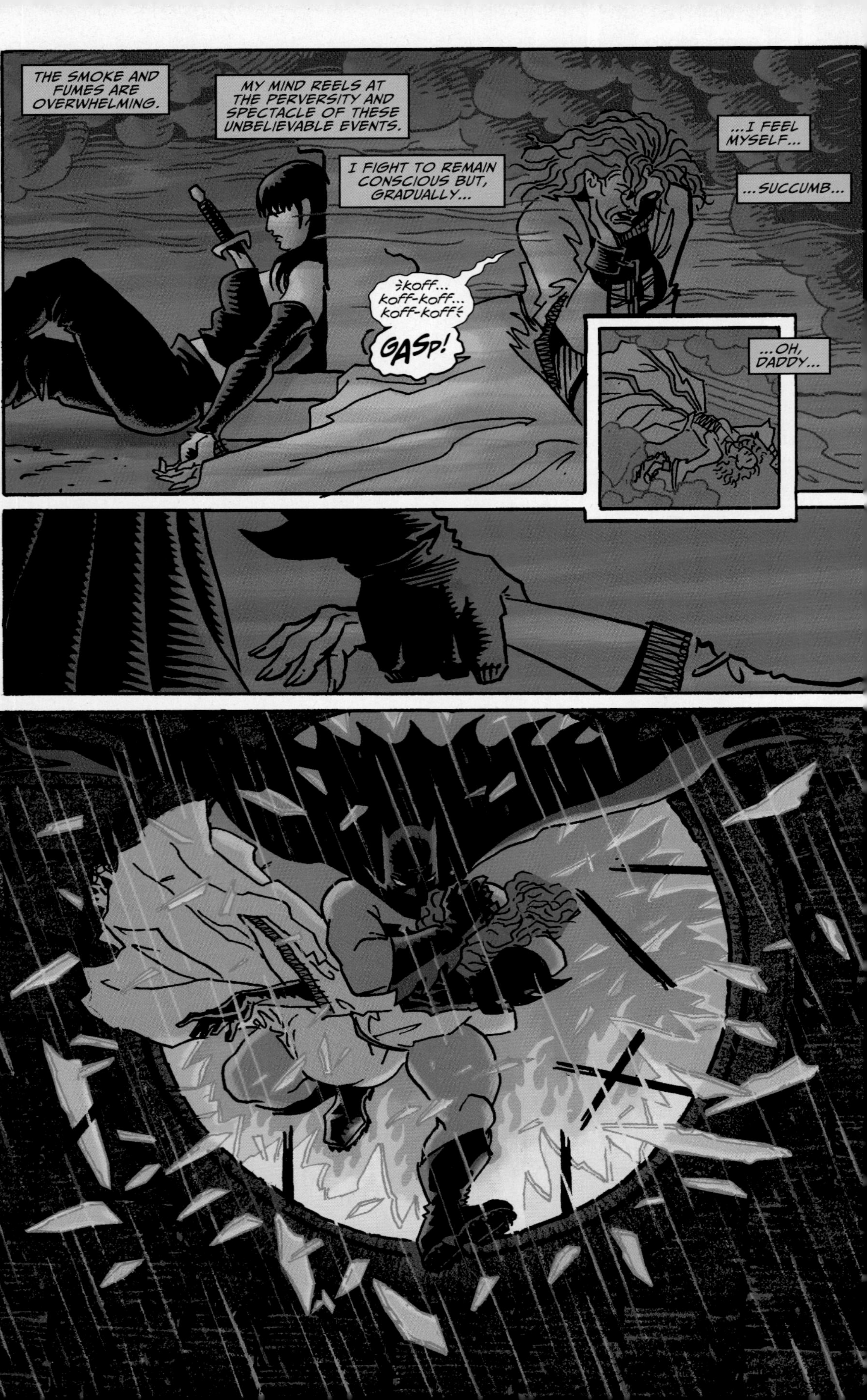
THE SMOKE AND FUMES ARE OVERWHELMING.
MY MIND REELS AT THE PERVERSITY AND SPECTACLE OF THESE UNBELIEVABLE EVENTS.
I FIGHT TO REMAIN CONSCIOUS BUT, GRADUALLY...
...I FEEL MYSELF...
...SUCCUMB...
koff... koff-koff... koff-koff
GASP!
...OH, DADDY...

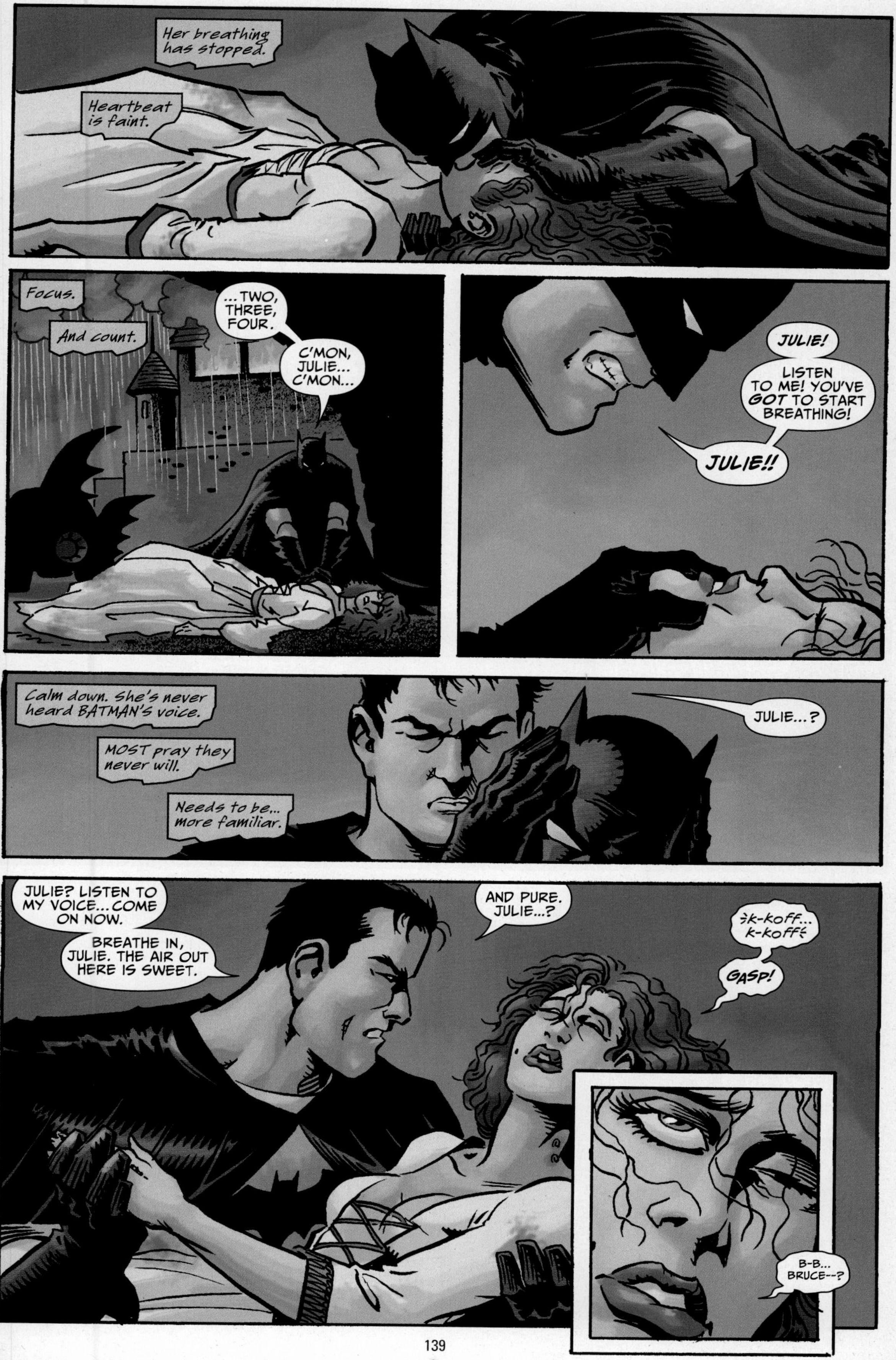
Her breathing has stopped.
Heartbeat is faint.
Focus.
And count.
...TWO, THREE, FOUR.
C'MON, JULIE... C'MON...
JULIE!
LISTEN TO ME! YOU'VE GOT TO START BREATHING!
JULIE!!
Calm down. She's never heard BATMAN's voice.
MOST pray they never will.
Needs to be... more familiar.
JULIE...?
JULIE? LISTEN TO MY VOICE... COME ON NOW.
BREATHE IN, JULIE. THE AIR OUT HERE IS SWEET.
AND PURE. JULIE...?
k-koff... k-koff
GASP!
B-B... BRUCE--?

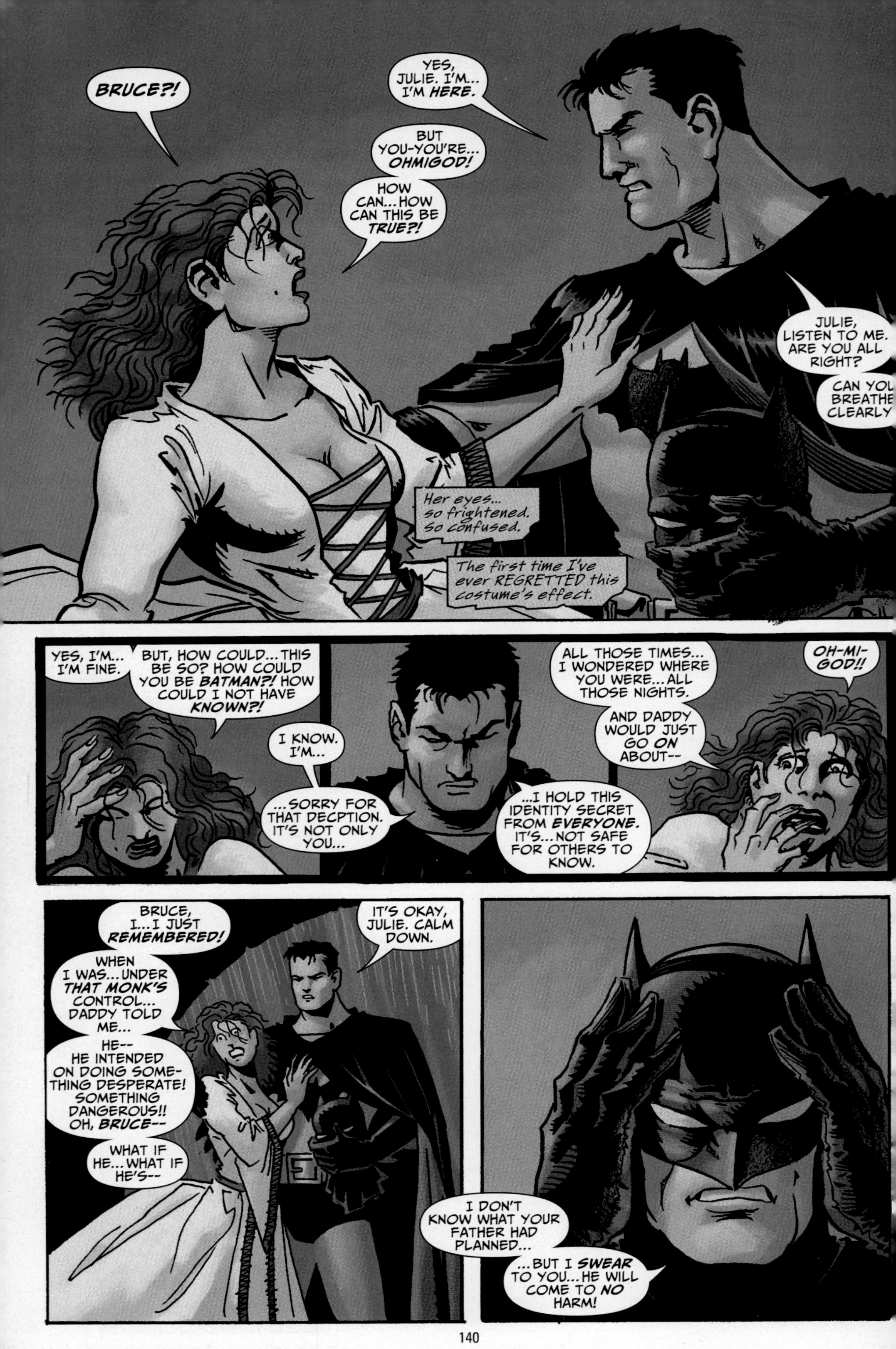
BRUCE?!
YES, JULIE. I'M... I'M HERE.
BUT YOU-YOU'RE... OHMIGOD!
HOW CAN... HOW CAN THIS BE TRUE?!
JULIE, LISTEN TO ME. ARE YOU ALL RIGHT?
CAN YOU BREATHE CLEARLY
Her eyes... so frightened. So confused.
The first time I've ever REGRETTED this costume's effect.
YES, I'M... I'M FINE.
BUT, HOW COULD... THIS BE SO? HOW COULD YOU BE BATMAN?! HOW COULD I NOT HAVE KNOWN?!
I KNOW. I'M...
...SORRY FOR THAT DECPTION. IT'S NOT ONLY YOU...
...I HOLD THIS IDENTITY SECRET FROM EVERYONE. IT'S... NOT SAFE FOR OTHERS TO KNOW.
ALL THOSE TIMES... I WONDERED WHERE YOU WERE... ALL THOSE NIGHTS.
AND DADDY WOULD JUST GO ON ABOUT--
OH-MI-GOD!!
BRUCE, I... I JUST REMEMBERED!
WHEN I WAS... UNDER THAT MONK'S CONTROL... DADDY TOLD ME...
HE-- HE INTENDED ON DOING SOME-THING DESPERATE! SOMETHING DANGEROUS!! OH, BRUCE--
WHAT IF HE... WHAT IF HE'S--
IT'S OKAY, JULIE. CALM DOWN.
I DON'T KNOW WHAT YOUR FATHER HAD PLANNED...
...BUT I SWEAR TO YOU... HE WILL COME TO NO HARM!

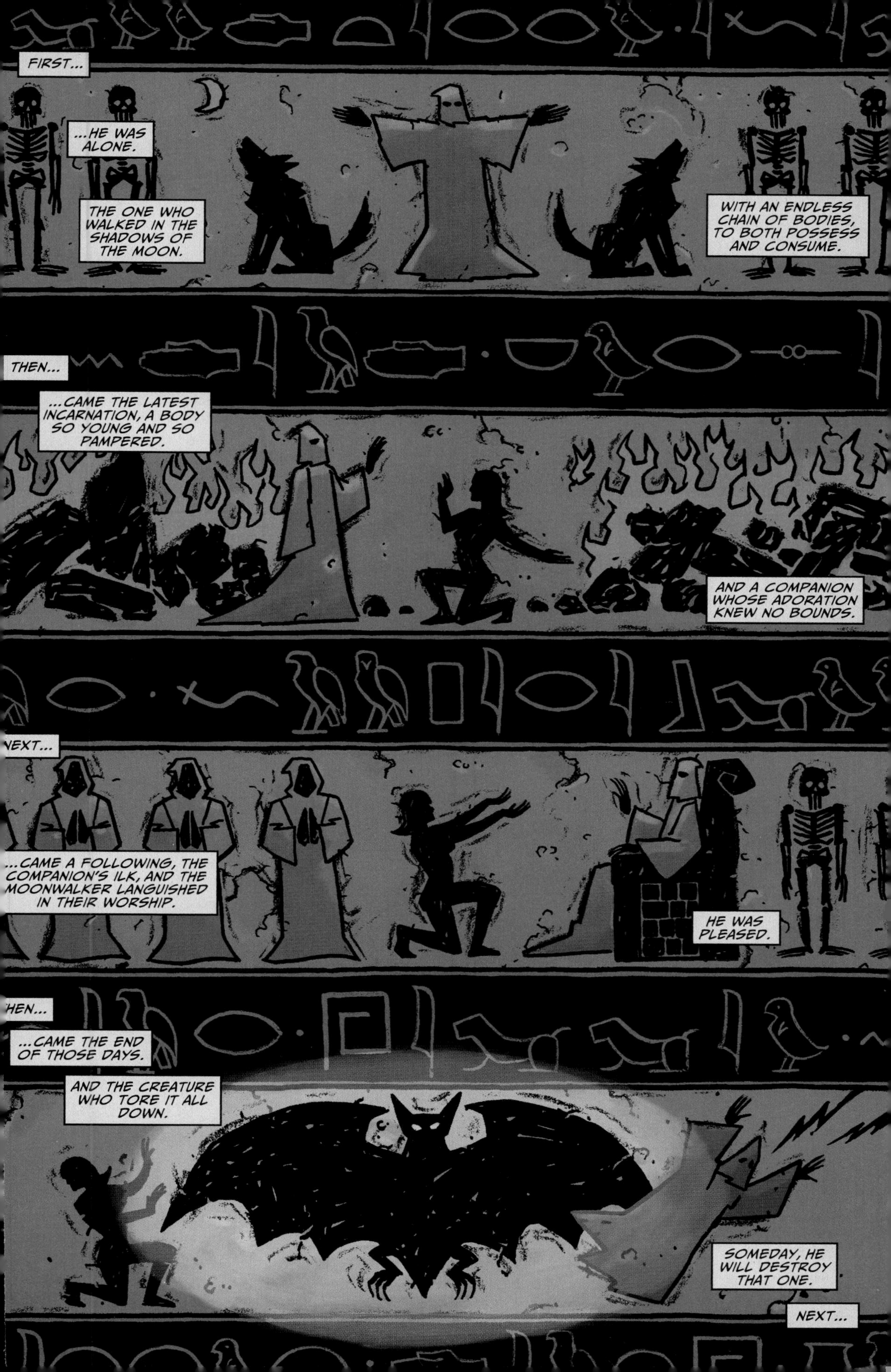
FIRST...
...HE WAS ALONE.
THE ONE WHO WALKED IN THE SHADOWS OF THE MOON.
WITH AN ENDLESS CHAIN OF BODIES, TO BOTH POSSESS AND CONSUME.
THEN...
...CAME THE LATEST INCARNATION, A BODY SO YOUNG AND SO PAMPERED.
AND A COMPANION WHOSE ADORATION KNEW NO BOUNDS.
NEXT...
...CAME A FOLLOWING, THE COMPANION'S ILK, AND THE MOONWALKER LANGUISHED IN THEIR WORSHIP.
HE WAS PLEASED.
THEN...
...CAME THE END OF THOSE DAYS.
AND THE CREATURE WHO TORE IT ALL DOWN.
SOMEDAY, HE WILL DESTROY THAT ONE.
NEXT...

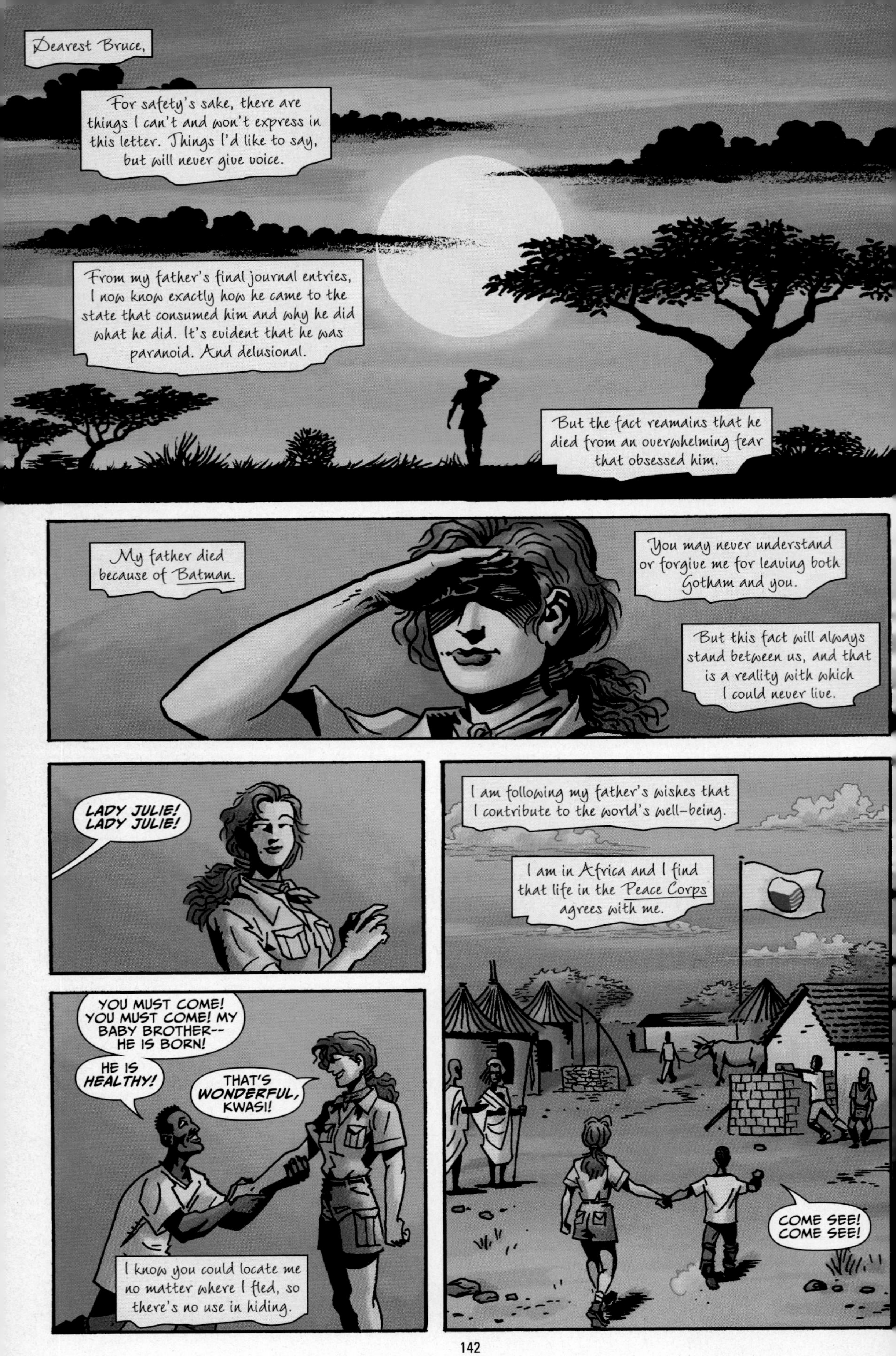

Dearest Bruce,
For safety's sake, there are things I can't and won't express in this letter. Things I'd like to say, but will never give voice.
From my father's final journal entries, I now know exactly how he came to the state that consumed him and why he did what he did. It's evident that he was paranoid. And delusional.
But the fact reamains that he died from an overwhelming fear that obsessed him.
My father died because of Batman.
You may never understand or forgive me for leaving both Gotham and you.
But this fact will always stand between us, and that is a reality with which I could never live.
LADY JULIE! LADY JULIE!
YOU MUST COME! YOU MUST COME! MY BABY BROTHER-- HE IS BORN!
HE IS HEALTHY!
THAT'S WONDERFUL, KWASI!
I know you could locate me no matter where I fled, so there's no use in hiding.
I am following my father's wishes that I contribute to the world's well-being.
I am in Africa and I find that life in the Peace Corps agrees with me.
COME SEE! COME SEE!

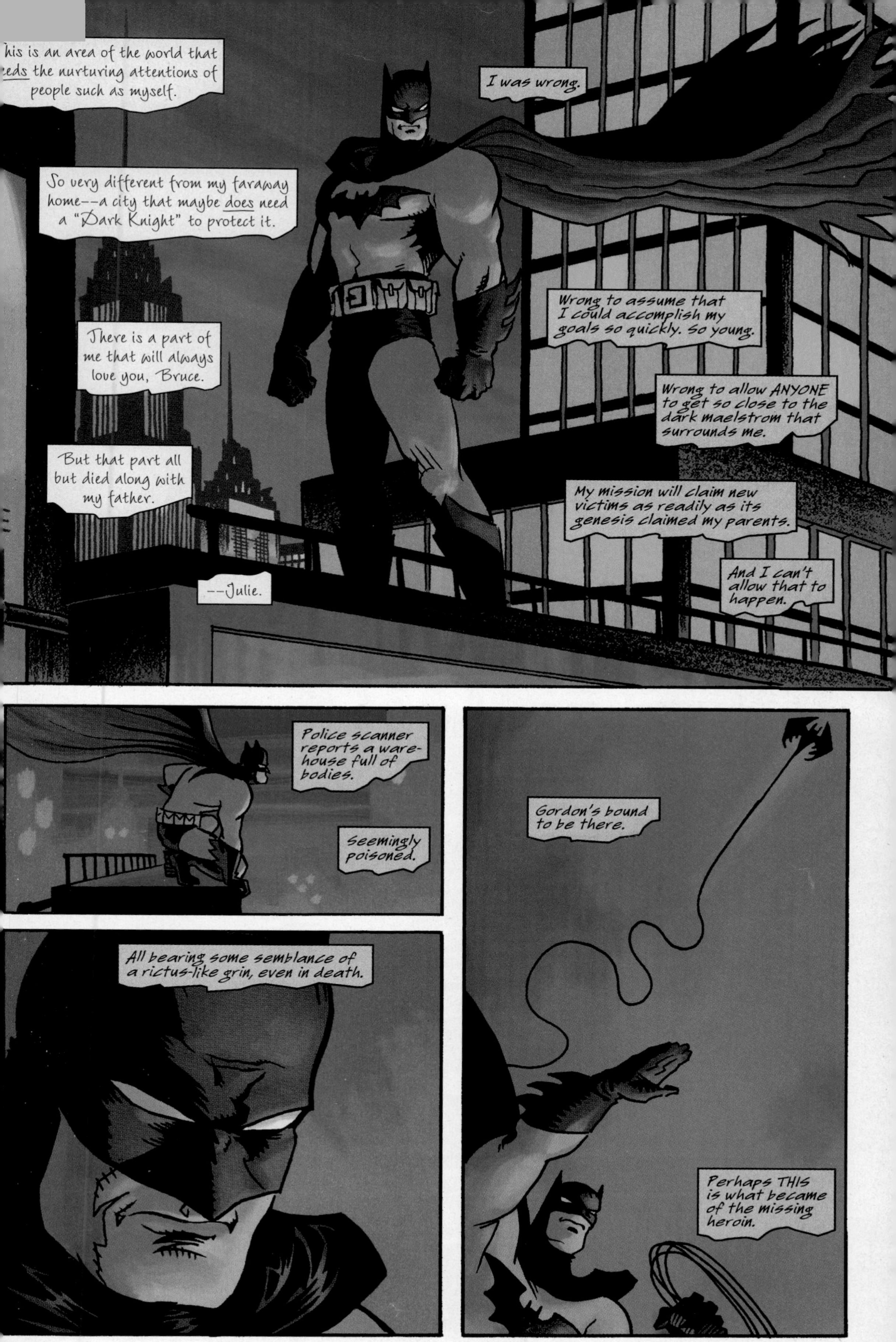
his is an area of the world that
eeds the nurturing attentions of
people such as myself.
I was wrong.
So very different from my faraway home--a city that maybe does need a "Dark Knight" to protect it.
There is a part of me that will always love you, Bruce.
But that part all but died along with my father.
--Julie.
Wrong to assume that I could accomplish my goals so quickly. So young.
Wrong to allow ANYONE to get so close to the dark maelstrom that surrounds me.
My mission will claim new victims as readily as its genesis claimed my parents.
And I can't allow that to happen.
Police scanner reports a ware-house full of bodies.
Seemingly poisoned.
All bearing some semblance of a rictus-like grin, even in death.
Gordon's bound to be there.
Perhaps THIS is what became of the missing heroin.

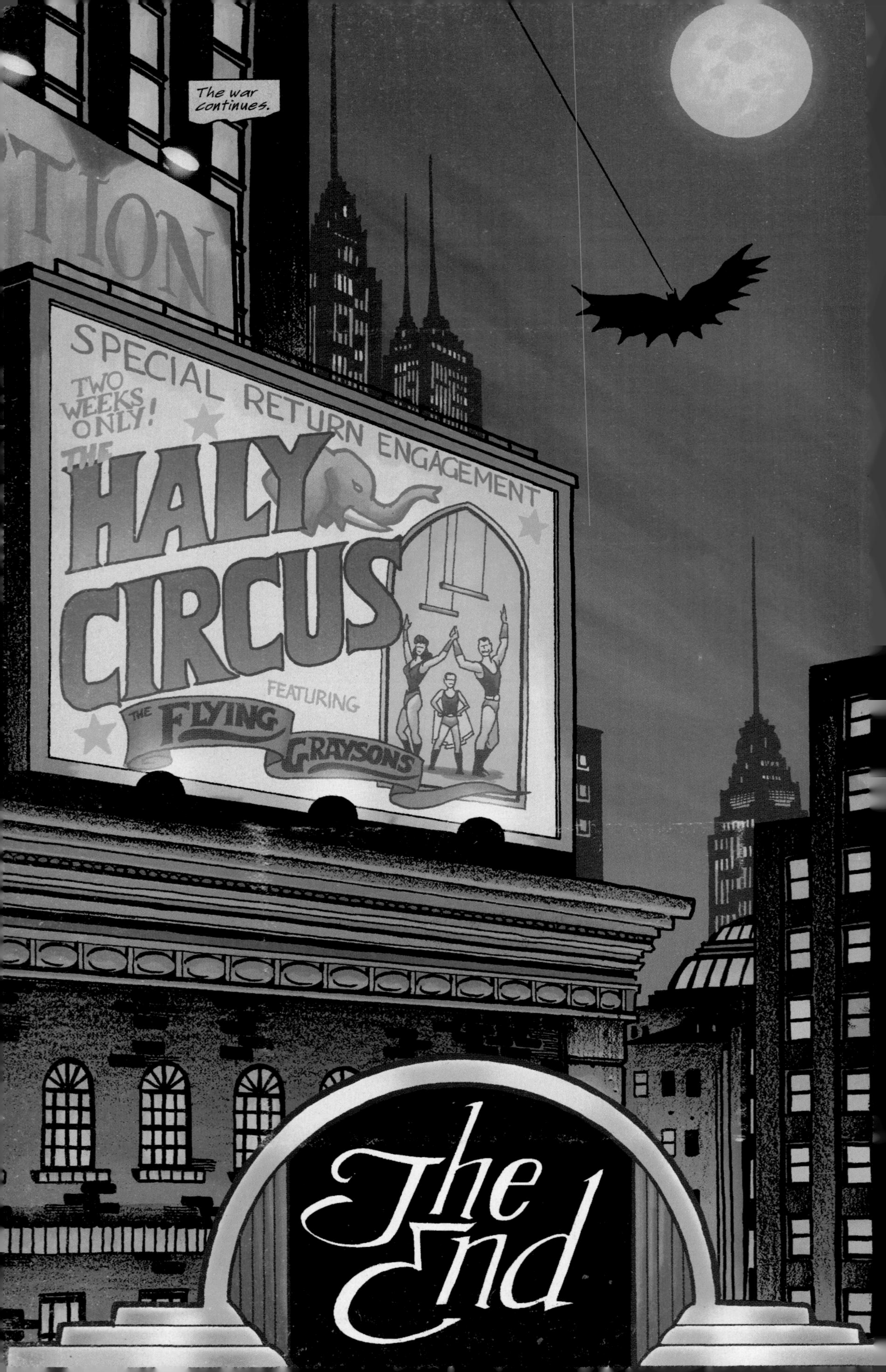
The war continues.
TION
SPECIAL RETURN ENGAGEMENT
TWO WEEKS ONLY!
THE HALY CIRCUS
FEATURING
THE FLYING GRAYSONS
The End